IN THE BALANCE

IN THE
BALANCE

Law and Politics on
the Roberts Court

MARK TUSHNET

W. W. NORTON & COMPANY · NEW YORK LONDON

For information about permission to reproduce selections from this book,
write to Permissions, W. W. Norton & Company, Inc.,
500 Fifth Avenue, New York, NY 10110

For information about special discounts for bulk purchases, please contact
W. W. Norton Special Sales at specialsales@wwnorton.com or 800-233-4830

Manufacturing by RR Donnelley, Harrisonburg
Book design by Dana Sloan
Production manager: Devon Zahn

Library of Congress Cataloging-in-Publication Data

Tushnet, Mark V., 1945–
In the balance : law and politics on the Roberts Court / Mark Tushnet.
    pages cm
Includes bibliographical references and index.
ISBN 978-0-393-07344-7 (hardcover)
1. Political questions and judicial power—United States.
2. United States. Supreme Court. 3. Roberts, John G., 1955–
4. Judges—United States. 5. Law—Political aspects—United States.
I. Title.
KF8775.T87 2013
347.73'26—dc23
                                        2013012744

W. W. Norton & Company, Inc.
500 Fifth Avenue, New York, N.Y. 10110
www.wwnorton.com

W. W. Norton & Company Ltd.
Castle House, 75/76 Wells Street, London W1T 3QT

1 2 3 4 5 6 7 8 9 0

To Leonard and Nora,
hoping that they and the Constitution
will flourish

CONTENTS

Striking the Balance on the Roberts Court

After the standard expressions of thanks to the senators, and a graceful reference to his mentor and predecessor William Rehnquist's "devotion to duty over the past year," John Roberts in 2005 launched into the substance of his opening statement in the hearings on his qualifications to be a judge of the U.S. Supreme Court: "Judges and justices are servants of the law, not the other way around. Judges are the umpires. Umpires don't make the rules; they apply them." Umpires and judges "make sure everybody plays by the rules," but "Nobody ever went to a ball game to see the umpire." Asserting that he had "no agenda" or "platform," he said that he did have "a commitment" to deal with each case "with an open mind," and—returning to his opening metaphor, "I will remember that it's my job to call balls and strikes and not to pitch or bat."

Five years later, Elena Kagan addressed the umpire metaphor at her own nomination hearing. Like most Supreme Court nominees these days, Kagan in July 2010 kept her cards close to her chest, refusing to answer questions about issues that might come before the Court. (This strategy, now routine, might make a skeptical mind question the purpose of these highly publicized hearings.) Yet she was somewhat more open than Roberts had been. She took on Roberts's "umpire" metaphor, saying that while "apt," it also "does have its limits." The metaphor made sense if all it meant was that the judge wasn't supposed to be rooting for one side: "If the umpire comes on and says, you know, 'I want every call to go to the Phillies,' that's a bad umpire." But, she continued, "the metaphor might suggest to some people that law is a kind of robotic enterprise, that there's a kind of automatic quality to it, that it's easy, that we just sort of stand there and, you know, we go ball and strike, and everything is clear-cut, and that there is—that there is no judgment in the process." That, she said, was "not right." Judges "have to exercise judgment."

Some academic critics suggested that her acknowledgment that judges exercise judgment was inconsistent with her statement, repeated so often that it must have been written in her talking points, that decisions were "law all the way down." I think she was making a subtle and pretty deep point: Law all the way down involves the exercise of judicial judgment. "It's not personal views. It's not moral views. It's not political views." But, importantly, it's not a "robotic" or "automatic" enterprise either.

Kagan's confirmation hearings foreshadowed her likely role on the Supreme Court as leading the intellectual opposition to Chief Justice Roberts. During the year that Kagan served as Solicitor General, Roberts seemed to understand the possibility that Kagan would join him on the Court and become a major force there. His tone with her was sometimes sharp. Responding to a question from Justice Antonin Scalia in a relatively obscure case, Kagan treated him as if he were one of her students, asking a question in response. The Chief Justice intervened, "Usually we have questions the other way." Kagan apologized. The tension between Roberts and Kagan was the most interesting feature of Kagan's tenure as Solicitor General. As Court observer Dahlia Lithwick noted, the tension doesn't come through clearly in the dry transcripts, but if you try to hear them in your mind as you read them, you can get some sense of what was going on. At the end of one sharp exchange, Roberts called the position Kagan took "absolutely startling." Kagan responded: "The United States Government is a complicated place." To which the Chief Justice replied dismissively, "I take your word for it."

The Roberts Court as it matured was closely balanced in partisan terms: five justices nominated by Republican presidents, four by Democrats. It was balanced intellectually as well, with Roberts and Kagan articulating their competing visions of constitutional law as a distinctive blend of law and politics—with the balance slightly different for each. Illinois senator (and former law professor) Barack Obama captured the distinction in announcing that he would vote against Roberts's confirmation:

> While adherence to legal precedent and rules of statutory or constitutional construction will dispose of 95 percent of the cases that come before a court, so that both a Scalia and a Ginsburg will arrive at the same place most of the time on those 95 percent of the cases—what matters on the Supreme Court is those 5 percent of cases that are truly difficult. . . . In those 5 percent of hard cases, the constitutional text will not be directly on point. The language of the statute will not be perfectly clear. Legal process alone will not lead you to a rule of decision. In those circumstances, . . . the critical ingredient is supplied by what is in the judge's heart. . . .

Obama understood that in the 5 percent of cases where the law left things open, "the critical ingredient" comes from outside the law. That ingredient is politics—not the everyday partisan politics we see on Capitol Hill, but a politics of principle, of competing visions about the best way to arrange our government so that it protects our liberty and our security. To say they are a matter of principle is not to say they are a matter of pure idealism, however. The larger structures that organize our politics—how presidents decide to lead their parties and how interest groups affect nominations and litigation, for example—generate and support those visions and their implementation by the justices.

In the Balance argues that the balance on the Roberts Court has been and will be affected by those political structures and political visions. Chief Justice Roberts and Justice Kagan are both products of those structures and authors of those visions. The future of the Court will be shaped not only by the nominations that President Obama and his successors will make, but by the competition between Roberts and Kagan for intellectual leadership of the Court, as each forcefully articulates differing views about the balance between law and politics. *In the Balance* suggests that we might find ourselves talking about a Court formally led by Chief Justice Roberts—a "Roberts Court"—but led intellectually by Justice Kagan—a "Kagan Court."

THE CLOSE balance on the Roberts Court today is reflected in its decisions: some "liberal," upholding the Affordable Care Act ("Obamacare") and invalidating some of the Bush administration's anti-terrorism initiatives, and some "conservative," upholding a federal ban on later-term abortions ("partial-birth abortions"), the *Heller* gun rights case, and the *Citizens United* campaign finance decision. Still, there's something odd about the Roberts Court's work when looked at as a whole. Judging from the personnel alone, you'd expect that the Roberts Court would be a reliably conservative Court. But, as conservative outrage at the Affordable Care Act decision indicates, it isn't.

Not *completely* reliable, that is—not a ventriloquist's puppet for the Republican Party. Yet, though the picture is mixed, the Roberts Court's decisions correspond to the main constitutional positions associated with the Republican Party of the early twenty-first century. Presidents Reagan, George H.W. Bush, and George W. Bush got pretty much what they were looking for when they appointed the men who make up the Roberts Court's core. So did Presidents Clinton and Obama on the other side.

This book offers an account of the Roberts Court that tries to make sense of the Court's work as part of contemporary politics, in a way that might make it easier to understand the mixed picture I've sketched. Part of the story involves the politics of appointments, which I examine in chapter 2. Another part of the story involves the *law* part of constitutional law. Throughout this book I argue that we have to take legal arguments seriously, and shouldn't simplistically blame "politics" for justices' decisions. We shouldn't take legal arguments too seriously, though. Judges use arguments tactically, as part of a larger campaign, and we need to focus on the larger strategy the tactics serve. The overall story is about conservatism and liberalism today.

In saying that I offer a political account, I don't mean that the justices take their cues from the platforms or leadership of the Democratic or Republican parties. What the justices do affects what presidents and Congress can do, and the justices know it. But usually the justices have a longer time frame for their form of politics than presidents or politicians do: the justices care about what's going to happen over the next few decades, the politicians about what's going to happen before the next election. A short-term balance can shift with the next appointment to the Court.

The politics of appointments means that justices are chosen because they have general outlooks on the Constitution that are consistent with the general views of the political parties *at the historical moment* when they were appointed. Political parties change. The longer a justice serves, the more likely it is that the "party" with which he or she was affiliated when appointed will change into something else. Most dramatically, Anthony Kennedy's Republican Party wasn't George W. Bush's, so Kennedy's "Republicanism" isn't the same as Samuel Alito's. The Republican Party in 2013 with an extremely strong Tea Party element was different from the Republican Party when Richard Nixon was elected, and different even from the party when Ronald Reagan was elected. John Roberts's constitutional philosophy was shaped before and during the Reagan years, and there's no reason to think that he's a partisan hack whose views change as new leaders come to the fore in the party. (As I explain in chapter 1, the timing issue matters a lot in understanding Chief Justice Roberts's "betrayal," as conservatives saw it, in the Affordable Care Act decision.)

No one should think, of course, that every decision of the Roberts Court can be explained in partisan terms. There are still the 95 percent of the cases that Senator Obama described where the best explanation for the decisions is what the justices think rules and precedent require. In 2012, for example, the Court decided a case asking whether children born eighteen months after their father had died (their mother had been inseminated with the father's frozen sperm) were entitled to "survivors' benefits" under the Social Security Act. Justice Ruth Bader Ginsburg wrote an opinion for a unanimous Court saying, "Not unless the children counted as heirs under state law." You can wring some politics from this case if you assume the liberals always want to make the social safety net as big as possible, but you'd be pretty foolish to do that. The case presented a straightforward problem in statutory interpretation and administrative law, with no real political overtones. The best explanation for the outcome is that most of the justices thought that "the law" supported Justice Ginsburg's analysis. That's what Chief Justice Roberts meant when he said that a judge's job was to call balls and strikes. He was right, but mostly about cases with no or only weak political overtones.

What about the cases that do have political overtones? I'm quite certain that the justices don't ask themselves what they can do to make the political future of the Republican or Democratic parties rosier (or gloomier). Yet what they *do* supports many of the positions on the Constitution's meaning that leading partisans take. That's not just convenient, as the Church Lady used to say on *Saturday Night Live*. It results from political structures and strategies that led to the selection of the five Republican appointees and the four Democratic ones, and to the political structures and strategies of the political parties and interest groups.

Yet, even if the justices did think of themselves in purely political terms—which they don't—knowing that wouldn't help us understand what the Court does. Suppose Chief Justice Roberts woke up the day the Court heard argument in the Obamacare case, and asked himself, "How can I decide this case to make it more likely the Republican candidate in November will beat President Obama?" He'd have no way of giving himself a satisfying answer. As one liberal blogger put it on the day the Court granted review in the case:

So what would be the political consequences of the court's ruling to uphold or strike down or punt on the mandate? If they uphold it, the Obama Administration will claim vindication—which, plus two dollars, will entitle them to a short ride on the Metro. Upholding the mandate means that the right will conclude the only way to get rid of "Obamacare" would be to repeal it legislatively by electing a Republican president, re-electing the Republican House and winning a GOP-controlled filibuster proof Senate. (Or even not filibuster proof, since a number of Democratic senators, under those conditions, would probably go along with repealing it.) The right, in other words, will go into the election even more stoked than it already is. The Democrats, meanwhile, from the president himself on down, bring no passion to Obamacare's defense. It's hard to envision Democratic get-out-the-vote campaigns centered on preserving a health care reform that never kindled the public's, or even the Democratic base's, imagination.

If, on the other hand, the court strikes down "Obamacare,"

Republicans will take it as vindication and feel more wind in their sails. Democrats will not campaign on battling to pass another version that does pass muster with the courts (as single-payer would, ironically, since it would be a universal governmental program like Medicare). In other words, a slight bump politically for the GOP; none for the Dems.

Basically, a justice thinking about the cases politically could figure that anything he or she was inclined to do would benefit his or her side. It's not like *Bush v. Gore*, where everyone knew that a decision one way would come close to guaranteeing that George W. Bush would take office on January 20, 2001. Under the circumstances of the Obamacare cases the only sensible thing to do would be to put political calculations aside and do whatever the justice's general view of the Constitution says to do.

Every justice has developed ways of thinking about the Constitution's meaning in partisan settings. But no political party tells them what to think, and sometimes the "party" is a messy coalition with factions adhering to accounts of the Constitution's meaning that overlap on many issues but diverge on some. The story of the Roberts Court as a pro-business Court, which I recount and qualify in chapter 5, is an example: many of the cases involve conflicts within the Republican Party, between its business supporters and its localists.

I describe the justices as "Republicans" or "conservatives," "Democrats" or "liberals," because they have differing constitutional visions—the term used in nomination hearings is "judicial philosophies"—that are systematically associated with the two parties. But judicial philosophies are capacious ways of thinking about problems, not checklists of partisan positions. John Roberts's decision to uphold the Affordable Care Act makes the point: as a justice thinks about what his or her judicial philosophy says about a specific case the Court has to decide, there's no guarantee that the justice's conclusions will fit the party's checklist. But, of course, as the votes of the conservative dissenters show, saying that there's no guarantee doesn't mean that there isn't a pretty good chance of such a fit.

More: The justices have to implement their constitutional visions through law and constitutional doctrine. The legal materials they have to work with are supple and manipulable, but they don't always fit easily into a purely partisan agenda. If the stakes are high enough, justices will set aside the limits that law puts on what a justice can do—as happened in *Bush v. Gore*. But I spend a fair amount of time in what follows laying out the structure of constitutional doctrine because law sometimes matters, and you can't tell when or, maybe more important, how politics dominates law unless you understand constitutional doctrine.

The Supreme Court is a small group of nine people, and law matters sometimes for each of them. My guesstimate is that 90 percent of the justices cast their votes in 80 percent of the politically salient cases in ways that could be read off from the party checklists. In the other cases a justice's position results from the justice's assessment of what the law requires. But we can't tell in advance which justice will "deviate" in which cases. When you aggregate the nine votes, sometimes you'll come up with results that someone who thought that the story was "Republicans versus Democrats" would find surprising. A colleague who does math better than I do calculates that, with the numbers I made up, you could expect on average about one fifth to one quarter of the politically salient cases to come out "counter"-ideologically—that is, on the Roberts Court, come out on the liberal side.

THE SUPREME Court's work rolls on, regardless of publication schedules. As I was writing this book the Court was considering important cases involving affirmative action, the Voting Rights Act, and gay marriage. The structures I describe give some clues to how to think about individual cases, but generate no solid predictions. The balance on the Roberts Court is close enough that no one should take large bets on specific outcomes. Still, as Ring Lardner put it, "The race is not always to the swift nor the battle to the strong, but that's the way to bet." So too for the Supreme Court.

IN THE BALANCE

CHAPTER 1

Off the Wall and Down the Rabbit Hole

The first news reports from the Supreme court on June 28, 2012, were that the Roberts Court had held the Affordable Care (ACA, or "Obamacare") unconstitutional. Those reports were wrong, corrected within a few minutes. As correctly reported, the central opinion, written by John Roberts, said that Congress didn't have the power to require people to buy health care insurance. But it also said that Congress could impose a tax on people who didn't buy health care insurance, and that was enough to make the Affordable Care Act the law of the land. Both parts of Roberts's opinion got five votes, and with the exception of the Chief Justice's, the votes tracked partisan lines. The other four justices appointed by Republican presidents agreed with the first holding but not the second, and the four justices appointed by Democratic presidents agreed with the second holding but not the first.

Immediately people began to speculate about why Roberts had split the difference to give President Obama a major policy victory. The speculation got added fuel when someone inside the Court leaked that Roberts had changed his vote from striking Obamacare down to upholding it. The most common view was that Roberts had chosen the path of statesmanship, politics in the largest sense. Upholding Obamacare was an act of statesmanship because it showed that the Court was not the creature of the partisan politics that dominates the rest of Washington.

Like the initial news reports, that view is wrong—or so I argue. The best interpretation of the Chief Justice's opinion is that he was doing law, not politics. The Obamacare decision had many other parts, and Justice Kagan joined the Chief Justice in holding that Congress couldn't threaten states that they would lose all their Medicaid funding if they didn't expand Medicaid dramatically. Perhaps she was the one acting as a politician inside the Court—or perhaps she too was simply doing what she thought the law required.

The Court's decision left Randy Barnett, the principal author of the case against Obamacare, in shock. "The outcome of this case still hurts," he wrote, "and it will for a very long time, unless Obamacare is repealed. . . ." Barnett, the proud "intellectual godfather" of the constitutional argument against Obamacare, probably felt a little like Charlie Brown: He ran up to kick the football but at the last minute Lucy pulled it away, and he ended up flat on his back.*

BOOKS HAVE been written, and more will be written, about how the Affordable Care Act came about. It would take us too far from the Supreme Court for me to describe the messy legislative process in detail—extensive and failed efforts to draw some Republicans into supporting some sort of health insurance legislation; the replacement of Senator Edward Kennedy by Scott Brown; and much more.

---

* As decision day approached, I heard liberal supporters of the ACA use the Charlie Brown metaphor: somehow, they believed, the Supreme Court was going to pull a deserved victory away from them as it had so often before. They were wrong this time.

Constitutional issues bubbled up to the surface and then disappeared. The ACA contained provisions requiring states to extend their existing Medicaid programs to a much larger group of the relatively poor. As a sweetener, Congress promised to pay the entire cost of the additional coverage for several years, then gradually reduce the federal contribution. At one point Senate majority leader Harry Reid was worried about getting Nebraska senator Ben Nelson's vote for the ACA. Reid inserted a provision saying that the federal government would pay Nebraska's additional costs permanently. Some observers derided this as the "Cornhusker fix," and suggested that it was unconstitutional to give Nebraska, no different in any relevant way from Iowa or any other state, a special benefit. Senator Nelson quickly protested that he'd never asked for the Cornhusker fix, it was dropped from the ACA, and Senator Nelson voted for the ACA anyway. Near the end of the process the Democratic leadership in the House proposed to use a process called "deem and pass" to enact the ACA. It's virtually impossible to explain "deem and pass" to anyone who isn't a specialist in congressional procedure. To many outsiders, the procedure—rarely used but not unknown before the ACA—looked like an end run around the Constitution's requirement that both the Senate and the House have to vote to transform a bill into a law. Again, "deem and pass" eventually fell by the wayside. But the episodes may have conveyed a sense that Democrats weren't really paying attention to the Constitution when they enacted the ACA.

The real constitutional issues arose out of the ACA's core provisions. President Obama pushed for legislation that would provide universal health care insurance. People could get that insurance in several ways. Some would get it through their employers, others through Medicaid. States had to expand their existing Medicaid programs to cover people with incomes up to 133 percent of the federal poverty level. If you were self-employed or your employer didn't provide health care insurance, and your income was too high for you to qualify for Medicaid, you had to buy insurance from private insurers. The ACA provided some subsidies to people who couldn't afford to pay what the insurance companies asked. But in the end the ACA required you to get insurance. This was described as the "individual mandate." If you didn't have health insurance, you'd have to make a "Shared Responsibility Payment," which was adjusted to income and topped out around $700. You'd fill out your income tax forms, where there would be a new section asking whether you had health care insurance. If you checked "No," you'd have to make the payment as part of your annual federal income tax.

To make this work, though, the privately provided health insurance had to be "affordable." The ACA sought to achieve that goal by regulating health care insurers. They had to issue insurance to anyone who applied for it ("guaranteed issue"), at a rate fixed by the cost of providing health care to the entire group of people who buy insurance ("community rating"). The ACA also requires insurance companies to issue insurance at the community rating to people with preexisting conditions.

That alone wouldn't help matters, and actually will make things worse, because of what economists call "moral hazard," and a related idea, "adverse selection." Moral hazard works like this: Consider a healthy young person. Insurance would cost her, say, $1,000. Rather than pay that to the insurance company, she'll wait until she gets sick or injured. Treating her illness will cost, say, $10,000. If the insurance company has to issue her insurance as she's brought into the emergency room, it's going to charge her full fare, $10,000. But she can't afford to pay that. So she becomes a charity patient and the hospital eats the cost of her care, passing the cost onto other patients through its insurance companies. And, of course, if the insurance company has to issue the insurance at the fixed $1,000 rate, it's going to go out of the insurance business pretty fast.

Adverse selection is similar. Here consider a person who already has an illness that is expensive to treat. He's going to buy health care insurance at the community rate, and consume health care that exceeds the amount he pays. But the young healthy person won't buy the insurance, seeing no need for it. So the pool of people who buy insurance consists only of people who already have high medical expenses. Again, investors in insurance companies are going to find better places for their money than companies from which money is draining every moment.

The ACA adopted a natural solution to the problems of moral hazard and adverse selection: make everyone, even the young and healthy, buy insurance. That's the individual mandate again. The young and healthy subsidize the ill, but that's how insurance always works. You buy fire insurance for your house and hope that it never burns down. If it doesn't, and the house of a family across town does, your insurance premiums subsidize the insurance payments to them. The individual mandate provided universal coverage, but it also solved the problems created by the combination of community rating, guaranteed issue, and required coverage for people with preexisting conditions.

Some states challenged the required expansion of Medicaid, but nearly all the public attention went to challenges to the individual mandate.

WHO CAME up with the most effective arguments against the mandate, and when, is disputed, but how they took hold is not. Along with many others, the idea of requiring people to buy insurance came up during the Clinton administration's effort to enact health care reform. Though the mandate didn't play a large part then—the effort collapsed for a host of reasons—two conservative lawyers, David Rivkin and Lee Casey, published an op-ed in the *Wall Street Journal* arguing that Congress didn't have the power to force people who were sitting around, "inactive," to do something. "If Congress thinks Americans are too fat, can it not decree that Americans shall lose weight?" they asked. Their argument was grounded more in libertarian thinking about the limits of all government power, not specifically that of the federal government. After all, the rhetorical force of the question, "If the Massachusetts legislature thinks Americans are too fat, can it not decree that state residents shall lose weight?" is just as strong as their question about Congress.

The quasi-libertarian argument dropped from view after the Clinton effort ended. But political interest in health care reform continued, and mainstream Republicans felt pressure to come up with something to counter Democratic proposals modeled on the Medicare program, in which the government pays doctors for the services they provide (and through the payment system controls those prices). At the conservative-leaning think tank the Heritage Foundation, Stuart Butler, born in Britain and charged with aspects of the foundation's domestic policy studies, came up with a plan that contained an individual mandate. As governor of Massachusetts, Mitt Romney made reform of health care insurance within the state a centerpiece of his policy agenda, and Romneycare included an individual mandate. As late as June 2009 Republican senator Charles Grassley of Iowa could say, "I believe that there is a bipartisan consensus to have individual mandates."

When Republicans adopted the tactic of obstructing every Obama administration initiative as part of their larger strategy of defeating President Obama in the 2012 elections, their approach to the individual mandate changed. Republicans began to say that Obamacare was not only bad policy but was unconstitutional—a common move in our public debates over issues that divide us politically. The libertarian argument that Rivkin and Casey had sketched resurfaced, and although Rivkin and Casey offered their argument again, Georgetown law professor Randy Barnett became the argument's most vigorous proponent.

The constitutional argument against Obamacare seemed nearly frivolous—"off the wall," in a phrase made popular among legal academics by Yale law professor Jack Balkin—to almost all scholars of constitutional law, or at least to almost all of those not deeply committed to libertarianism. Even some conservative scholars who thought the argument had some merit were quite skeptical about the possibility that today's judges would accept it.

The argument was off the wall because the Supreme Court had adopted extremely expansive views of Congress's power to regulate the national economy since the New Deal, and with health care forming such a large part of the national economy it seemed obvious that Congress had the power to regulate *it* too. In the most celebrated precedent, the Court held that Congress could prohibit a wheat farmer from growing more than a specified amount of wheat even when he planned to use the wheat on his farm, as feed, rather than place it on the market for general sale. True, the Rehnquist Court had placed some limits on Congress's power, but only twice, and neither case involved anything as substantial as the health care sector. And more recently, the Court upheld Congress's power to prohibit a person who used marijuana to alleviate her crushing pain from growing marijuana at home solely for her own use—in a case where Randy Barnett represented the sick woman.

These precedents did make an argument that Obamacare was unconstitutional because Congress didn't have the power to adopt the individual mandate seem frivolous to many scholars. But there was more. Everyone agreed that Congress had the power to adopt the "guaranteed issue," preexisting coverage, and other regulations of insurance companies. Whatever might be said about individuals who didn't have insurance, no one thought that insurance *companies* were outside the scope of Congress's power to regulate interstate commerce. Then the adverse selection and moral hazard problems kicked in. The Constitution gives Congress the power to adopt laws that are "necessary and proper for carrying into Execution the foregoing powers," one of which was the commerce power. So, the argument for Obamacare went, even if Congress didn't have the power to impose the individual mandate as a freestanding requirement unconnected to anything else, surely the individual mandate was a "necessary and proper" method of executing the insurance company regulations, given the adverse selection and moral hazard problems. The Supreme Court said in 1819 that the word "necessary" means something like "convenient" or "reasonably thought to be effective," which the individual mandate certainly was. It had never really focused on the word "proper" as a separate limitation, though there were hints that "proper" meant something like "not designed to accomplish something Congress couldn't do directly." Still, the individual mandate wasn't imposed simply to get around a supposed limit on Congress's power (the limit, again, being that Congress couldn't regulate inactivity), but really was designed to implement the insurance regulations.

In retrospect, one scholar called Barnett one of law's most successful entrepreneurs of rhetoric because Barnett came up with a rhetorical maneuver that swept the field. Barnett had been a libertarian since college. After graduating from law school he became a prosecutor in Chicago, attracted to prosecution, he said, because criminals violated their victims' rights, and preventing rights violations was the government's only proper role. After a few years he moved into the legal academy, where he taught and wrote about contract law, the natural home for libertarian thinking because contract law involves thinking systematically about the agreements people voluntarily make with each other. He gradually moved toward constitutional law, eventually publishing an important compilation of articles on the Ninth Amendment and then a well-regarded book called *Restoring the Lost Constitution*. The "lost" Constitution was a Constitution with a strong libertarian presumption of liberty, which could be overcome only when the government's supporters could make a very strong showing that restricting one person's liberty was truly necessary to protect another's. As he put it, "originalism" meant that the quality goes in before the name goes on. He also produced a more focused originalist study compiling all the uses of the term "commerce" he could find during the framing period, which showed almost conclusively that during that period people used the word as part of a phrase, "manufacturing, commerce, and agriculture" (with "navigation" sometimes thrown in). That showed, Barnett argued, that as understood in 1789, the word "commerce" used in the Constitution didn't have the expansive meaning the Supreme Court had given it since the New Deal.

Barnett's great move was the broccoli argument. The conservative journalist Terence Jeffrey was apparently the first to bring broccoli into the discussion. I assume that Jeffrey came up with broccoli rather than, say, Brussels sprouts because he recalled President George H. W. Bush's statement that he never liked broccoli, and understood that the vegetable was an object of cultural disdain. If the government could make you buy health insurance, it could make you buy broccoli, Jeffrey said, and that was obviously ridiculous. Note, of course, that in this form the broccoli argument is clearly libertarian—it's *the government*, not Congress, that's the oppressor here. Romneycare is as vulnerable as Obamacare to the broccoli argument.

Barnett translated the libertarian objection into a federalism one. Rivkin and Casey had already restated their argument, and Senator Orrin Hatch of Utah used it at a hearing in October 2009. Barnett combined broccoli with Rivkin and Casey's argument about inactivity, in a paper published in December 2009, and the argument took off. Congress has the power to regulate "commerce," and "commerce" involves doing something. As long as you're just sitting around, you're not engaged in commerce. And it didn't matter that someday you might be involved in commerce—that is, that someday you might, indeed were almost certain to, use health care services for which insurance would pay if you had it. After all, if Congress could make you buy health insurance because someday you might actually use health care services, it could make you buy broccoli because someday you might buy some green vegetables.

This argument left Obamacare supporters in the legal academy sputtering. They focused on the obvious differences between health care insurance and broccoli. If you put off buying health care insurance until the moment you need it, the cost is going to be quite high (unless the government regulates the price of insurance). Indeed, at that moment you're not buying insurance, you're simply paying for health care. But lots of people aren't going to be able to afford to pay the full cost. We could be hardhearted and say, as law professor Andrew Koppleman put it in describing Barnett's approach, "Tough luck." That is, if you can't pay for health care when you need it, you're just not going to get treated. We're not that hardhearted, though, and so what we do is subsidize your health care through charity or government payments. Yet the money has to come from somewhere, and it comes from the people who do have health care insurance. That means that the price of health care insurance goes up because you didn't buy it for yourself. For Obamacare supporters, that's what made broccoli different from health care insurance: if you put off buying broccoli, the price of broccoli doesn't go up when you get around to buying it.*

Even more, Obamacare's supporters didn't see how the broccoli argument had anything to do with the constitutionality of the Affordable Care Act under the "necessary and proper" clause. Maybe, they said, "not buying insurance" was inactivity that Congress couldn't regulate, but even Barnett agreed that the insurance regulations—"guaranteed issue" and the like—were within Congress's power. The individual mandate was necessary for those regulations to be effective.

Barnett had to come up with something more. And he did. The individual mandate wasn't a "proper" means of implementing the insurance regulations. Why? In part, because the mandate was completely

---

* Technically, economists will say that the price will go up a tiny amount because, with a fixed supply of broccoli, your desire to buy it increases demand and broccoli suppliers will increase the price they charge. The price increase is likely to be small, of course, unlike the price increase for health care. Maybe more important, if it turns out that you can't afford the broccoli when you go to the market, we are going to say, "Tough luck," something we just won't say when health care is involved.

unprecedented. That wasn't enough, though, as Barnett acknowledged, because there's a first time for everything. Novelty alone doesn't tell you that a statute is "improper." Barnett added a libertarian component. The individual mandate wasn't proper because it worked a major change in the relation between Americans and their government, a change inconsistent with deep assumptions we've always held—as shown by the mandate's novelty.

Barnett's argument, when presented in full, is actually rather complicated. The broccoli metaphor is quite simple, and it captured the imagination of Republicans looking for a way to explain their constitutional objections to Obamacare. The nascent Tea Party took a return to what its members understood to be fundamental constitutional principles as one of their major planks. Believing Obamacare profoundly misguided, the Tea Party took the broccoli argument on board. Once enough Republicans accepted the broccoli argument, Jack Balkin said the argument moved from off the wall to "on the wall," though that metaphor really doesn't work well. Rather, an argument that had been off the wall was now on the table—not because of its intrinsic merits but because it had substantial support by an important political party.

With the argument now a credible one, judges—mostly Republican appointees—started paying attention. Federal judges Roger Vinson in Florida and Henry Hudson in Virginia bought it, with Judge Vinson expressly mentioning a minor variant on the broccoli argument. The argument was no longer frivolous. The federal court of appeals affirmed Judge Vinson's judgment, and the case headed for the Supreme Court.

THE COURT set aside three full days for oral argument in March 2012, more time devoted to any one problem than it had for decades. Aside from the issue's public importance, the reason was that the Court might have to decide a slew of issues. There was a hurdle right near the starting line. A federal statute, the Tax Injunction Act of 1867, says that you can't bring a lawsuit to prevent the government from collecting taxes (you're supposed to wait until the Internal Revenue Service asks you to pay, then pay, then sue for a refund). The individual mandate was administered by the IRS through a complicated new set of lines on income tax returns. But no one was going to have to fill out those forms until 2014. Maybe the challenges were premature. The Obama administration wanted the courts to decide that the statute was constitutional as quickly as possible, so it didn't raise this technical issue. And, of course, neither did the challengers. The Court appointed a private lawyer as amicus curiae (friend of the court) to argue that the Tax Injunction Act did bar the suits.

If the lawsuits got over that hurdle, there were a bunch of additional issues. The constitutional challenge focused on the individual mandate.

- Did Congress have the power to require people to buy health insurance or pay a penalty? Randy Barnett's argument was that Congress didn't have the power under the commerce clause to require it.
- Was the individual mandate a "necessary and proper" means of implementing the rules saying that health insurance companies had to offer insurance to people with "preexisting conditions" at the same rates they charged everyone else?
- Even if the Court agreed with Barnett, maybe Congress had the power to impose the penalty as a "tax." Yet, even if it did have *that* power, had Congress exercised it? Was the penalty really a tax because it was administered by the IRS?
- And, if it was a tax, another constitutional provision came into play. The Constitution says that Congress can't impose "direct" taxes— meaning, roughly, a tax of a specific amount levied on every individual—except in a way that Congress hadn't even tried to use. So, if the penalty was a tax, was it a direct tax? And, incidentally, if the penalty was a tax, why wasn't the lawsuit barred by the Tax Injunction Act?

- Then there was the Medicaid extension. Everyone agreed that Congress can make states do some things if they accept federal money, but the Supreme Court had said that these "conditions" placed on sending the states federal money couldn't "coerce" them into accepting the money, though it hadn't found any conditions actually coercive since the New Deal. Every state had accepted federal money to finance part of the Medicaid program. The ACA said that they would have to give up all that money if they didn't expand their Medicaid programs to cover a large new group of uninsured people. The act promised that the federal government would send a whole lot of additional money to pay for the expansion, but was the threat to take away the money it had already committed "coercive"?

- Finally, after all this, there was the question of "severability." The ACA had a lot of provisions other than the individual mandate and the Medicaid extension, some of which had something to do with health care, others of which were basically "sweeteners" designed to get the vote of one or another senator or representative. If the Court found the individual mandate unconstitutional, what would happen to all those other provisions? Could they be "severed"—cut loose from—the unconstitutional provision and still be legally effective? Or, if the ACA's core supporters wouldn't have voted for the sweeteners unless they got the individual mandate in return, should the sweeteners fall along with the individual mandate?

No surprise that the Court needed to hear hours of argument on the cases.

"A train wreck" for the Obama administration—that was the legal commentator Jeffrey Toobin's characterization of the oral arguments about the individual mandate. Solicitor General Donald Verrilli hadn't shown justices skeptical about the mandate a "limiting principle" they could invoke were they to uphold it. Verrilli stumbled over his words; his opponent Paul Clement was smooth and polished. Political scientists counted the number of questions asked each side—many more to Verrilli than to Clement—and pointed to studies showing that the side that has to answer more questions and interruptions tends to lose.

Actually, Verrilli did quite well. Tom Goldstein, who had started the influential SCOTUSblog, called both arguments brilliant. Verrilli had a frog in his throat when he started, but inside the courtroom that hardly mattered. And he had indeed offered a limiting principle—that markets for insurance are different from other markets. The next day, when Clement argued the Medicare part of the case, the liberal justices were loaded for bear. Justice Kagan let him say two sentences before she jumped in with a series of questions, ending with, "Now, suppose I'm an employer and I see somebody I really like and I want to hire that person. And I say I'm going to give you $10 million a year to come to work for me." When Clement refused to agree that "that's not coercive," Justice Kagan could only shake her head, "Wow, wow." Justice Stephen Breyer went after Clement's famed manner of arguing without notes. "Where does it say that?" he asked about a statutory provision Clement had described. Clement referred to a specific page in his brief. "And that cite section is what?" Justice Breyer asked. Clement: "I don't have that with me." Breyer: "Well, I have it in front of me." Clement: "Great. Perfect. Thank you." All in all, an embarrassing exchange for Clement.

What the oral arguments chiefly showed was that Justice Antonin Scalia wasn't at his best. Despite his well-known opposition to televising Supreme Court arguments, he seemed to be playing to the audience outside the Court, who would hear the oral arguments only hours after they finished. In the Medicare argument, he tried to develop a riff on "the old Jack Benny thing, Your Money or Your Life, and you know, he says, 'I'm thinking, I'm thinking.'" The riff was to say what if "the choice were your life or your wife's." Clement did his best to take the question seriously, but Scalia lost the thread of his own cleverness. Roberts tried to get him out of it by saying, "Let's leave the wife out of this," but Scalia kept going for another round before Roberts said firmly, "That's enough frivolity for a while."

Scalia tried something similar in the severability argument. He asked: "What happened to the Eighth Amendment [which prohibits cruel and unusual punishments]? You really want us to go through these 2,700 pages? And do you really expect the Court to do that? [Laughter] Or do you expect us to—to give this function to our law clerks?" A few moments later Justice Kagan picked up on the reference to law clerks: "For some people, we look only at the text. It should be easy for Justice Scalia's clerks. [Laughter]" Justice Scalia was offended: "I don't care whether it's easy for my clerks. I care about whether it's easy for me. [Laughter]" A justice in greater control of his cleverness would have let the sting pass.

Justice Scalia repeatedly went for sound bites reproducing common conservative talk radio lines. In the individual mandate argument, after the Chief Justice and Justice Samuel Alito had formulated serious questions about the reach of the government's arguments, Justice Scalia lowered the level of the discussion by asking the "broccoli" question (and then reverted to the point, no better when repeated, asking about mandatory car purchases). In the severability argument he felt compelled to introduce a serious question by invoking "the corn husker kickback," the provision singling Nebraska out for special treatment but not included in the statute (to make the question coherent, he had to introduce a non-existent "constitutional proscription of venality"). Again, it's trivially easy to come up with an example from the statute that raises the same question (Justice Breyer did it at, as usual, great length). And, finally, he went for "The President said it wasn't a tax" line—to which the U.S. Solicitor General had the good sense not to invoke Abraham Lincoln on how many legs a horse has ("How many legs does a horse have if you call its tail a leg?" "Four—calling it a leg doesn't make it a leg").

Liberals and conservatives started to prepare the battlefield they would fight on after the Court's decision. President Obama expressed confidence that "the Supreme Court will not take what would be an unprecedented, extraordinary step of overturning a law that was passed by a strong majority of a democratically elected Congress." Democratic senator Pat Leahy of Vermont said to the Senate, "I trust that [Chief Justice Roberts] will be a Chief Justice for all of us and that he has a strong institutional sense of the proper role of the judicial branch." Conservatives responded by attacking liberals for attempting to "intimidate" the Court.

Toobin captured the "gloom-and-doom" view of the oral argument among liberals and most constitutional scholars, who thought—not mistakenly—that existing case law made the mandate's constitutionality an easy question. Barnett and other conservatives started taking victory laps, with Barnett's version—basically, I told you my argument wasn't frivolous—the most temperate. Even President Obama seemed to agree that the arguments showed that the statute was in trouble. After a formal statement saying that he was confident the Court would uphold the mandate, he joked at the White House Correspondents' Dinner on April 28, "In my first term, we passed health care reform; in my second term, I guess I'll pass it again."

As JUSTICE Scalia is fond of saying about *Bush v. Gore*, a case that resembles the ACA decision in reverse, liberals who don't like parts of the Court's analysis and conservatives who don't like the Court's result in the ACA case should just get over it. But to understand the relation between politics and the Court, you have to have at least a short description of what the justices said at enormous length. The opinions total 187 pages. The Court's own summary, called "the Syllabus," runs to six. CNN and Fox News were embarrassed when they went on the air with the "breaking news" that the Court had held the

ACA unconstitutional, based on their reporters' reading only the first three pages of the Syllabus.

- *The Tax Injunction Act.* All nine justices agreed that the case wasn't barred by the Tax Injunction Act, because the individual mandate was enforced by a penalty, not a tax.
- *The commerce clause.* Five justices said that Congress didn't have the power under the commerce clause to regulate inactivity. Chief Justice Roberts devoted 12 pages to explaining his reasons for that conclusion. Justices Scalia, Kennedy, Thomas, and Alito delivered a "joint opinion," spending the same number of pages to lay out what was essentially the same argument. Justice Ginsburg wrote a long dissent, which the other liberals joined.
- *The necessary and proper clause.* Here too the conservative justices agreed on the result, but offered separate opinions. Chief Justice Roberts said that the individual mandate might be "necessary" to make sure that the regulations dealing with preexisting conditions and community rating would be effective, but it wasn't "proper," because—and here the opinion gets fuzzy—it was a novel approach and, if allowed, would "work a substantial expansion of federal authority." Justice Ginsburg replied that not all markets involved "moral hazard," so basic economics provided a limit to that expansion of authority.
- *Penalty or tax?* The individual mandate was enforced by a "Shared Responsibility Payment." Chief Justice Roberts wrote that the most natural reading of the provisions creating that mechanism was that it imposed a penalty on people who didn't have health insurance. But, he continued, judges should try to find plausible interpretations of statutes that would make the statutes constitutional. And, he argued, you could plausibly interpret the provisions to impose a tax. The four liberals agreed with the bottom line here, though not the

interpretation that was needed to get around finding the individual mandate unconstitutional. The other conservatives' joint opinion said that it wasn't even plausible to say that the payment was a tax.

- *The tax power.* Roberts and the liberals agreed Congress could impose the individual mandate through the tax power, so the ACA survived. From the point of view of ordinary citizens, who cared about whether the ACA would take effect or not, this was the central holding, even though the Chief Justice at least backed into it through an odd route. The conservatives' joint opinion didn't address the tax power because they didn't think that the ACA imposed a tax.

- *Direct tax?* Roberts's opinion concluded that the tax the ACA imposed wasn't a direct tax. The other conservatives noted that that issue had barely been noticed during the arguments, and shouldn't be resolved so casually.

- *The Medicaid extension.* Seven justices agreed that Congress went too far when it threatened states that they would lose all their Medicaid funds if they didn't extend Medicaid to a substantially larger population. At the oral argument, Justice Breyer had struggled to come up with some way to limit the threat of taking away all Medicaid funding, and he ended up agreeing with the Chief Justice. Perhaps acting diplomatically, and seeing that the Medicaid extension was going to be struck down anyway, so did Justice Kagan. Dissenting Justices Ginsburg and Sotomayor argued that when states agreed to accept the core Medicaid funding years ago, they had also agreed to accept "modifications" in the program, and that the Medicaid expansion in the ACA was just such a modification. The Chief Justice responded that the expansion was so large that it amounted to a "new" program, not a modification of the existing one.

- *Severability.* The conservatives' joint opinion would have held that the individual mandate and the Medicaid extension couldn't be cut out of the ACA, leaving its other provisions intact; rather, none of the ACA's provisions should take effect. Justices Breyer and Kagan joined Roberts's opinion on severability. When you looked at the set of votes, the only thing a majority of the Court held unconstitutional was the Medicaid extension, and the reason for that was that Congress's threat to the states was too big. So, the Chief Justice wrote, you could salvage everything by severing only the threat: states could extend Medicaid if they wanted to, but they wouldn't lose their existing Medicaid funding if they didn't. Everything else in the ACA survived.

The outcome showed that drawing inferences from oral arguments is hazardous. True, a majority of the Court bought the broccoli argument and held that Congress didn't have the power—under the commerce clause—to impose the individual mandate. But despite the tenor of the oral argument seven justices, including Justices Breyer and Kagan, held that threatening states with the withdrawal of all federal Medicaid funds was unconstitutionally coercive. And, from out of left field, Chief Justice Roberts and the Court's liberals upheld the individual mandate as an exercise of Congress's power to impose taxes. The Obama administration had made the tax power argument, more or less, in its briefs, and it was made more clearly by some of the amicus briefs. Solicitor General Verrilli spent a fair amount of time in his oral argument defending the individual mandate as a tax. But, as the conservative dissenters pointed out, the administration had said almost nothing to explain why the mandate wasn't a "direct" tax. Barnett might well have felt that the Chief Justice had sent them down the rabbit hole, accepting the arguments he and others had devoted so much time to developing but then coming up with something completely unexpected to take their victory away from them.

And, even more, Roberts's opinion began by holding that the Tax Injunction Act didn't block the lawsuit at the outset. But if the mandate imposed a tax, how on earth was it possible to say that the Court could reach the merits—it's a statute called the *Tax* Injunction Act, after all. Roberts said, "Well, there's a difference between a statute and the Constitution. Congress can say that something isn't a tax for purposes of the Tax Injunction Act, but can also say that it's a tax for purposes of figuring out whether we have the power to enact the thing." Charles Dickens's Mr. Bumble gave the classic non-lawyer's response to that sort of thing: "If the law supposes that . . . the law is a ass."

WHAT HAD happened? Well before the decision was announced, rumors circulated within informed circles about the outcome: that the Court had decided to strike down the Medicaid extension (true, sort of), and that it had voted to strike down the individual mandate (probably true at the time the rumors were circulating). After the decision rumors became "leaks," Jan Crawford reported, as the headline on her story on CBS News put it, that "Roberts Switched Views to Uphold Health Care Law." And she followed up, "Conservatives feel a sense of betrayal. They feel that Roberts changed his mind for the wrong reasons."

Speculation broke out over who Crawford's source was. Few observers began their analysis by asking who had an interest in leaking information, and in leaking this particular version of the story about what happened. Crawford had good sources on the conservative side of the Court, developed when she reported and then wrote a book on Bush's nominations to the Court. It would have been an extraordinary breach of confidentiality for a justice to have leaked the information to her, although if passions were high, maybe one of them did. The other possibility is that the leak came from a law clerk, most likely a conservative law clerk. That too would be a breach of confidentiality, but at the end of June when the leak occurred the law clerks were halfway out the door and didn't have to worry, as the justices did, about maintaining good relations inside the Court over the long run. Some conservative law clerks had the right combination of interests and knowledge to be plausible candidates for "source."

At this point no one outside the Court knows whether Roberts really did "switch his views," nor—if he did—why. But I'm going to offer some speculations, based not on any inside knowledge about what happened in the ACA cases but rather on a long time spent watching the Court. I'm going to argue, perhaps surprisingly, that Chief Justice Roberts probably never "changed" his mind, but rather "made up" his mind. His opinion upholding the ACA on tax power grounds—and finding it outside Congress's commerce power—expressed his best judgment about what the law as he understood it required. He called it as he saw it: one ball and one strike.

The argument has a lot of moving parts, combining general features of the opinion-writing process with features specific to the ACA case.

First comes the fluidity of opinions. The justices meet at "the Conference," as they call it, shortly after they've heard oral arguments. The Conference is completely private. If someone has to get in touch with a justice for some urgent reason, the message is sent to a member of the Court's staff sitting outside the closed door of the Conference Room; he or she knocks on the door; the junior justice—now Justice Kagan—goes to the door, takes the message inside, and hands it to its recipient. The justices talk about the cases they have to decide. How much they talk varies a lot. As Chief Justice, William Rehnquist was something like a military drill sergeant, getting each justice to say what he or she thought in a sentence or two, then moving on to add up the votes and see who "won" the case. Chief Justice Roberts reportedly runs the Conference with a somewhat lighter hand, but no one has reported that the justices really try to persuade each other to move away from their initial views. The Conference ends with an informal but usually reasonably stable vote on what the outcome is going to be.

Next comes the task of assigning opinions—figuring out which justice is going to write which majority opinions. The Chief Justice gets to assign the opinion if he is in the majority. If he isn't, the senior associate justice in the majority—these days, usually Anthony Kennedy—makes the assignment. The Chief Justice's assignments are mildly limited by a loose and informal set of guidelines: If possible, try to give each justice at least one majority opinion from each two-week session of arguments, and, again if possible, try to work things out so that by the end of the term each justice will have written the same number of majority opinions. These guidelines also influence assignments by the senior associate justice, but even more loosely.*

The justice assigned the majority opinion then gets down to work drafting it, aided by a small personal staff of law clerks. The law clerks tend to do more initial drafting as the term goes on, because "their" justice gets to know how able—and reliable—they are. As the term winds down, drafting pressures increase. Opinions have to be circulated in time for any dissenters to respond with their own arguments. The dissenters can of course start writing their opinions right away. They know what their own positions are, and they are sometimes pretty sure they know the general lines the majority opinion is going to take. But dissents typically aren't finished until the majority opinion is circulated within the Court. And, again, timing matters. The justices expect the Court to rise for the summer at the end of June. A majority opinion circulated in mid-May can leave the dissenters with a very short time to respond, particularly in a case as complex as the ACA.†

But—and I think this is key to understanding what happened in the ACA case—the votes taken at the Conference, which are the basis for the opinion assignments, are only tentative. Each justice can

---

* The senior associate justice almost inevitably has fewer opinions to assign, and so is less able to determine whether a particular assignment fits into the overall pattern of equality that guides the Chief Justice.

† The fact that the law clerks have to work hard and fast when opinions are circulated late or responses have to be written quickly in reply to such opinions may have some bearing on how the Court's leakers characterized what happened. Annoyed law clerks might have characterized reactions by the conservative justices more sharply than was actually warranted.

switch from supporting the defendant to supporting the government in a criminal case, for example. And, importantly, even the justice who is assigned the majority opinion can "change sides." In 1992 the Court decided a case involving the delivery of a religious invocation and benediction at a high school graduation ceremony. At the Conference the Court divided five to four over whether the practice was an "establishment of religion" that violated the Constitution. Anthony Kennedy was what political scientists call the "least persuaded" justice in the majority—the justice closest to the middle. Chief Justices sometimes make strategic opinion assignments to the least persuaded justice, both in the hope that the justice's position will firm up in the process of drafting an opinion, and to make sure that the draft is moderate enough to keep the least persuaded on board with the majority's result. Chief Justice Rehnquist made a strategic assignment of the graduation prayer case to Justice Kennedy. But, as Kennedy put it, as he worked on an opinion allowing the prayer, it "looked quite wrong" when put down on paper. So he circulated a draft opinion finding the prayer unconstitutional—changing the result.

John Roberts himself described the "decisional process" as "very fluid." Speaking to law students in February 2005, and describing his experience as a court of appeals judge, he said: "It is not unusual in my experience to have one view of the case when you finish reading the briefs, a different view . . . when you debate it with your clerks, another view . . . after oral arguments, and you're back again at a different view after the conference. . . . Then as you go through the writing process, you come up with either the original view, a third view [or] the second view."

My best judgment is that something like that happened to Chief Justice Roberts in the ACA case, with one tweak. Having focused on Barnett's commerce clause argument, he went into the oral argument inclined to think that the ACA was unconstitutional, and nothing in the argument or in the justices' discussion at the Conference changed his mind. So he tentatively voted to strike the ACA down. He knew that the tax power argument was rattling around in the case, but—I think—he wasn't sure what he thought about it. The justices all agreed that the individual mandate wasn't a tax for purposes of the Tax Injunction Act, and maybe Roberts thought that was going to be enough to solve the constitutional problem as well. So, I think that he probably indicated that he didn't think that the tax power argument was going to save the ACA.

Walking out of the Conference, all the justices probably thought that the vote was five to four to strike the statute down, in an opinion centering on the commerce clause. Justice Ginsburg certainly did because, as she said later, she immediately began to work on the opinion she published as a dissent from the conclusion reached by five justices that the ACA wasn't within Congress's power to regulate interstate commerce. According to Crawford, the justices expected that Roberts would circulate his proposed opinion by June 1.

As I've indicated, after the Conference the next step is assigning the opinion. If I'm right, Chief Justice Roberts was in the majority, and so had the power to assign the opinion. As commentators had been saying all along, the case was so important that Roberts would almost certainly assign the opinion to himself if he was in the majority. He and his law clerks got to work.

But on what exactly? The cases were argued at the end of March, leaving a relatively short time for opinion writing. And there were a number of issues to deal with. Here my speculations are rather less grounded. My guess is that the Chief Justice decided to parcel out the issues. He would take the Tax Injunction Act issue and the tax issue. My guess is, he asked Justice Kennedy to draft the portion of the opinion dealing with the commerce clause.*

---

* I can't even speculate on how he might have parceled out the other issues, such as the Medicaid expansion and severability. If I'm right, eventually we'll find out who wrote which parts of the "joint dissent."

Why Justice Kennedy? Here we enter the realm of modern Krem-linology—deriving what happened inside the Court from manifes-tations only the truly obsessive pay attention to. The week before the Court heard argument in the ACA cases, it heard argument in two cases challenging the constitutionality of requiring that defendants who committed murder when they were juveniles be sentenced to life imprisonment without the possibility of parole. Along with gay rights, juvenile sentencing was one of Justice Kennedy's signature issues. He had written the Court's opinions holding it unconstitutional to impose the death penalty on those who committed murder when they were juveniles, and holding life without parole unconstitutional for juveniles who committed violent crimes other than murder. The Chief Justice ended up voting to uphold mandatory life without parole for juvenile murderers, which means that Justice Kennedy almost certainly had the power to assign the opinion. But instead of taking it for himself, he assigned the opinion to Justice Kagan. One reason might have been that he expected to be writing something substantial in the ACA case, either for himself alone or as part of a majority.

The suggestion that the Chief Justice parceled out the issues gets some modest support from the structure of the joint dissent. The con-servative dissenters offer an extensive analysis of the commerce clause question, which certainly reads as if it had been prepared as a majority opinion. And, if they started working only on June 1, when they learned what Roberts's opinion looked like, they and their law clerks would have had to work really hard to get the joint dissent done by the end of the month.

The conservatives had an extensive discussion of the Medicaid exten-sion and severability. Of course, Roberts's opinion deals with the Med-icaid extension and severability. But he *had* to write something about those issues, because he needed to write the opinion in a way that would keep Justices Breyer and Kagan on board.

What did Roberts circulate in early June? I think it was an opinion pretty much like the one he ended up publishing. That's what surprised the Court's conservatives.* They had expected an opinion saying that the individual mandate was a penalty, not a tax. That opinion would be combined with the other portions being written in the other conservatives' chambers to produce a comprehensive treatment of all the issues. Instead, they got a full-scale opinion, reaching the conclusion they had all agreed on about the commerce clause but saying, to their dismay, that the statute could be construed to impose a tax, and if so construed it was constitutional.

The weakness in my argument involves Roberts's treatment of the commerce clause. Maybe he included his discussion hoping that the other conservatives would go along with the tax power argument, and then his opinion would carry the whole Court on the tax power and maybe even the Medicaid expansion. If so, it was a risky calculation, in part because (on my theory) Roberts would be throwing the work the other justices had done into the garbage can. But maybe I'm wrong in thinking that Roberts divvied up the issues. Maybe he thought he was writing a full-scale opinion for the majority. That too would explain why he discussed the commerce clause.

Jan Crawford has a different account, as does another commentator, the law professor Paul Campos. According to Crawford and her sources, when the other conservative justices discovered in late May or early June that Roberts was writing to uphold the ACA's constitutionality under the tax power, they "deliberately ignored Roberts' decision, . . . as if they were no longer even willing to engage with him in debate." All I can say about that is that it sounds pretty childish to me—something that a youngish law clerk might say, but not the way grown-ups behave. Campos quotes "a source within the court with direct knowledge of the drafting process" as saying that "most of the material

---

* The conservative commentator Ramesh Ponnuru on June 2 stated that he had heard from inside the Court that the initial vote was five to four, but that the Chief Justice "seems to be going a little bit wobbly."

in the first three quarters of the joint dissent was drafted in Chief Justice Roberts' chambers in April and May." That could be: Roberts circulates an opinion dealing with the commerce clause and the tax power; the other conservatives like what he says about the former and hate what he says about the latter; they cut-and-paste his commerce clause discussion into the joint dissent, and have the time to develop their criticisms of his surprising position on the tax power. The problem, though, is to explain why Roberts would then write something new about the commerce clause: Why not say, "Gee, I agree with the joint dissenters on the commerce clause; indeed, it sounds almost like something I could have written"? It's rare when one justice simply appropriates the words of another, but it does happen, and most of the time the true author leaves the plagiarism unmentioned. Not to parse phrasings of leaks too closely, Campos also says that his source "insists that the claim that the joint dissent was drafted from scratch in June is flatly untrue." Now, *that* could be right—after all, that's my claim too.

Finally, there's bargaining among the justices. After one justice circulates a draft, the others have a chance to respond. Mostly they just sign off, with a brief "I agree" or, using the Court's jargon, "Join me." Sometimes they suggest minor changes in phrasing. Some phrases in the joint dissent clearly come from Justice Scalia, for example. Its overall style seems to me Justice Kennedy's, though. And sometimes they actually try to change something substantial in the draft.

According to Crawford, that's what happened in the ACA case. My argument is that Roberts didn't "change" his mind on anything, because that phrase suggests that he had made up his mind one way and then changed it. Instead, I think that Roberts made up his mind for the first time, or substituted a different conclusion for the one he had tentatively—and clearly only tentatively—reached after the oral argument. Crawford said that the exchanges between Roberts and Kennedy were particularly intense, with Kennedy "relentless" and with some "arm-twisting" going on. The language is dramatic but almost certainly overstated. Lyndon Johnson might be able to twist arms by threatening a senator that he'd stop spending on a project the senator favored, but what can one justice do to another? Just give reasons and arguments. So, presumably, Justice Kennedy tried to persuade Roberts that Roberts's effort to describe the individual mandate's penalty provision as a tax just didn't make sense, and Roberts tried to persuade Kennedy that the commitment they both had to judicial restraint supported what he had written.

In the end, of course, no one seems to have budged.

All this raises some additional questions. For example, why has the "changed his mind" story taken hold? The answer might be simple: The story has legs because it's true. I've argued that it isn't. If I'm right, the question I've posed here may be interesting.

One reason the story that Roberts changed his mind has legs is that it's simple. That's not a virtue, though, when we're dealing with complicated issues of personal decision making within institutions dealing with complex matters. No one writing about foreign policy would think it enough to say, "The Secretary of State changed her mind," without giving a much thicker description of the information she had, the bureaucratic pressures she faced, and more. References to "pressure" from President Obama and Senator Leahy get you somewhere, but not far.

Another reason "Roberts changed his mind" has some appeal is that both conservatives and liberals like it. Conservatives like it because they treat what Obama and Leahy did not as preparing the battlefield for the days after the decision came down but more like working the refs. It was "low" politics, and it worked. That shows why the Chief Justice was wrong when he changed his mind. He succumbed to the worst kind of politics aimed at influencing the Supreme Court. In a sense, for conservatives the "changed his mind" story is a continuation of their efforts to work the refs, this time treating the American people as the referees in a contest over respect for the Supreme Court.

Liberals like the story because it helps them with an argument they've been making against conservatives who insist that politics should never affect the Supreme Court. For liberals, politics in the large should matter. Justices should be chosen for the larger visions they hold of the Constitution's meaning and its relation to short-term and long-term politics. If the Chief Justice changed his mind because he came to a greater appreciation of the impact on the Court's ongoing role in American political life were the Court to strike the ACA down, that's all to the good. It showed how "high" politics can work.

A YOUNG Harvard law student, and Federalist Society leader, Joel Alicea, has written one of the most insightful comments on the differences among the Court's conservatives. Alicea described two traditions of conservative thought about judicial restraint. The older tradition held that judges should exercise self-restraint so that legislatures could give their constituents the policies the constituents wanted. As Alicea put it, "judicial restraint used to mean that a judge should bend over backwards to avoid striking down a law." Judges should step in, not when they thought those policies were mistaken, and not even when they thought that there were decent arguments that the policies violated the Constitution, but only when it was absolutely clear that the policies violated the Constitution—"palpably unauthorized by law," as one judge put it in 1905. Alicea quoted Roberts citing a case from 1883, " 'Proper respect for a co-ordinate branch of the government' requires that we strike down an Act of Congress only if 'the lack of constitutional authority to pass [the] act in question is clearly demonstrated.' "

Another doctrine embedded in this older tradition ended up playing a key role in the ACA decision. The doctrine is called "the avoidance of constitutional questions," and it comes in two versions. The older version says that if the most natural reading of a statute makes it unconstitutional, a judge should look for a plausible alternative reading that makes the statute constitutional. The newer version says that if the most natural reading *might* make the statute unconstitutional, a judge should avoid deciding the constitutional question if there's a plausible alternative reading that makes the statute constitutional.

Roberts linked the "avoidance" doctrine to the older tradition of judicial restraint in the first paragraphs of his opinion: "It is not our job to protect the people from the consequences of their political choices." Unless they really have to, judges shouldn't displace policy choices the people and their representatives made through the statutes Congress enacts. And—this is important—the traditional idea of conservative judicial restraint took into account the fact that legislators don't pay much attention to the constitutional basis for what they do. They just want the policy, and if there's some basis in the Constitution for getting it, that's all that matters to them. The doctrine about interpreting statutes to make them constitutional followed from this: Congress as the people's representative wanted the policy embodied in the ACA, and judges should let the policy go into force if there was some plausible way to do so. This older tradition lives on at Senate confirmation hearings. Senators use the language of judicial activism and restraint when they criticize Supreme Court decisions like *Roe v. Wade* for keeping a majority of the American people from having restrictions on the availability of abortion that, they contend, a large majority wants.

Activists in the conservative legal movement—such as the lawyers who pushed the Court to strike down strict gun regulations—regard the senators' language as quite naive, though perhaps good enough for mere politicians. They created a different tradition. For the political scientist Keith Whittington, the older tradition was not restraint but "passivism." The newer tradition defined restraint as holding the judges' own impulses in check. Rather than focusing on majority rule, it focused on the possibility of judicial overreaching. Judges should always be aware that they might come up with constitutional interpretations that were congenial to their policy preferences. The way to avoid that was to look to some objective sources for constitutional interpretation. Alicea located an effective statement of the position, again by Whittington: the newer approach "requires deference only to the Constitution and to the limits of human knowledge, not to contemporary politicians."

The two traditions weren't unrelated, but they differed in emphasis. Though the newer one focused on keeping judges' impulses in check, the reason for worrying about judges' impulses was a concern that judges following their instincts would deny the people the power to make their own choices. The older tradition emphasized letting the people get what they wanted as often as possible; the newer one emphasized that the Constitution sometimes really did stand in the way of what the people wanted.

Chief Justice Roberts invoked both traditions of judicial restraint in the first paragraphs of his opinion in the ACA case. The first tradition: "Members of this Court are vested with the authority to interpret the law; we possess neither the expertise nor the prerogative to make policy judgments. Those decisions are entrusted to our Nation's elected leaders, who can be thrown out of office if the people disagree with them." And in his opinion's concluding words: "But the Court does not express any opinion on the wisdom of the Affordable Care Act. Under the Constitution, that judgment is reserved to the people." The second tradition: "Our deference in matters of policy cannot, however, become abdication in matters of law. . . . Our respect for Congress's policy judgments . . . can never extend so far as to disavow restraints on federal power that the Constitution carefully constructed. . . . And there can be no question that it is the responsibility of this Court to enforce the limits on federal power by striking down acts of Congress that transgress those limits."

The difficulty, of course, is figuring out when restraint in the newer sense should take over for restraint in the older one. As the Chief Justice saw the matter, the constitutional limits on Congress's power to regulate commerce and to impose conditions on spending were completely clear, bringing the newer tradition of judicial restraint into play; it would have been willful, not lawful, to find that Congress had the power to impose the individual mandate under the commerce clause. But it also would have been willful to strike it down under the tax power, because there the legal arguments weren't nearly as clear (in the Chief Justice's eyes).

Roberts's experience in the Reagan administration and then in conservative legal circles shaped the way he thought about the issues in the ACA case. As Joel Alicea pointed out, Roberts had absorbed the rhetoric of judicial restraint as meaning leaving things to democratic majorities. One place where that rhetoric had bite was on federalism issues. Those issues have two faces. One deals with congressional power; that was what the ACA involved. When you say that Congress doesn't have the power to regulate, from a federalism point of view the second face emerges. You're saying, "But the states—or more precisely, the people in the states, acting through the legislatures and governors they elected—do."

The Reagan administration's commitment to federalism was a commitment to democratic decision making on the state and local level. And, importantly, it focused almost exclusively on the commerce clause. Its playbook, the Justice Department publication on *The Constitution in the Year 2000*, dealt with the commerce clause and the spending power, and said nothing about the tax power. Coming to the ACA case, Roberts had a firm intellectual grounding in both versions of conservative judicial restraint. At the level of detail, though, conservatives had good intellectual resources when they thought about the commerce clause, and basically none when they had to think about the tax power. The other version of judicial restraint—let majorities do what they vote for—was fully developed, and weighed against the vacuum in dealing with the tax power. Conservative legal theorists were fond of saying, "You can't beat something with nothing," and perhaps that's how

Roberts saw the tax power argument: something—judicial restraint as deference to majorities—on one side, and nothing on the other.

The way the constitutional challenge to the ACA arose matters here. Snarkily: Roberts came out of the Reagan-Bush Justice Department; the challenge to the ACA came out of nowhere—or, out of the Tea Party. More substantively: legal conservatives were committed to federalism. Republicans in Congress hated Obamacare. The latter found some legal conservatives willing to pursue a federalism-based challenge to Obamacare through the broccoli argument even though that argument doesn't really get its rhetorical force from federalism. The argument wasn't exactly made up for the sole purpose of defeating Obamacare, but the distinction between activity and inactivity on which it rested hadn't been a substantial element in conservative rhetoric about federalism until Obamacare. The argument gained traction because it fit into the politics of the day. But in the conservative discourse about Obamacare, the only discussion of the tax power was, basically, that even President Obama didn't defend it as a tax. Put another way, the broccoli argument had become embedded in the wider discourse of legal conservatism and federalism, but nothing similar had happened in connection with the tax power. If Roberts thought that judicial restraint counseled caution in striking legislation down, he might have thought as well that rejecting the tax argument would provide support for the view, which he certainly rejected, that legal conservatism was simply a fig leaf for doing what the Republican Party at the moment wanted done.

Yet the Court's other conservatives emerged from the same intellectual background, and they obviously didn't see the problem in the same terms. Either legal conservatism was a wider movement than they appear to have thought, or Roberts saw some things differently.

One of the things Roberts saw differently was the judicial role in interpreting statutes to avoid constitutional problems. Most of the time when judges have to decide whether a statute is constitutional, figuring out what the statute means is the easy part, doing the constitutional analysis the hard part. The Stolen Valor Act of 2005 (chapter 6) said that it was a crime to claim falsely that you had received a military award. The words alone seem to make it a crime for an actor to play a character who says, "I won the Medal of Honor," because the actor didn't. Judges don't interpret statutes that way. They give them their most natural readings. Then they decide whether the statute is constitutional. Chief Justice Roberts said that the most natural reading of the provision imposing a "penalty" for not having health insurance—the way the individual mandate was enforced—was that it directly regulated what people could do. As a regulation, its only justification could be the commerce clause. And, the Chief Justice said, Congress couldn't impose a penalty on people who merely did not have health insurance, because it couldn't regulate inactivity.

Roberts used the older version of the "avoidance" doctrine in the ACA case. It wasn't the first time. He and Justice Alito used it in an early case, and his first stab in *Citizens United* used it as well, though there he abandoned the effort when no one else would go along. The Chief Justice used the newer version in his first year. In the elegantly named *NAMUDNO* case (Northwest Austin Municipal Utility District No. One), the constitutionality of the Voting Rights Act was at stake.* Conservative legal activists had made the act one of their most important targets; liberals treated it as an unassailable legacy of the civil rights movement. The Chief Justice managed to get everyone but Justice Clarence Thomas to agree on a single opinion. He gave the conservatives a sympathetic rendering of the case against the act's constitutionality, and the liberals a result they could live with. How? By using the doctrine of avoiding constitutional questions through interpreting a statute.

---

* Technically, the constitutionality of extending the lifetime of the act in 2006 for another twenty-five years.

The task wasn't easy in *NAMUDNO*. The act deals with state and local rules in several states with a history of racial discrimination in voting. With an elected board of directors, the municipal utility provided several forms of services around Austin, Texas, one of the covered states. One important provision requires all governing bodies in covered states to get permission—called "preclearance"—from the Department of Justice for changes in their voting rules. Congress eventually came to understand that preclearance for every rule didn't always make sense. Sometimes cities and towns stopped discriminating long ago, and getting preclearance was a pointless burden. So Congress adopted a "bailout" provision letting a "political subdivision" eliminate the preclearance obligation by getting a court to find as a matter of fact that it hadn't engaged in racial discrimination for a long time. *NAMUDNO* had an even stronger case against preclearance: created in 1987, it hadn't existed when Congress included Texas as a covered state in 1965, and no one contended that there had ever been any racial discrimination in voting for its board.

All well and good, but *NAMUDNO* ran up against the precise terms used in the statute to define "political subdivision." In the provision creating the bailout, the term is defined in these words: "any county or parish, . . . [and] any other subdivision of a State which conducts registration for voting." *NAMUDNO* wasn't a county or parish, of course, and it didn't register voters either, relying instead on the state's general registration process. The natural reading of the statute would lead to the conclusion that *NAMUDNO* couldn't use the "bailout" provision. Chief Justice Roberts reached into some of the Court's cases interpreting other provisions of the Voting Rights Act using the words "political subdivisions," and found language that let him say that any subdivision could invoke the bailout provision. So, the definition in other provisions displaced the specific definition in the bailout provision. Pretty creative, but consistent with the doctrine about interpreting statutes to avoid finding them unconstitutional.

After the first year some observers treated *NAMUDNO* as a case illustrating Roberts's ability to bridge ideological differences within the Court—an act of statesmanship, a term that came up again after the ACA case. But put it together with all the cases I've mentioned, and it begins to look as if the idea of interpreting statutes so that they are constitutional is a fundamental principle of Roberts's approach to constitutional interpretation.

The Chief Justice's argument in the ACA case didn't stretch the statute's language nearly as much as he had in *NAMUDNO*. Here's how the argument went. Treated as a penalty, the enforcement mechanism made the ACA unconstitutional. But, he said, you *could* read the enforcement mechanism to be a tax. It was enforced by the Internal Revenue Service, for example, and once the mandate took effect, there would be a line on tax returns asking whether you had health insurance. The government estimated that it would collect about $4 billion a year from people who didn't have health insurance. The Chief Justice agreed that treating the penalty as a tax wasn't the most natural reading of the ACA, but the doctrine about avoiding holding statutes unconstitutional if you could interpret them the right way required only that the reading be plausible. And, he said, it was.

Invoking older conservative ideas about judicial restraint, then, Chief Justice Roberts found that the ACA was unconstitutional when you gave the enforcement mechanism its most natural reading, that you could plausibly read the enforcement mechanism as imposing a tax, and then, anticlimactically, when you read the enforcement mechanism as imposing a tax the ACA was constitutional.* His conservative colleagues on the Court agreed with the first point, vehemently disagreed with the second, and so didn't have to say anything about the third.

Why, then, did Chief Justice Roberts vote the way he did?

---

* Even more anticlimactically, the Chief Justice went on to hold that, treated as a tax, the "penalty" wasn't a direct tax prohibited by the Constitution.

Commentators from the left and the right agreed on the explanation for his position. He was being a statesman. For liberals, that was praiseworthy: Roberts protected the Court from the charge that its conservatives were simply the mouthpieces for whatever positions the Republican Party happened to hold. His action interrupted the sequence that liberals feared: from *Bush v. Gore* to *Citizens United* to the ACA case, all decided along ordinary partisan lines.

For conservatives, judges who tried to be statesmen were abandoning the judicial role. Judges were supposed to interpret the Constitution, period. Trying to protect their institution from criticism wasn't part of their duty. Conservatives also emphasized the narrative they had begun to develop before the decision. Democrats from President Obama on down had made statements suggesting that they would try to do something bad to the Court—if only make it an issue in the 2012 elections—if the Court held the ACA unconstitutional. For conservatives, far from being a statesman, the Chief Justice had caved in to those threats.

Maybe upholding the ACA was statesmanlike because it showed that the Court wasn't a narrowly partisan body. Maybe striking it down would have been statesmanlike because it would have showed that the Court could resist threats. Maybe upholding the ACA was bad statesmanship because it damaged the Court's reputation among conservatives who—perhaps—were going to take over the presidency and the Senate in a few months. Maybe striking it down would have been good statesmanship because it would have forced both parties to come together to design a health insurance program that could have broad public support. Who knows?

Conservative observers of the Court were outraged at Roberts's bottom line. One fulminated against the "awful" performance of Republican presidents in appointing conservatives with spine. They didn't get over their defeat. Legal challenges to the core of the ACA persisted: now that we knew that the ACA rested on Congress's power to impose taxes, did it violate the constitutional requirement that "Bills for raising Revenue" originate in the House of Representatives? In states that didn't set up health care insurance "exchanges," you could go to a national exchange, but would you get favorable tax treatment if you did? A small provision—at least as part of the entire package—attracted the most attention, when corporations run by people with religious objections to contraceptive services said that requiring them to provide their employees with insurance covering such services violated their rights to religious liberty. But the big constitutional fight was over.

Conservatives had made "No more Souters" a rallying cry in the nomination process, and yet Roberts seemed to have turned out to be another David Souter in the case that conservative legal activists thought would set constitutional limits on liberal reforms. And, of course, the fact that the four other conservative justices took a different course showed that conservative legal thinking didn't dictate what Roberts did.

Yet part of the conservative lament about Roberts clearly misunderstood the politics of judicial appointments. Obamacare wasn't on the horizon when the Bush administration picked John Roberts for the Supreme Court. If the judge-pickers had tried to find out what Roberts thought, they'd get something general about "too much power in Congress over the states," with some allusions to the commerce clause, but nothing about the tax power. The judge-pickers were awful only because they didn't anticipate how the Republican Party's positions would change—or because they didn't look for someone who would be a partisan hack who would read the morning papers to find out what the Republican Party leadership thought and then write that into the Constitution.

What the judge-pickers were looking for was someone whose approach to constitutional interpretation was likely over the long run to generate results consistent with the views of important constituencies within the Republican Party. The ACA decision aside, that's certainly

what they got with John Roberts—notwithstanding the inevitable resonance of that sentence with the joke about the question to Abraham
Lincoln's wife, "That aside, Mrs. Lincoln, how was the play?"

Justices Scalia and Kennedy saw the issues one way. Chief Justice
Roberts saw them differently. From his vantage point, he wasn't being
a conservative or a statesman. He was being an umpire who called balls
and strikes.

Finally, it's worth thinking about the possibility that the Obamacare
decision is something of a blip despite the intense attention it attracted
in 2012. Justices know that politicians come and go, but they have life
tenure and are going to be there for a long time. They can have a longer
"time horizon" than politicians who worry about the next election. Even
if we treat John Roberts as a politician in robes, we have to think about
what he wants to achieve over the course of his career. Here, too, the
assumption that he wants to promote Republican goals over the long
term wouldn't tell him—or us—what he should do.

Judicial conservatives nurtured in the Reagan-Bush era and located
in the Federalist Society's intellectual universe care about a package of
issues. The most important are campaign finance reform (they think it's
unconstitutional), the Voting Rights Act (ditto), and affirmative action
(ditto again). These are long-standing matters of interest in conservative
legal circles. Obamacare is basically a blip. It happened to matter a lot
in 2012, but no conservative legal thinker had devoted much time to
developing arguments against national mandates to individuals until
Obamacare came along. Conservative legal thinkers did care about
federalism in some vague and general sense, but no one had a good
sense of what that meant in specific cases.

Continue with the assumption that John Roberts was just a Republican politician in robes. What should he do in the Obamacare case,
taking the long view? As with the short-term view, the answer is, Who
knows (including John Roberts)? A Republican politician in robes
could think that electoral demographics were trending against his

party. Anybody alert to news reports and blogs knew the argument that Republicans were permanently alienating the growing bloc of Hispanic voters, and polling in early 2012 seemed to confirm that. From that analysis, the politician in robes could think that in the long run Roberts's colleagues were going to be appointed by Democratic presidents. He and his conservative colleagues might as well take their best shot while they had it—invalidating Obamacare, getting rid of affirmative action, gutting the Voting Rights Act.

Or they might hold their fire, conserving their resources for issues more deeply entrenched in their intellectual universe. The Democrats were setting up their story about the Court even in 2012. *Bush v. Gore* and *Citizens United* were already part of that story. Its narrative line was that partisan Republicans on the Supreme Court were acting as politicians who took their job to be preventing Democrats from implementing policies at their platform's heart. Striking affirmative action down and limiting the Voting Rights Act would slip easily into that narrative. No one, Democrats would say, could think that John Roberts was simply calling balls and strikes when everything he did favored Republicans and hurt Democrats.

Why should our imagined Republican politicians in robes care whether that narrative took hold? Again, because of the long-term view. They would want their decisions to have some staying power—some legal and moral resonance even when the Court had a majority of justices appointed by Democrats. The more often they visibly abandoned the umpire role, the less staying power their decisions might have. Because conservative legal thinkers hadn't cared much about the precise question raised by Obamacare—and had cared for a long time about the questions raised by affirmative action and the Voting Rights Act—the politicians in robes might use Obamacare as an occasion to show that they "really" were umpires.

But, again, who knows what the long run holds? And so, deciding a case in 2012 one way to make it easier to decide an unrelated case in

2017 in the way you prefer doesn't make much sense. You might as well decide the case in 2012 by using the legal arguments you think best.

THE OUTCOME fully satisfied almost no one. Democrats worried that the Court's holdings would eventually put sharp limits on Congress's power under the commerce and spending clauses. Neal Katyal, who had served as Acting Solicitor General after Elena Kagan was appointed to the Supreme Court, called the decision "a pyrrhic victory," because "the fancy footwork that the court employed to view [the Medicaid expansion] as coercive could come back in later cases to haunt the federal government." He observed that Congress had used its spending power to tell schools and universities that they had to adopt privacy regulations if—as inevitably occurred—if they accepted federal education aid. Were these statutes "now unconstitutional"? As to the individual mandate, "The court employed language that could be read to suggest that whenever statutes are novel, they are unconstitutional."

Republicans were devastated by the fact that the Court didn't strike down the ACA completely. Law professor Jonathan Adler tried to find a "silver lining" in the opinions: "the Court's embrace of justiciable [that is, judicially enforceable] limits" on Congress's "ability to impose conditions on the receipt of federal funds." That "may open a new front in the war to reinvigorate constitutional federalism" and "occasion a reexamination of statutes from No Child Left Behind to the Clean Air Act."

Exasperated at the liberal response to the decision, law professor and human rights activist David Cole lamented, "Why can't we recognize a win when it is handed to us on a silver platter?" The Court's commerce clause holding was "unlikely to have much practical impact," and the decision about the Medicaid expansion "was very fact-specific, and turned on the vast amount of money involved and the radical changes effected by the ACA." It wasn't likely to "present any serious obstacle to Congress's ability to craft future spending programs." His conclusion: "At least sometimes, the rule of law, and fidelity to precedent, constrain conservative judges to reach liberal results."

Law professors have the job of imagining new cases to test the limits of what the Supreme Court has said. The Chief Justice summarized the commerce clause holding: "The Court today holds that our Constitution protects us from federal regulation under the Commerce Clause so long as we abstain from the regulated activity." What does that mean for the future?

Suppose Congress enacts a statute requiring that employers reasonably accommodate the needs of their transgendered employees. An employer doesn't provide an accommodation, and defends by saying, "I didn't do anything—I abstained from the activity of providing accommodations." Does the employer win? Worse, the owner of a restaurant refuses to serve African Americans, and defends against a charge of racial discrimination by saying, "I didn't do anything—I just abstained from the activity of serving meals." Those are the liberal nightmares. The conservative one is easy. If there's a next time around, Congress imposes an individual mandate on anyone who engages in an activity that exposes himself or herself to the risk of injury or illness—which is to say, anyone who doesn't live inside a plastic bubble.*

You can do the same thing for the Court's spending power analysis. Threatening to eliminate 100 percent of existing funds for a very large program is coercive. What if the threat is to cut 10 percent? What if the program isn't all that large relative to the state budget, but is quite large relative to the budget of some specific component (state universities, for example)? What makes a program "new" rather than a modification of

---

* As a law professor I can't hold myself back: Does Congress have the power to say, "Once you buy some green vegetables, you have to buy a stalk of broccoli twice a year for the next five years. You get one free pass on uninsured health care, but after that you have to buy insurance or pay a penalty"?

an old one? Justice Ginsburg's dissent pointed out that, had Congress known of the "modification/new" distinction the Court was going to use, it could have written the ACA to repeal the existing Medicaid program, thereby eliminating all the money states were getting, and reenacted a Medicaid program with the ACA's expanded coverage. States could then "choose" whether to participate in this new program. The Chief Justice responded feebly that it would be harder for Congress to repeal and reenact than to adopt the expansion in the first place. Well, sure, as of 2012, when the political landscape had changed, but less clear as of 2010. Maybe President Obama and Harry Reid could have pushed through a repeal-and-reenact statute if they had known that that was what they had to do.

Perhaps my examples are extreme and unrealistic, but my point is simple. A case like the ACA decision doesn't "mean" anything at the moment it's decided. Certainly it resolves the immediate controversy: the ACA is now legally effective. But what its doctrines mean—the activity/inactivity distinction, the modification/new program distinction—will be determined by courts in the future. What they decide depends on the appointments the next presidents make.

CHAPTER 2

Making the Roberts Court

Close observers of the Roman Catholic Church describe some cardinals as *papabile*—among the front-runners for becoming Pope. John Roberts and Samuel Alito were *papabile* for the Supreme Court. Nothing is done in Washington until it's done. Yet it's telling that Roberts and Alito headed the list of potential nominees compiled at the outset of the Bush administration's deliberations, which began before Sandra Day O'Connor announced her retirement, and that at the end of the process Roberts and Alito were the nominees. Day to day, dramatic incidents occurred, new names surfaced, activists on the right and left went to work; but in the end the drama didn't matter because the nominations resulted from the operation of a political logic—what I'm calling the structures of constitutional politics—that went deeper than any of the daily meetings, phone calls, and conversations over dinner. Structures don't always win out over events and personalities. This time they did.

John Roberts was the Bush administration's presumptive nominee before any vacancy occurred. After a stellar career at Harvard Law School, he served as a law clerk to William Rehnquist, then went to work in the Reagan administration, first as a special assistant—speechwriter, legal adviser, and general factotum—to Attorney General William French Smith, and then as an associate counsel in the Office of White House Counsel Fred Fielding. He left the administration in 1986 for the high-powered Washington law firm Hogan & Hartson, but returned to public service as the "political" Deputy Solicitor General to Ken Starr in the George H. W. Bush administration.* As a reward for his service and in recognition of his talent, President Bush nominated him for a seat on the District of Columbia Circuit Court, a Triple-A league for judges being primed for a Supreme Court appointment. The nomination came at the very end of the Bush administration's term, and no one expected it to go through before the 1992 election. With Bush's defeat, the nomination lapsed and Roberts returned to Hogan & Hartson, where he headed the firm's specialized appellate practice, focusing on Supreme Court advocacy. He became one of the "go-to" lawyers for corporations seeking the best representation they could get at the Supreme Court, arguing thirty-nine cases and winning twenty-five.

Roberts's nomination to the circuit court was revived in 2001. There was one problem. The bitterness occasioned by *Bush v. Gore* and the fact that the Senate was controlled by Democrats meant that the administration had to tread carefully. Its first package of nominees balanced some moderate conservatives with some judges Bill Clinton had sought to promote to the circuit courts. That package went through. Then the administration started to present nominees who fit its preferences about judicial philosophy more closely, and Democrats balked. They refused to hold a hearing on Roberts's nomination. But when the Republicans gained control of the Senate in 2003, the nomination went forward. The

---

* The Office of the Solicitor General has several career deputies and, usually, one "political" deputy who serves as a liaison to the administration generally, ensuring that political concerns are brought to the attention of the career lawyers doing the day-to-day work on politically charged cases, and available to serve, with appropriate political credentials, when the Solicitor General is recused from a case.

administration and Roberts generated a letter from a bipartisan group of Washington lawyers, including Lloyd Cutler, known as the "chair" of the Washington Democratic establishment, and Seth Waxman, who served as Bill Clinton's Solicitor General. They urged a quick hearing, saying that they were "united in our belief that John Roberts will be an outstanding federal court of appeals judge." Roberts was confirmed by voice vote and took his seat on the circuit court.

Chief Justice William Rehnquist developed a severe case of an ordinarily quite aggressive form of throat cancer in 2004, and its treatment kept him out of the Court's center seat for several months. When he returned, he was visibly weakened. Once Rehnquist's illness became known, insiders generally assumed that Rehnquist's seat would be the first one President Bush would have the opportunity to fill. The symbolism of appointing Roberts would be strong—Rehnquist's law clerk replacing Rehnquist. And, of course, Roberts's qualifications couldn't reasonably be challenged except on the ground that he was "too conservative." That case would be hard to make. Democrats had successfully portrayed Robert Bork as a wild-eyed radical conservative, abetted by Bork's appearance and, it must be said, by his views. Roberts's years as an appellate advocate meant that he was extremely smooth in his personal presentation. And although Democrats were unlikely to draw careful distinctions among conservatives, Roberts's mentors in the Reagan and Bush administrations—William French Smith, Fred Fielding, and Ken Starr—were "only" moderately strong conservatives, not the hard-liners associated with Edwin Meese.

O'Connor approached Rehnquist to find out whether he planned to retire. When he told her that he planned to serve one more term, O'Connor decided to go first, so that she could deal with her husband's increasing disorientation from Alzheimer's disease. On July 1, 2005, she announced her intention to retire, but only when a successor was ready to join the Court. That O'Connor announced her retirement first didn't derail the apparent plan to make Roberts the Chief Justice. The administration strategy became: Appoint him to her seat, then promote him when, as would inevitably occur, Rehnquist left the Court. The Chief Justice is the Supreme Court's public face. Within the Court the Chief Justice's role is limited but important. He manages the Court's workload—Warren Burger did it badly, William Rehnquist quite well—and sometimes acts as the formal coordinator of social activities within the Court. As I noted in chapter 1, the Chief Justice also has the power to assign opinions when he's in the majority, and sometimes can try to use that power to accomplish strategic goals. The Chief Justice can have personal relationships with other justices that are the Court's glue. He can be an intellectual leader. Because of his personality and his talent, Republicans saw Roberts as someone who could be both the social glue and intellectual leader on the Supreme Court. Whether either would be true depended on what the Court would look like over the course of his career.

Roberts's path to the nomination was reasonably smooth, though it had some characteristics of a comic opera. The public announcement of Rehnquist's diagnosis—and its likely course to his demise within a relatively short time—triggered White House planning for a successor. As Rehnquist's health declined, the search intensified. And John Roberts was the first and—for quite a while—only person given serious consideration as Rehnquist's successor. According to Jan Crawford Greenburg's account, based on extensive interviews with White House insiders, Roberts was first screened by Attorney General Alberto Gonzales, then by a group including Vice President Dick Cheney, White House counsel Harriet Meirs, and Cheney's chief of staff Scooter Libby. Roberts was pressed to describe his judicial philosophy, but always careful about the words he chose, gave answers the group thought unrevealing.

The insiders were looking for the Holy Grail of Republican nominations: reliability. They wanted to be sure that the person they advised Bush to nominate would embed a shared conservative constitutional

vision in constitutional law for decades. As they understood recent
history, Republican presidents had made mistakes: Sandra Day O'Connor, Anthony Kennedy, and of course David Souter turned out to be
unreliable. Roberts's cautious answers didn't provide strong assurances
of reliability.

Still, the list of potential Chief Justices was relatively short. It included
two judges from the federal court in Richmond, J. Harvie Wilkinson
and Michael Luttig. Both were clearly conservative and well regarded
in conservative legal circles. Everyone described Wilkinson as "courtly."
He had clerked for Justice Lewis F. Powell, Jr., during the term *Roe
v. Wade* was decided (Powell voted with the majority to recognize a
right to choose), and during his brief academic career had co-authored
an article that cautiously endorsed a theory of constitutional privacy
with resonances that troubled conservatives. Wilkinson was thought
a bit erratic, not sufficiently reliable for the White House. He also was
near the upper end of the age range acceptable for a Supreme Court
appointment. Luttig had a different set of problems. No one doubted
his conservatism, but from the time he had served in the Reagan and
Bush Department of Justice he had a reputation for sharp elbows in
his personal relations. The new Chief Justice, the White House hoped,
would be able to consolidate a conservative majority through personal
leadership, and they worried that Luttig couldn't do that. Edith Brown
Clement from the court of appeals in Louisiana had some support, but
she wasn't well known in Washington, she had specialized in admiralty
in her practice, and she was a graduate of Tulane Law School. All that
added up to a "meh" feeling about her—good enough, but surely there
were better possibilities.

Finally, there was Samuel Alito. Tweak John Roberts's résumé, and
you get Alito's: Yale Law School rather than Harvard; an interview for
a Supreme Court clerkship with Byron White but wasn't offered the
job, probably because he was too shy at his interview with White; first
job as an assistant U.S. Attorney; then a position in Washington as an

assistant to Solicitor General Rex Lee in the first years of the Reagan administration; then deputy to Attorney General Edwin Meese. He returned to his home state of New Jersey as the chief U.S. Attorney there, then in 1990 got an expected appointment to the Third Circuit Court of Appeals, headquartered in Philadelphia. Over the next decade and a half Alito became one of the most prominent conservative federal judges, particularly active at Federalist Society national meetings. Notably, he wrote an opinion raising questions about the constitutionality of the federal statute banning private possession of submachine guns, in light not of the Second Amendment but the commerce clause's limitation on national power.

Roberts had strong support at the staff level just below the main players, and they kept his name alive even after the first round of interviews left Cheney unimpressed. Second in line was Alito. Crawford Greenburg makes it clear that just before Court rose in June 2005, Roberts was reasonably confident that he would be nominated to succeed Rehnquist. Even the surprise announcement that O'Connor, not Rehnquist, would be the first to retire didn't shake things up much. Outsiders speculated that President Bush would face pressure to name a woman to the Court. Bush didn't have to worry about that. No matter what Rehnquist's intentions—and the White House didn't know that he had told O'Connor he wanted to serve one additional term, then leave the Court—his seat would certainly open up during Bush's time in office. O'Connor's replacement could sit in her seat, then be promoted to Chief Justice. Only then would the issue of appointing a woman really arise.

Events unfolded in ways resembling a low-level theatrical farce. Roberts went to London to teach at Georgetown Law School's summer program, then basically had to turn around to fly back to Washington to yet another interview, this one with President Bush, who had also spoken with Wilkinson and Luttig—and Samuel Alito. In the background was staffwork telling Bush that were he to nominate Roberts, he could defend the selection without equivocation as the choice of the most qualified person for the job. The interview went well, but Roberts still had his academic obligation in London, so he flew back—and then returned almost immediately to join President Bush for the announcement of his nomination for O'Connor's seat.

Then Rehnquist passed away, and the administration's long-term strategy was deployed. Roberts's nomination for O'Connor's seat was formally withdrawn, and he was nominated as Rehnquist's replacement. The administration now had to find a new nominee for O'Connor's seat. The judge-pickers had just gone through one search exercise, and they had concluded that, after Roberts and Alito, the pickings were rather thin. No woman had impressed anyone during the first search. A couple of additional names surfaced. Maureen Mahoney was somewhat equivalent to Roberts as a leading figure within the specialized Supreme Court bar. Mahoney, though, had argued the case for the constitutionality of the University of Michigan's affirmative action program, and apparently agreed with the position she took for her client. That was enough to put her out of contention. Another possibility, Miguel Estrada, was Hispanic and so would have satisfied advocates for a "diversity"-based appointment. But Estrada had recently gone through a bruising fight over his nomination for the court of appeals in Washington, ultimately withdrawing his name, and he didn't want to go through anything like that again, even with the possibility of a Supreme Court seat at the end.

Within the White House a new name came up: Harriet Meirs, the White House counsel. Harry Reid, the Senate Democratic leader, suggested her nomination, because he liked the idea that a lawyer with real-world experience, rather than a judge, would be put on the Supreme Court. An evangelical Christian, Meirs had had a quite successful career as a commercial lawyer in Dallas, and had developed a close relationship to President Bush first as a member of the White House staff and then as White House counsel. Bush trusted her judgment and knew from personal contact that she shared his conservative views: "I know her heart," Bush said.

Meirs was not part of the wider community of conservative lawyers associated with the Republican Party. Bush may have known her heart, but conservatives were reluctant to take his word for it. They began to question the nomination almost immediately. Unlike Bush, they did not know what she thought about the issues they were passionate about, and they didn't accept assurances from Bush and Meirs's friends, such as Texas judge Nathan Hecht, that she really was quite conservative. They disparaged her background—a legal education at the third-tier law school at Southern Methodist University, a legal career focused on commercial litigation, an absence of writing—either academic articles or substantial legal briefs—from which her judicial philosophy could be extracted.

As the controversy developed outside the White House, Meirs was going through the second stage within the White House of the nomination process—"murder boards" in which White House staffers quizzed her aggressively in anticipation of questions she might get from the Judiciary Committee. In the staffers' view, she didn't do well. In the end Bush withdrew her nomination, using the face-saving excuse that the hearings would have degenerated into a quarrel about access to memoranda she had written as White House counsel. Pretty much everyone believed that he withdrew the nomination because it had become a political liability. Nominating a woman might have gained him some political points. Even a failed nomination might have been all right, if the failure could be pinned on Democrats. But a nomination that failed because of Republican opposition wasn't worth the political cost, especially because diversity-based appointments weren't nearly as high a priority for Republicans as reliability on the issues that mattered.

And so Samuel Alito got the nomination.

THE JOURNALISTIC tick-tock with the details of the nomination process reveals a good deal, of course, but the welter of details also conceals the structures that the daily events both reflect and create. The judge-pickers—White House and Justice Department staff and, of course, the president—face one serious problem: to the extent that they care about what a nominee will do once appointed, they are making a prediction about which they can't extract promises, even unenforceable ones. No one would ask Samuel Alito whether he would vote to overrule *Roe v. Wade*, or even whether it should be overruled. The question would be insulting and, if the judge-pickers have good proxies, unnecessary. Rather, the judge-pickers followed Abraham Lincoln's advice: "We cannot ask a man what he will do, and if we should, and he should answer us, we should despise him for it. Therefore we must take a man whose opinions are known." The structures generate the proxies that the judge-pickers use.

The largest structure is one so obvious that it's easy to overlook. Presidents use Supreme Court nominations to create a legacy. That legacy, though, isn't only the record the nominees will compile after the president leaves office; in the end, after all, there aren't any guarantees. What the president can control is the immediate effect of a nomination (not even an appointment). Nominations can strengthen the president's political party, and the legacy the president leaves is a party stronger because of his nominations. Justices are a president's legacy in the narrow sense that they are sure to be in office after the president departs. But they are his legacy as well when their nomination strengthens the party.

Party building through judicial nominations can take place only when the nomination satisfies one part of the party's coalition without annoying another too much. The structure of the modern Republican Party means that the two aspects of a legacy—the effect on the Court and the effect on the party—converge. The Republican coalition combines economic and social conservatives. Republican presidents

Reagan and the two Bushes promoted business-oriented policies through tax cuts, but adopted relatively few concrete policies to advance the social conservative agenda. Instead, they gave social conservatives strong rhetorical support—nothing to sneer at for pushing a long-term agenda—and, most important, control over the Department of Justice and judge-picking. Harriet Meirs's basic problem was that she couldn't assure social conservatives of her "reliability," from their point of view, and so her nomination turned out to be a liability rather than a contribution to party building. (As we'll see later, President Obama's party-building strategy for picking judges didn't focus as centrally on liberal reliability, although Republicans appeared not to understand that, because the Democratic Party is a different kind of coalition.)

For social conservatives, reliability didn't consist of litmus tests administered directly. They wanted to have a good sense of the way potential nominees would think about constitutional law generally. Opinions on specific issues are less important—for party-building purposes—than a general orientation or judicial ideology (the Democrats' preferred term for Republican judges' orientations) or philosophy (the Republicans' preferred term). Social conservatives needed to know—in Lincoln's sense—Roberts's and Alito's way of thinking. And they did, based on the following features of the structures of decision making, starting with two minor ones.

First, the interviews. The tick-tock includes two kinds of interviews, with the White House's judge-pickers and with President Bush. The interviews with the staffers are only mildly interesting. The staffers are usually the journalists' best sources, and they understandably tell the story in ways that inflate their own importance. Roberts's interview with the staffers would have had to have been disastrously bad, not just a bit off key, for him to lose his status as the presumptive nominee. But the staff interviews matter within the White House. They give the staffers a chance to jerk the nominee's chain—by insisting on urgency, for example, and disrupting the interviewee's life, as in the two trips

Roberts had to make from London. The power to do that lets the staffers think they are important players in Washington—and presidents probably want to keep staffers happy by letting them think so. And, of course, nothing is ever set in stone in politics before it happens. The staffers do have *some* power, just not as much as the tick-tock's focus on the details of interviews might suggest.

Reporters today don't remark on the now routine practice in which presidents interview a short list of potential nominees, because it's a "dog-bites-man" story. It's not entirely clear what a president actually can get out of a one-hour interview. Any reasonably competent staff will have done the vetting the president wants, and won't put anyone on the short list who doesn't satisfy the president's basic requirements for a nominee—in the Republican case, reliability on questions of approaches to constitutional interpretation. Only presidents can give the full answer; but from the outside it looks as if presidents get a sense of who the person is and a few anecdotes to tell when introducing the nominee. And from the outside one wonders whether that's worth the time it takes—although enough presidents have done the interviews that they must think they get something out of them.

Certainly in historical perspective these interviews are a relatively new practice. John F. Kennedy didn't have to interview Byron White because he already knew White personally: White had chaired Lawyers for Kennedy during the campaign, and was Bobby Kennedy's Deputy Attorney General. In general, most presidents have known their nominees long before they were placed on a short list. What counts as "knowing" a nominee can vary, of course. Richard Nixon had met William Rehnquist before nominating him, but he seems to have remembered only Rehnquist's sideburns and hippielike tie, and once referred to Rehnquist as "that clown Rehnchburg."

What the interviews show is a change in the selection process. Nominees used to be people who moved within Washington insider circles, or at least within the political circles the president moved in. They aren't outsiders now, but they are insiders in a different way—insiders to a culture of distinctively judicial politics. Some of the problems Harriet Meirs faced came about because she fit into the older model of a nominee personally known to the president rather than the newer one of a nominee who has positioned him- or herself to catch the attention of Washington's "Great Mentioners," the columnists and reporters who come up with lists of potential nominees.

Supreme Court reporters were surprised when Harriet Meirs's name surfaced. She hadn't been mentioned for earlier judicial nominations, and the lists of potential nominees contained the usual suspects— Republican judges well known in the Federalist Society network. Meirs's emergence resulted from another underlying feature of the nomination process. All else equal, presidents prefer to nominate their own people to the Supreme Court. John Roberts's selection was overdetermined, but even he was Bush's "own man," placed on the court of appeals by George W. Bush. Harriet Meirs was even more of a Bush person, serving in the White House in daily contact with the president.

Presidents don't prefer their own people because they think that the nominees will have some sense of personal loyalty, or will be particularly grateful for the appointment. As Abraham Lincoln is supposed to have said, the problem with patronage of that sort is that every nomination creates ten disappointed enemies and one ingrate. The occasions on which a Supreme Court justice might be called upon to demonstrate personal loyalty are rare. Perhaps one can count Paula Jones's case against Bill Clinton as such a case, and many historians suggest that Fred Vinson's position in a case involving Harry Truman's seizure of steel plants during the Korean War was influenced by Vinson's personal ties to Truman. Those examples involved situations where the appointing president's actions were directly and centrally at issue. But most presidents don't get involved in such cases, and putting someone on the Court as insurance against that possibility doesn't make much sense. More likely, presidents prefer their own people because they want to be as confident as they can be that the nominee's actions will cast the president in a good light over the next decades, even after the president has left office.

Of course, things aren't always equal. A nomination might open up early in a president's term, when he doesn't yet have his own people to shift from one position to the Supreme Court. Or, as the failure of Meirs's nomination shows, other structural features of the nomination process can block an "own person" nomination.

Ultimately, the interviews and the "own person" preference are fairly small features of the nomination process, and they're not distinctive to the Republican nominations. Several other features are more important and distinctively Republican.

Justice Department experience mattered to George W. Bush. In 1988 the Office of Legal Policy in the Department of Justice, which operated in part as an in-house think tank for Edwin Meese, published a pamphlet, *The Constitution in the Year 2000*. It laid out the conservative constitutional vision that pervaded the Justice Department. That vision was produced and absorbed by the department's young, politically attuned lawyers like John Roberts—as special assistant to Attorney General Smith and in the White House Counsel's Office—and Samuel Alito, in the Solicitor General's Office and as Meese's assistant. The pamphlet ran through a list of constitutional issues and decisions, mostly liberal, and laid out the positions that, it maintained, represented the Constitution's true meaning and would if all went well *be* the Constitution in 2000. The idea that the Constitution meant today exactly what it meant when it was adopted—a theory of constitutional interpretation known as "originalism"—was at the pamphlet's heart.

Most of the pamphlet's targets were obvious ones for those who came at the Constitution with a conservative philosophy: affirmative action was unconstitutional; *Roe v. Wade* was wrong from the start; Congress's powers had to be reined in. One target was less familiar outside conservative circles: the federal regulatory bureaucracies that had grown up since the New Deal and had been endorsed and even expanded through Richard Nixon's administration. Reagan's Justice Department contended that some of the federal regulatory apparatus was unconstitutional because it wasn't under the president's direct control.

The Reagan administration mounted its challenge to the regulatory apparatus for reasons that blended practical politics with constitutional theory. Reagan and his allies sought to redirect federal regulatory efforts, but they discovered, as a common metaphor within their circles put it, that changing the direction of bureaucracies was like trying to turn an ocean liner around. It was a difficult and slow process. The bureaucracies were staffed by civil servants who had come to Washington in a era when being public servants meant regulating pretty vigorously. The bureaucrats were committed to their missions, and obstructed Reagan's deregulatory efforts, if only by "slow-walking" them. Protected by civil service rules, the bureaucrats couldn't be fired easily. Worse, the bureaucracies were part of what political scientists called an "iron triangle" of policy making in Washington. The three legs of the triangle were the interest groups affected by each regulatory agency, the congressional committees responsible for agency budgets and policy, and the agency bureaucrats. Note what's missing: someone from the executive branch.

These structures stood in the way of many Reagan policy initiatives. They weren't insurmountable obstacles. The iron triangle weakened in the late twentieth century, as the ideology of deregulation gained strength and as interest groups proliferated to the point where they were often at odds with each other, thereby weakening one of the triangle's legs. The president appointed some agency heads, such as the administrators of the Environmental Protection Agency (EPA) and the Food and Drug Administration (FDA). But, in addition to these "executive branch" agencies, there were "independent" agencies like the Securities and Exchange Commission (SEC), with several members whose terms extended beyond a president's and who could be removed only "for cause," which meant, effectively, that they couldn't be removed at all. And even a weakened iron triangle gave some protection to agency heads who could resist the directives of the president who had appointed them and threatened to remove them, by pointing out that congressional committees and interest groups would exact a substantial political price for pushing out an agency head.

Reagan's legal theorists wanted to give the president a more firm hand over the agencies. They did so with a constitutional theory that came to be known as the theory of the unitary executive. In its early formulations, the theory dealt only with presidential control of the regulatory bureaucracies. The executive branch was unitary, according to this theory, because the president had the constitutional duty to "take care that the laws be faithfully executed." He couldn't fulfill that duty unless he could insist that *his* interpretations of the laws prevailed over the interpretations offered by bureaucrats, even his own bureaucrats. So, the theory went, the president had to have the complete power to appoint and fire agency heads, and to discipline civil servants who resisted his policy directives.

The unitary executive theory would have a strong effect on the independent regulatory agencies, though only a few of them—the Federal Communications Commission, the Nuclear Regulatory Commission, the Consumer Product Safety Commission—had much to do with the administration's primary regulatory goals. The theory had only modest purchase in connection with executive branch agencies like the EPA and the FDA, where the statutes clearly gave the president the power to direct policy and to fire an agency head who resisted direction. Even there, accepting the theory would weaken some claims made from the iron triangle. Something of a political brushfire broke out when George W. Bush "fired" a number of U.S. Attorneys, for example. From a strict legal point of view, Bush pretty clearly had the power to do that—or, at least, the legal arguments supporting him were easy to make, the ones against his actions difficult and complicated. Had the unitary executive theory been widely accepted inside the Beltway, the controversy wouldn't have had any legs at all.

The unitary executive theory made essentially no progress during the Reagan years and after. The Supreme Court dealt it a near-fatal blow when it upheld the statute creating "Independent Counsels," appointed by federal judges to investigate allegations of criminal activity by high-level administration officials. As Justice Scalia said in a biting dissent, decisions to prosecute criminal activity were at the heart of the power—and duty—to see that the laws were faithfully executed, a duty, he said, the Constitution placed on the President alone. But Justice Scalia stood by himself, with William Rehnquist (appointed Chief Justice by Reagan) writing for the other eight justices to uphold the statute.

The unitary executive theory awakened from the dead, seemingly strengthened by its rest, after September 11, 2001. Vice President Dick Cheney and his counsel David Addington came out of the Reagan years firmly convinced that Congress and the bureaucracies had prevented Reagan and George H. W. Bush from implementing the conservative policies they thought the nation stood behind. Al Qaeda's attack on the United States gave them the chance to push a reinvigorated unitary executive theory. Now the theory wasn't just about the president's power to fire agency officials. According to the new version, the president's duty to take care that the laws be faithfully executed covered *all* the laws—including the Constitution. In its strongest version, the theory held that the president could disregard statutes that he believed intruded on his executive powers, including his power as commander in chief of the armed forces. So, for example, if the president believed that he had the power as commander in chief to order that terrorists be tortured to obtain military information, the Constitution prevented Congress from enacting a statute restricting the interrogation techniques he could use.

Coming out of the Reagan Department of Justice, Roberts and Alito were familiar with and probably sympathetic to the early, weak version of the unitary executive theory. The second Bush administration's version of the theory was much stronger, of course, and agreeing with the weak version didn't guarantee agreement with the strong version. Still, there *was* a constitutional argument connecting the two versions through the "take care" duty, and smart lawyers might be willing to make the connection. "Worked in the Reagan Department of Justice" was a proxy for views about executive power: Roberts and Alito might be open to the strong version of the unitary executive theory when lawyers without their experience in the Reagan Justice Department might not have been. And, in fact, some studies find that a judge's experience in the executive branch is a decent predictor of that judge's willingness to uphold claims of executive authority.

Roberts and Alito haven't yet dealt with issues central to claims about expansive presidential power in the so-called war on terror. In 2013 Justice Alito wrote for the usual conservative majority denying journalists and lawyers a chance to show that part of the post-9/11 system of looking for suspicious phone calls from overseas was unconstitutional.

Roberts did write an opinion endorsing a rather mild example of the early version of unitary executive theory. Reacting to the Enron and WorldCom scandals, in 2002 Congress enacted a statute tightening the regulation of stocks. One provision created a new federal board to oversee the development of accounting rules: the Public Company Accounting Oversight Board (PCAOB), known to cognoscenti as "Peekaboo." The board's members were appointed by the Securities and Exchange Commission, and the statute said that the SEC could remove board members only for cause. The SEC is an independent commission, which means that the president can remove *its* members only for cause. Writing for the Court's conservatives, Roberts said that two layers of insulation from the president violated the Constitution, basically by limiting the president's control over delegated lawmaking and enforcement "too much." Roberts deployed a version of his "enough is enough" principle: "two layers are not the same as one."

Compliance Week, which describes itself as "the leading information service on corporate governance, risk and compliance," reacted to the Peekaboo decision with the headline: "Much Ado About Nothing." It called the decision "a victory for conservative activists who had been trying to undermine" the new regulatory system. But, the story continued, "For compliance and financial reporting officers, life continues, and you might as well get back to your usual routines for testing internal controls over financial reporting. There's not much else to see here." The Reagan Justice Department's campaign for a unitary executive ended, at least so far, by bringing forth a mouse in the Peekaboo decision.

After Justice Department experience in the list of structural features comes another kind of legal experience. Republican presidents aren't merely presidents, of course. They are also Republicans, which means that they are typically proponents of business interests. Shortly before Richard Nixon appointed him to the Supreme Court in 1971, Lewis F. Powell, Jr., then a leading corporate lawyer, wrote a memorandum to the U.S. Chamber of Commerce complaining that liberal lawyers had outgunned the corporate bar, in part by establishing public interest law firms with the long-term goal of shifting the law in a liberal direction. Powell's memorandum contributed to conservative interest in developing a counterforce to liberal lawyers.

Conservatives created their own public interest law firms, with the goal of challenging what they regarded as excessive regulations. These firms had some relatively minor success, but they couldn't do much for large corporations. It was easy to target minor regulations that harassed small businesses, but large corporations had to work within the regulatory system rather than against it. Conflicts between profit-oriented business people and ideologically oriented lawyers broke out. Conservative public interest law firms soldiered on, supported not by large-scale corporations but as the pet ideological projects of the occasional multimillionaire.

America's major corporations needed something else, and the reorganization of the bar in the 1980s and 1990s gave it to them. From the late nineteenth century to the middle of the twentieth, large corporations used a successful model for legal representation. They had in-house counsel, lawyers paid salaries by the corporation itself, for routine work, such as managing everyday labor relations and routine regulations. And they hired a single outside counsel—a BigLaw firm, as the group came to be known in the late twentieth century—for all the large projects the corporation had, such as mergers, antitrust litigation, and representation in the Supreme Court. The BigLaw model began to change as corporate managers came to understand that they could get better results by hiring specialized law firms for specialized work, rather than by relying on the departments within a single BigLaw firm: faced with a major antitrust suit, the corporation would hire an antitrust specialist. And faced with an important Supreme Court case, the corporation would look for a specialist in Supreme Court advocacy.

Richard Lazarus was an environmental lawyer (and John Roberts's law school roommate), sometimes referred to as the "Solicitor General for the environmental movement." He knew from that experience that the liberal public interest bar had several lawyers who appeared before the Supreme Court with some regularity. And he knew that there had always been a handful of lawyers scattered around the country who were Supreme Court specialists, sometimes academics, sometimes lawyers like Floyd Abrams, a lawyer for the *New York Times*, a client that brought cases to the Supreme Court with some regularity. In the 1990s, Lazarus observed something that seemed new, at least in modern times: the rise of an elite Supreme Court bar consisting of a handful of Washington lawyers who argued several cases each year at the Supreme Court, on behalf of corporations. The reorganization of corporate legal practice was the predicate for this development.

Lazarus published a pathbreaking article identifying the new

Supreme Court bar. His story begins with Rex Lee, Reagan's first Solicitor General. Spotting the transformation of corporate legal practice, Lee joined the Chicago-based law firm Sidley & Austin after he left the Justice Department. He headed a department within the firm specializing in corporate representation at the Supreme Court. Other "refugees" from the Solicitor General's Office followed; some went to Sidley, others to found their own specialized departments in different large law firms.

The lawyers in these departments had accumulated a good deal of experience in the Solicitor General's Office, and they got more as the specialized bar grew. As lawyers who had worked for a conservative Republican administration they were comfortable with representing corporate interests, and their clients appreciated their experience and talent. Members of the specialized bar knew how to pitch their cases to the Supreme Court. As the bar became well established, law clerks reported that they gave special attention to petitions for review with the name of an elite Supreme Court lawyer on them. Together with the justices' own views about what cases mattered, the elite lawyers contributed to a change in the mix of cases the Supreme Court considered —more business cases, fewer pure constitutional.

John Roberts was a leading member of the new Supreme Court bar. Between his first failed nomination to the circuit court in 1992 and his successful nomination in 2003, Roberts argued thirty-nine cases in the Supreme Court. His Supreme Court clients included two major coal companies, a health management organization, and Toyota. Roberts's membership in the elite Supreme Court bar mattered when he was nominated to the Supreme Court. People expected that Roberts's experience would let him hit the ground running, and they were right.

Successful Supreme Court advocates are able to present their clients' positions forcefully and as required by existing law. Their rhetorical posture is that they will win if the justices simply call balls and strikes fairly. And they are able to present client-favoring positions in ways that can appeal to judges who might initially be inclined against their clients. Good Supreme Court advocates can speak to people across the ideological spectrum. That clearly is an asset in the nomination process. So is the smoothness that comes from being a successful appellate lawyer. President Bush's judge-pickers expected Roberts to be equally smooth inside the Court, able to attract votes from the other side of the ideological divide.

Members of the elite Supreme Court bar are also something of a fraternity (mostly men, with a few women). They deal with each other all the time, as friendly rivals. A member of the elite bar nominated for a judicial position by a Republican can count on testimonials from members of the fraternity with ties to Democrats in the Senate, and vice versa. Announcing Roberts's initial nomination, President Bush quoted the letter written to the Judiciary Committee in 2001 when Roberts was nominated for the court of appeals, signed by "a former counsel to two Democratic Presidents—and former high-ranking Justice Department officials of both parties."

Lawyers don't necessarily come to believe that their clients are always right. Indeed, the best lawyers probably are indifferent to whether their clients are right or wrong, because that lets them see clearly the strength of the positions on the other side. But a lawyer who consistently represents large corporations can easily end up thinking that the legal positions large corporations assert are the truly sensible positions, the ones the law *should* adopt. Just as experience in the Justice Department provided some indication that Roberts and Alito would be reliable on matters of executive power, so Roberts's experience as a member of the elite business-oriented Supreme Court bar gave some indication of his reliability on matters of concern to the business community.

Membership in the elite Supreme Court bar isn't a prerequisite for a Supreme Court nomination, of course, but it's an "inside the Beltway" asset that can ease the path to the Supreme Court.

So can connection to the Federalist Society network. Liberals outside of legal circles tend to regard the Federalist Society as a cabal that dictates legal and constitutional policy to the Republican Party. As they see it, the Federalist Society chooses judges for Republicans, then supplies those judges with law clerks who write conservative legal theories into constitutional law, sometimes even blocking squishily conservative judges from deviating from the party line.

This is a fantasy. The Federalist Society is made up of chapters of law students and lawyers. It's what social scientists call a "network," whose function is not to do anything in particular, but to connect people to each other so that *they* can do things. The society's heart lies in its student chapters, though its "practice groups" of lawyers are increasingly important within the organization. Its most important members are federal judges and law students, with Republican politicians in Congress and—when Republicans occupy the presidency—in the executive branch playing smaller roles. That makes the Federalist Society network a job placement service for conservative law students. Membership tells conservative judges that a student shares their views—not a guarantee of a job, but a helpful credential. For judges, active participation in the Federalist Society is a helpful credential too. It burnishes their résumés, putting them on lists for advancement to higher positions in the judiciary from the trial courts to the appellate courts, and then—the brass ring—from the appeals courts to the Supreme Court.

Three law students created the Federalist Society in 1982. Feeling themselves politically isolated in a sea of liberal law students and law professors, unable to obtain intellectual validation for their views, Steven Calabresi, Lee Liberman, and David MacIntosh simply invented the society, then sought academic sponsors, including Professor Antonin Scalia of Chicago—and through those sponsors sought financial support from conservative-leaning foundations. The society went national, hiring an executive director, Eugene Meyer, who has run it ever since. As the political scientist Stephen Teles has detailed, Meyer and other

early Federalist Society leaders guided the society through the hazardous waters of intraconservative factional fighting by insisting that it
refrain from direct involvement in politics and maintain its posture as
an organization primarily dedicated to intellectual debates about law.

The Federalist Society's headline events are annual meetings for
students and lawyers. Panels of judges, academics, and lawyers discuss
the hot constitutional issues of the day. The panels are salted with the
occasional liberal academic but the overall line is decidedly conservative. The discussions are sometimes interesting, because conservatives
sometimes disagree among themselves in interesting ways, especially
when libertarian conservatives confront social ones on issues like gay
rights. The point of the meetings, though, is not advancing conservative legal thought. The panels serve to validate that way of thinking,
showing conservative law students and others who might feel politically
isolated in their daily encounters that they actually have decent arguments behind them, no matter what they hear from their liberal law
professors and colleagues.

And what about the judges? They are the rock stars of the Federalist
Society meetings, in part because they actually hire recent graduates as
their law clerks, but also because their appearances at Federalist Society
meetings are tryouts for higher office.* A judge can establish his or her
conservative credentials simply by showing up at a Federalist Society
national meeting. Even more, the judge can push to the head of the
pack by "doing well" on a panel—that is, by engaging seriously with
conservative legal thinking. As one regular attendee put it, Samuel
Alito's appearances showed that he was "wicked smart." So did John
Roberts's. Harriet Meirs wasn't part of the Federalist Society network,
and though Edith Clement was a Federalist Society member, she didn't

---

* Judges have always campaigned for promotion. Sometimes the campaign involved getting
friends of politicians to write letters on the candidate's behalf, sometimes it involved getting
other judges to weigh in. Those forms of campaigning persist.

generate the kind of buzz she would have needed to displace the enthusiasm for Roberts and Alito.

Roberts and Alito didn't get their Supreme Court appointments because they were members of the Federalist Society. Their appearances at society events simply provided the Bush administration's judge-pickers with another set of proxies for reliability, and a network of people already in place who would enthusiastically endorse their nominations.

The quest for reliability is difficult. The core problem is that Republican presidents and their advisers hold somewhat conflicting ideas of what reliability is. They begin with reasonably solid thoughts about what an ideal justice would think and do: for President Bush, executive power mattered a lot, as did abortion; immigration less so. And they would expect the justice to interpret the Constitution based in some sense on its original meaning. Presidents and their advisers aren't, and shouldn't be, systematic constitutional theorists of the sort that populate the law schools, but these general ideas are enough to give them a decent sense of what a reliable justice would do.

Republican presidents have been interested in something beyond today's constitutional controversies. They hope for reliability over the long term, articulating constitutional conservatism in 2010, 2020, and 2030, which they hope—though without much basis—is going to help the Republican Party in 2010, 2020, and 2030.

The problem is that things change. Some of the issues that George W. Bush was most concerned about in choosing his nominees have basically disappeared from the Supreme Court, most notably questions about presidential power and terrorism. Roberts and Alito might be completely reliable on those issues, but they haven't had much of a chance to show it. And as new issues emerge, exactly what the judge-pickers of 2005 would think reliable behavior becomes increasingly obscure.

Perhaps more important, the Republican Party changes. From the Republican point of view, David Souter was probably unreliable from the very beginning. Not so Sandra Day O'Connor and Anthony Kennedy. Over their careers they were pretty consistent Reagan Republicans. But despite Ronald Reagan's iconic status within the Republican Party, the Republican Party at the end of the century wasn't Reagan's party. As Justice O'Connor put it just before she left the Court: "What makes this harder is that it's my party that's destroying the country." Even more so with the Tea Party–inflected Republican Party of 2012: John Roberts was reliable as reliability was understood within the Republican Party in 2005, when he was chosen. When he voted to find the Affordable Care Act constitutional in 2012, he was unreliable as seen by the Republican Party *at that time.*

The quest for perfect reliability may well be futile. Changing issues and political interests may convert a wholly acceptable appointment when made into a disappointing one a few years later. Still, the cases of Antonin Scalia, Clarence Thomas, and Samuel Alito show that sometimes the Republican quest for reliable judges can succeed.

OF COURSE, the more a nomination does to strengthen the president's party, the more the opposition party will resist. Everyone knew that Roberts and Alito were chosen because they thought about the Constitution in the way that social conservatives did, but openly acknowledging that would give Democrats ammunition for their charge that President Bush was "politicizing" the Supreme Court. So, Roberts and Alito bobbed and weaved during their hearings.

The hearings were typical examples of contemporary politics in action. Thinking that the only way to justify a vote against a nominee they opposed on ideological grounds was to find some personal or ethical failing in the nominee's history, Democrats dredged up incidents from Roberts's and Alito's early years. But all the Democrats managed to do was to confirm, to no one's surprise, that both were standard college, law school, and Justice Department conservatives.

Some of Roberts's memos as a White House staffer had a sharper tone to them than people who met him only during the nomination process expected. He called the idea that men and women should receive comparable pay for comparable work "a radical redistributive concept," and rephrased the classic Marxist dictum as "From each according to his ability, to each according to her gender." Solicitor General Ted Olson wrote a memo arguing against the constitutionality of proposed statutes taking the power to hear cases involving abortion and school prayer away from the Supreme Court, mentioning that a decision to oppose the statutes would "be perceived as a courageous and highly principled position, especially in the press." Roberts noted of this, in longhand, "Real courage would be to read the Constitution as it should be read and not kowtow to the [Laurence] Tribes and [*New York Times* columnist Anthony] Lewises."

The memos were easily dismissed as the kinds of things smarty-pants young whippersnappers say, and as failing to reflect Roberts's current views. Yet they suggested that there might be a more explosive John Roberts held under tight control by the more polished persona Roberts had developed. Over the course of his tenure as Chief Justice, there was some chance, not that the hidden John Roberts, were there actually to be one, would emerge, but that the inner John Roberts might shape what the outer one did.

Democrats tried to use Alito's membership in Concerned Alumni of Princeton against him; the group consisted of alumni who were fighting a rearguard action against the admission and integration of women into Princeton's culture. They found a case that Alito helped to decide about the Vanguard Fund, a large mutual fund in which he held shares. Alito said that his staff had overlooked his standing orders to keep him off cases involving Vanguard; that the amount at stake was so small that even if he had sat on the case it would have been ethically permissible; and that in any event, when he discovered the problem he had the chief judge put the case before another panel of judges. All this was small beer. Senator Lindsey Graham of South Carolina used a standard trial lawyer's technique to defend Alito by repeating the Democrats' charges, followed by the equivalent of "That's not true, is it?" Hearing the charges in rapid succession so bothered Alito's wife Martha-Ann that she left the committee room in tears.

Many legal scholars, including Elena Kagan, have criticized confirmation hearings as failing to inform senators about the nominees' views, or the public about what it means to interpret the Constitution. Instead of discussing the Constitution, senators inflate minor ethical questions into major issues. Robert Bork was candid, and it did him little good. Most nominees do their best to avoid saying anything of substance, and for good reason. If you say something, it's unlikely that it's going to convert an opponent into a supporter; there's a risk that you'll commit a gaffe; and, probably most important, all you're likely to do is give your opponents ammunition to use against you. Yet academic studies indicate that there has been only a slight decline in nominees' candor during hearings.

The most enduring episode occurred in the first moments of Roberts's hearing, when he read his opening statement, with its "balls and strikes" metaphor. Roberts had obviously thought a lot about the "umpire" metaphor, using it not in a spontaneous answer to an unexpected question but rather in his very first minutes before the Senate. But for people informed about either law or baseball, the metaphor fell flat. It was designed to show that judges didn't just make things up, or come up with constitutional interpretations based on their personal values—the standard conservative critique of liberal judges. It traded on the image of an "objective" reality, independent of the umpire's values: a ball was either in the strike zone or it wasn't. So, too, the Constitution either meant that a woman had a right to choose with respect to abortion, or it didn't.

Critics immediately challenged the metaphor from both its sides.

Judges, they argued, couldn't avoid making decisions that others might disagree with. That's why we call them judges, after all. There wasn't an objective "reality" about the kinds of legal issues that got to the Supreme Court. Some decisions might be easy, just as sometimes it's easy to know that a fastball down the middle is a strike; Roberts's metaphor fits those decisions. But sometimes decisions are hard, just as it's sometimes hard to know whether a curve ball cut the corner just inside or just outside the strike zone. The Supreme Court's most important decisions are like that. And when decisions are hard, judges have to look somewhere—to a judicial philosophy, for example—for help.

From the other direction, critics came up with examples showing that umpires don't "just" call balls and strikes. The three umpires were trotted out: the objective umpire who says, "I call 'em as they are," the subjective one who says, "I call 'em as I see 'em," and the realist, "They ain't nuthin' until I call 'em." The suggestion was that the first two were silly, the third on point. Baseball fans explained that umpires differed about the size of the strike zone, just as, they suggested, judges differed about the Constitution's meaning. Even more, they explained that an individual umpire adjusted the strike zone's size depending on how big a lead a team had, or how important the game was.*

As a skilled oral advocate, of course, Roberts knew his audience, and it wasn't legal sophisticates—or hard-core baseball fans. He was speaking to the American people, or at least a large part of them, who believed—or wanted to believe—that whenever they, their family, or their friends went to court, their chances of winning didn't depend on who the judge on the bench happened to be. They *knew* they were right about the law, and all they needed was a judge who acknowledged that reality—or at least a judge who would hear them out with the open mind Roberts said he would have. The political scientist William

---

* Before and after Roberts's hearing, legal scholars and political scientists explored the umpire metaphor, usually concluding that the realist umpire had a better grasp of his job—and so of the judge's—than the objective or subjective umpires.

Blake has observed that the umpire metaphor is helpful to him as a teacher, because his students, representative of the public generally, do think that deciding what the Constitution means is a merely formal and objective task. By teaching them what umpires actually do, he can teach them what judges do as well. Most Americans, though, don't get that kind of lesson, and Roberts's metaphor reassures them about the American legal system.

The umpire metaphor has dogged Roberts for years, and he has said that he has some mild regrets about using it. The metaphor did its work when it needed to. Once Roberts was confirmed, the metaphor might have faded away, except that Roberts's critics keep bringing it up whenever they want to argue that he makes the law up no less than his liberal opponents do.

As politics around the Supreme Court changed, so did norms about the reasons senators could openly use in opposing a nominee. Here's what the votes were on the recent nominees: O'Connor—99/0; Rehnquist (as Chief Justice)—65/33; Scalia—98/0; Robert Bork—42/58; Kennedy—97/0; Souter—90/9; Thomas—52/48; Ginsburg—96/3; Breyer—87/9; Roberts—78/22; Alito—58/42; Sotomayor—68/31; Kagan—63/37. A new norm may have emerged, at least for now. A substantial number of senators from both parties appear entirely comfortable with voting against a nominee solely because of disagreement with the views he or she has. The search for ethical failings has dropped away, and the days of near-unanimous confirmations may have passed.

As Senator Barack Obama put it in announcing that he would vote against Roberts's confirmation:

> There is absolutely no doubt in my mind Judge Roberts is qualified to sit on the highest court in the land. Moreover, he seems to have the comportment and the temperament that makes for a good judge. He is humble, he is personally decent, and he appears to be respectful of different points of view. . . . it became apparent to me in our conversation

that he does, in fact, deeply respect the basic precepts that go into deciding 95 percent of the cases that come before the Federal court. . . .

[W]hat matters on the Supreme Court is those 5 percent of cases that are truly difficult. . . .

The problem I had is that when I examined Judge Roberts' record and history of public service, it is my personal estimation that he has far more often used his formidable skills on behalf of the strong in opposition to the weak.

Obama's focus on the 5 percent of cases where the law left things open, and his insistence that "the critical ingredient" comes from outside the law, now seems to be widely shared in the Senate. They know that they are not simply hiring umpires.

EVERY PRESIDENTIAL election year reporters call law professors who watch the Supreme Court to get their predictions about who each of the nominees would appoint to the Supreme Court if elected. In 2008, the answer for Barack Obama was blindingly obvious: Sonia Sotomayor. In October, *Esquire* magazine listed her as one of "the 75 Most Influential People of the 21st Century" because she was going to be Obama's first nominee to the Supreme Court. The magazine reported my analysis: "As a Hispanic woman with 16 years of court experience, Sotomayor would slay two of the court's lack-of-diversity birds with one swift stone. 'These are criteria that matter these days. Even Laura Bush was disappointed that her husband didn't name a woman to replace Sandra Day O'Connor.' . . ." A federal judge since 1991, Sotomayor would be the first Hispanic American justice. Indeed, Republicans had been wary about Sotomayor early on. She was nominated by the first President Bush as part of an arrangement, impossible to imagine today, in which Republican presidents allowed New York's Democratic senators to name their fair share of federal district judges. She was advanced to the Court of Appeals by President Clinton, and at that point Republicans began to take notice. They stalled her nomination a bit, not wanting to burnish her credentials as a Supreme Court nominee. But, in the end, they couldn't block the promotion. She plainly was qualified in standard terms; indeed, one academic study placed her solidly in the group of judges whose performance and reputation made them potential Supreme Court nominees. After Clinton's presidency ended and eight years of Republican control of the presidency, Judge Sotomayor's time had come.

Democratic presidents use Supreme Court nominations to build their party differently from Republicans. The Democratic Party is a coalition of groups identified by their demography and affiliations—African Americans, Hispanic Americans, union members, many members of cultural elites—but not by deep ideological commitments in the way social conservatives are part of the Republican coalition. So, Democratic presidents tend to pursue a demographic strategy rather than an ideological one for Supreme Court nominations. Baseline ideology matters, of course. No Democratic president is going to nominate someone who thinks that *Roe v. Wade* should be overturned. But ideological activism is far less important—probably it's completely unimportant—to Democratic presidents, in stark contrast to Republican ones. To put it bluntly: no matter how much conservative and liberal activists think otherwise, liberal supporters of judicial activism aren't an important constituency in today's Democratic Party.

The Democratic demographic strategy is tempered by three other considerations: age, securing confirmation, and timing.

Taking a page from the Republicans, Democrats now seek relatively young nominees, with an eligible age range from the early forties to the late fifties. When Chief Justice Roberts welcomed Elena Kagan to the Court, saying that he looked forward to working with her for the next twenty years, Justice Kagan is said to have replied, "Why only twenty?" (more a comment about her expectations than his, and a hint of tensions to come). When the president doesn't have a deep pool of his own appointees to draw on but has to rely on candidates who were legal activists under a predecessor's administration, it can be difficult to find people who are young enough. Judges appointed under President Clinton have basically aged out by now.

Simply nominating a justice has some political benefits, but getting him or her confirmed has more. Sometimes even losing a nomination fight can strengthen the party, as with Richard Nixon's failed effort to nominate two southern judges to the Supreme Court, which fit well into his party-building strategy for the South. Usually, though, winning is better than losing: Nixon got more out of putting Lewis Powell on the Supreme Court than in failing to get Clement Haynsworth confirmed.

Finally, early in a president's term it might be difficult to find your own people. Presidents then have to draw from a pool developed by someone else.

Sonia Sotomayor was as close to a pure demographic nomination as you can imagine, and even better for her, the nomination was coupled with the difficulties of making an "own person" nomination in President Obama's first year. Elena Kagan's nomination was only weakly demographic, though the fact that she was a woman mattered. Rather, hers was an "own person" nomination—she was serving as the Solicitor General in the Department of Justice when nominated—of someone who the President's advisers knew could be confirmed without too much real difficulty.

Republicans developed the "Pinpoint strategy" to defuse Democratic opposition to Clarence Thomas's nomination in 1991. The strategy emphasized the compelling life story Thomas told. The demographic strategy that led to Sotomayor's nomination led almost naturally to a similar approach to her confirmation. Her nomination placed Republicans in a difficult position. Hispanic support for Republicans was something of a Holy Grail for national Republican candidates, but the Republican constituency that paid attention to the courts was deeply suspicious of any potentially liberal addition to the Supreme Court. Sotomayor's confirmation was inevitable—in the end, the vote was 68–31, with nine Republicans voting to confirm her—but Republicans had to say something against her. The Democrats' "Sonia from the Block" strategy (as some snarkily called it) actually gave them a hook on which to hang their opposition.

Sotomayor's story was as compelling as Thomas's. The daughter of parents who left Puerto Rico for New York, Sonia Sotomayor was raised in a Bronx housing project. She got a full scholarship to Princeton University, where she won the school's undergraduate prize for the student who best combined scholarship and student activity. She went on to Yale Law School, where she was a good student, though not a superstar. She took a seminar with Yale's general counsel, José Cabranes, who had himself been born in Puerto Rico, and he took her under his wing. He gave her a job in his office during the summer, then recommended her for a job as an assistant district attorney in the high-powered office of Robert Morgenthau in Manhattan. After working there for a few years, she joined a small commercial law practice, where she specialized in intellectual property and international litigation. With Morgenthau's support, she began to be given political appointments, which in turn brought her to the attention of Senator Daniel Moynihan of New York, who chose her for one of the federal trial court appointments he had. She had been a district judge for five years when President Clinton nominated her for the court of appeals in 1997, a promotion of the forty-three-year-old that was widely viewed as foreshadowing a future Supreme Court nomination.

Searching Sotomayor's record as a trial and appeals court judge, you can't find a quotable phrase. She was sometimes aggressive in questioning the lawyers in front of her, some of whom anonymously disparaged her as "bullying" them. One notable case involved a challenge to Connecticut's practice of subjecting to a strip search every young woman brought into its juvenile justice system. Sotomayor dissented from her colleagues' decision upholding the policy, meticulously mining the record for the tiny amount of evidence, as she saw it, supporting the state's position that strip searches were necessary to detect child abuse and discover contraband such as drugs. Her decisions were always competent, always reasonable, and always pedestrian applications of the relevant precedents.

Campaigning for the presidency, Barack Obama said that he would choose judges who had "the heart, the empathy, to recognize what it's like to be a teenage mom. The empathy to understand what it's like to be poor, or African-American, or gay, or disabled, or old." Republicans naturally assumed that he meant what he said, and that Sotomayor had just that kind of empathy. As Republican senator Jeff Sessions of Alabama put it, "empathy for one party is always prejudice against another." Or, in Federalist Society founder Steven Calabresi's words, deciding cases based on empathy would "replace justice with empathy." That, they thought, was obviously a bad thing.

Republicans pushed two somewhat inconsistent lines. They criticized Obama's empathy standard because it was selective: he wanted empathy for the poor and disabled, but not for the small businessperson hobbled by government regulations. More important, they criticized the standard because, as they saw things, empathy had nothing whatever to do with the law. John Roberts's umpire wouldn't empathize with the runner he called out, or with the left fielder who bobbled a fly ball just inside the foul line.

Discussion of empathy pervaded Sotomayor's confirmation hearings. The tension within the Republican critique of empathy put them in a difficult position. Clarence Thomas's "Pinpoint strategy" drew pretty expressly on the idea that a person with his background would be a particularly good judge. Thomas's statement that when he saw the jail bus passing outside his office window, he said to himself, "There but for the grace of God go I," was about as clear a statement that he was an empathetic person as you can get.

Republicans pushed the "selective empathy" line in criticizing a circuit court opinion in a case on which Sotomayor sat. The city of New Haven, Connecticut, had historically discriminated against African Americans and Hispanics in promoting firefighters to captain. The city hired a consulting firm to devise a test for promotion. When the test was administered, the city discovered that no minorities would be on the list for promotion. It canceled the test results, and wanted to start over. Firefighters who would have been on the promotion list sued. The trial judge wrote an extensive opinion allowing the city to cancel the test results, and the court of appeals affirmed that decision, in a one-paragraph opinion that Sotomayor joined. That opinion elicited a long and passionate dissent by her mentor José Cabranes.

The Supreme Court had heard but not decided the case while Sotomayor's confirmation hearings were going on, and the case became a focal point for the "selective empathy" point. As the Senate was considering her nomination, the Court reversed her decision, by a five-to-four vote. Justice Alito's concurring opinion explained why Senate Republicans thought the case a good one for their argument against Sotomayor. Frank Ricci was the lead plaintiff against the city. "In order to qualify for promotion, [Ricci] made personal sacrifices. . . . Ricci, who is dyslexic, found it necessary to 'hir[e] someone, at considerable expense, to read onto audiotape the content of the books and study materials.' He 'studied an average of eight to thirteen hours a day . . . , even listening to audio tapes while driving his car.' " Like Thomas's references to the jail bus, this is an invocation of empathy. But, the challenge to Sotomayor went, she had so little empathy for Ricci that she didn't push her colleagues to write anything more than a paragraph in his case.

The Republican concern with selective empathy sat uneasily with their claims about how judges should interpret the Constitution. As we'll see in chapter 4, Republicans today think that judges should interpret the Constitution by finding out what a reasonable person at the time the Constitution was written would have thought the Constitution's words meant. Nothing in that inquiry calls for empathy with litigants, whether selective or universal. The Republicans' conflicted message was: "You shouldn't be empathetic to anyone, but when you are, you ought to be even-handed about it." Not quite a logical contradiction, but an awkwardness.

Democrats defending Sotomayor had an easier time of it. President Obama's campaign statement might have lent itself to the "selective empathy" charge, but there was precious little in Sotomayor's record to support it. Democratic senator Charles Schumer of New York recited cases involving applicants for asylum, victims of an airplane crash, a low-income woman who claimed that she had been denied a home equity loan because of her race, in all of which Judge Sotomayor ruled *against* the seemingly sympathetic litigants. Yet she repeatedly referred to her experience as a prosecutor, where, as she said in her opening statement, she "saw children exploited and abused . . . [and] felt the suffering of victims' families torn apart by a loved one's needless death."

The Democrats were able to work empathy smoothly into their account of constitutional interpretation. Empathy—for both sides—was a way judges could understand what Republican senator Lindsey Graham described as "the real-world implications of their decisions and the effects on regular Americans. . . . " Within the framework of the Republicans' preferred constitutional theory, though, consequences didn't matter. For Democrats, consequences mattered a lot, and a judge with empathy would come up with better interpretations of the Constitution than one who, like Roberts's umpire, was completely indifferent to the outcome.

The Democratic demographic strategy for nominations put Sotomayor's ethnicity up front in her confirmation hearings. As with the "Pinpoint strategy," the demographic strategy required injecting appealing details into their presentation of Sotomayor. The fact that she had diabetes came up, for example, not as a matter of concern but to show how she had overcome adversity (unrelated to her ethnicity), and we were told how she once rode a motorcycle to raid someone dealing in fake luxury goods.

Republicans thought they could turn the demographic strategy to their advantage. In part they capitalized on an undertone always present in discussions of affirmative action, that those who benefit from it aren't fully qualified—or, as the legal reporter Jeff Rosen put it, Judge Sotomayor was "not that smart." The demographic strategy opened the way for *Washington Post* columnist Dana Milbank to write that President Obama had chosen "biography over brains."*

Republican critics jumped on a statement Sotomayor had made several times in speaking to law students. Justice O'Connor was fond of quoting a state supreme court justice that a wise old man and a wise old woman would reach the same decision. Sotomayor used that quotation too, but said that it was wrong: "I would hope that a wise Latina woman with the richness of her experiences would more often than not reach a better conclusion than a white male who hasn't lived that life."

Sotomayor was drawing on some strands in an academic theory, more fashionable then than now, known as critical race theory, and it's not surprising that she made these comments most prominently at a symposium sponsored by a journal on race at the University of California Law School at Berkeley. In a weak version, critical race theory argued, pretty unexceptionably, that the kinds of experience a person has affects the way she, or he, sees a case. Every case comes to court with a background that doesn't appear fully in the record. Judges fill in the background by drawing on their understanding of the way the world works. That understanding draws on their experiences. As Sotomayor tried to explain, the statement was designed to say that her life experiences helped her to "listen and understand," not to "command the results in the case." Samuel Alito said the same thing: "When I get

---

* An academic study relying on Judge Sotomayor's work on the court of appeals concluded that on many plausible measures of quality she was in the top quarter of all federal court of appeals judges, and that on some she was in the top 10 percent.

a case about discrimination, I have to think about people in my own family who suffered discrimination because of their ethnic background or because of religion or because of gender. And I do take that into account."

Sotomayor tried to take some of the sting out of her "wise Latina" statement by referring to Justice Alito's comment, but it didn't work. Critical race theory in some stronger versions claimed that judges should shape what the law is—not merely understand what the facts are—by drawing on their experience-based knowledge of an unstated background. Sotomayor never really made that claim, but her use of the word "wise" brought her into the territory of the stronger claim. Justice O'Connor's statement was that wisdom was a virtue available to men and women. Sotomayor's suggested that it was available more easily to Latinas than to white men.* She said that she used the line in inspirational speeches aimed at encouraging minority students to take their studies seriously and work for social justice. She ended up by claiming that her words were a "rhetorical flourish that fell flat"—pabulum that sounded good to the immediate audiences but that could fairly be read to say more than she intended.

Sotomayor replaced her earlier line with a mantra that the judge's job was to apply the law to the facts. While perhaps a decent description of what she had been doing before, it was laughably inaccurate as a description of what a Supreme Court justices does. To be fair, "apply[ing] the law to the facts" is John Roberts's umpire metaphor translated into descriptive prose. It had worked for him, but it didn't work well for Sotomayor. Her "wise Latina" statement forced her into a defensive crouch, from which she said as little as possible about how she would actually figure out what the law was—or, as a more candid

---

* Technically, she never said that Latinas were generically wiser than white males. O'Connor juxtaposed a wise old man to a wise old woman, while Sotomayor juxtaposed a wise Latina to a white male, omitting the modifier.

nominee would put it, how she would decide what the law should be. Candor, though, might have led to defeat.

As a justice, she continued to pay attention to factual details. Sotomayor was perhaps the Court's closest—and arguably its best—analyst of the records in criminal cases, probably as a result of her years as a prosecutor and trial judge. She was neither invariably pro-prosecution nor invariably pro-defendant in criminal cases, writing a noteworthy opinion putting some limits on Justice Scalia's foray into pro-defendant rulings on the confrontation clause. Her personal demeanor on the bench and in her public appearances conveyed the message that she was a person of real substance, even when she showed up on *Sesame Street* to settle the dispute between Goldilocks and the Three Bears. But, overall, Justice Sotomayor left a small footprint after her first years on the Court.

SENATOR LINDSEY Graham was questioning Elena Kagan on the second day of her confirmation hearing when he asked, "Now, as we move forward and deal with law of war issues, [the] Christmas Day bomber, where were you at on Christmas Day?" Kagan assumed, correctly, that Senator Graham planned to ask her whether she thought that government investigators had acted properly when, after an hour of interrogation, they gave the accused bomber his *Miranda* warnings.* Like a runner jumping the gun, she started to answer that question, and then fumbled to figure out a way in which she might say something that would satisfy Senator Graham: "Senator Graham, that is an undecided legal issue, which—the—well, I suppose I should ask exactly what you mean by that. I'm assuming that the question you mean is whether a person who is apprehended in the United States is. . . . " Senator Graham

---

* Umar Farouk Abdulmutallab, the Christmas Day or "underwear" bomber, pleaded guilty to eight criminal charges on October 12, 2011.

replied, "No, I just asked you where you were at on Christmas." Kagan broke out with a genuine laugh that lasted several seconds, a long time as these things go, and then came back with the perfect answer: "You know, like all Jews, I was probably at a Chinese restaurant." That punctured Senator Graham's balloon, and the hearings moved on.

Kagan had a conventionally successful career as a student and young lawyer and academic, with a few bumps. Raised in a liberal Upper West Side family in New York, she graduated from Princeton University, where she edited the college newspaper, and won a university-sponsored scholarship to Oxford before attending Harvard Law School. There she was a successful law student, becoming an editor of the *Law Review* and graduating *magna cum laude* along with a handful of other top students. There are hints, but only hints, in her personal and family history of some more than conventionally liberal-leftish leanings: a brother's career trajectory from college to working on a shop floor as a union and political organizer to teaching in the public schools; a senior thesis she wrote at Princeton on the socialist movement in New York City; career guidance she received from Morton Horwitz, a leader of the left-leaning critical legal studies movement at Harvard, after she got a low grade from him in her first-year Torts class.

After the announcement of her nomination, some liberal interest groups and legal academics worried that she wasn't going to be a liberal in the mold of William Brennan and Thurgood Marshall. Paul Campos of the University of Colorado wrote a highly critical profile of Kagan that described her as "a blank slate." That misread both Kagan and the changing nature of the Democratic Party's liberalism. Kagan's early career choices suggest that as a young lawyer she did indeed fit the older mold. She clerked for Abner Mikva, a liberal icon in Congress and—after redistricting reduced his reelection prospects—on the District of Columbia Court of Appeals, where, notably, he once almost had a fist fight with conservative icon Laurence Silberman. Then she clerked for Thurgood Marshall. Marshall left a great deal of the work of drafting opinions to his law clerks, and Marshall and the committee of former clerks who screened their successors were careful to ensure that the clerks would be instinctively attuned to his views about the Constitution. If you really were basically an ambitious liberal in the late 1980s, the Mikva-Marshall path was about the best that you could follow.

Kagan's career after her clerkships was, again, reasonably conventional. She worked for Williams & Connolly, a large Washington law firm well connected to Democratic politicians, though as a young lawyer she had no significant involvement in any politically important cases. After a few years there, she decided to go back to the legal academy. Harvard's faculty considered her for a position, but decided to hire her classmate and friend Carol Steiker instead—because, as one colleague put it, in 1991 Harvard Law School simply couldn't hire two women at the same time. She went instead to the University of Chicago Law School.*

In the early 1990s Chicago's law school had a conservative reputation, only partly deserved. The school had a strong group of conservative-leaning scholars interested in law and economics, but it also had a strong group of liberal-leaning scholars of constitutional law, led by Geoffrey Stone, the school's dean from 1987 to 1994 and a leading scholar of the First Amendment.

Mostly, the law faculty was an intellectual hothouse. Kagan's interests were more diffuse than the purely intellectual ones generally favored by the Chicago faculty. Her untenured colleagues accumulated long lists of publications by churning out short paper after short paper. Kagan wrote relatively little. One essay was a dyspeptic discussion of the Supreme Court nomination process in the 1980s and 1990s, which came back to bite her. Senator Graham alluded to the article when he asked—again to laughter—"Are we improving or going backward? And

---

* I first met Kagan when she was on the Chicago faculty. I organized a dinner for some friends at the annual meeting of the academic association for law professors, that year in San Francisco, and someone brought her along.

are you doing your part?" Kagan answered diplomatically but with a twinkle, "I think you have been exercising your constitutional responsibilities extremely well," to which Graham responded, "So it's those other guys that suck, not us, right?" (After laughter from the audience, Kagan's answer was, "I'm not going to . . . ," with the rest—probably something like "get into that" or "try to answer that"—cut off.) Kagan also wrote an article on First Amendment theory, bringing into focus some ideas rattling around in the literature that the Court's concern in free speech cases centered on the reasons legislatures had for attempting to regulate speech.

Kagan's scholarly record was thin for a Chicago faculty member, and her tenure case was a close one, as Chicago faculty members later put it. Chicago's law faculty also was not an easy place for women, which may have affected the tenure decision both in its closeness and its outcome. After getting tenure, Kagan took a leave from the faculty to work in Bill Clinton's White House, initially on the staff of the White House counsel and then as a major adviser on issues of domestic policy. Her work and her intelligence impressed everyone around her. Late in his term, President Clinton nominated Kagan to a seat on the District of Columbia Court of Appeals. The Senate was controlled by Republicans, and Senator Orrin Hatch didn't schedule a hearing for Kagan and another nominee to the same court. Kagan's nomination in 1999 met the same fate as had John Roberts's nomination in 1992: coming too late in the administration of a president the opposing party expected to replace, both nominations lapsed when the president's term ended. For both, the setback may have been the best thing that happened to them, though it surely did not seem so at the time.

Chicago's faculty limited the length of leaves for government service, and Kagan had had to resign from the faculty during her time at the White House. The faculty decided against rehiring her, and she was at academic loose ends. Harvard had passed her over for a position twice—once when she was just going on the job market, and then a few years later when she was proposed as part of a package that included a law-and-economics scholar, a package that fell apart when the law school's internal politics led to a negative vote on the other candidate and then to the withdrawal of Kagan's proposed appointment. The third time was the charm, though it did not come easily. Kagan got a two-year appointment as a visitor at Harvard, on the understanding that she would be considered for a permanent appointment if she produced a major scholarly article during the visit.

As human resources people say, Kagan exceeded expectations. She was a spectacularly good teacher, whose unforgiving questions somehow led students to love her. More important for her career, she drew on her experience in the Clinton White House for a brilliant article in the *Harvard Law Review* on what she called "Presidential Administration." The article pulled together a lot of strands about politics and administrative law in the 1990s, giving a clear view of what, relying in part on Kagan's work, I called in 2003 "the new constitutional order." The article defended as entirely constitutional what others regarded as questionable innovations in presidential power. For Kagan, these innovations resulted from persistent divided government, and our understanding of the Constitution ought to adapt to that political environment. Although she didn't phrase it in this way, the article was an example of "living Constitution" reasoning—another indication that liberal misgivings about Kagan's possible position on the Court were misplaced.

"Presidential Administration" was enough to get Kagan a job at Harvard. Perhaps more precisely the article, her teaching evaluations, and her personality were enough to get her the job. As she showed in her nomination hearings, Kagan is an extrovert, happy to schmooze with anyone. Justice Ginsburg reportedly remarked at the end of Kagan's first year on the Court that if you asked each justice who was Kagan's closest friend on the Court, each one would have said, "Me."

Kagan had many friends at Harvard before she arrived, and made more while she was visiting. She moved rapidly into the law school's informal leadership, and then got an important administrative assignment. The law school's faculty was worried about Harvard's plans to expand its campus "across the river" from Cambridge. Two plans emerged as the main candidates. One would have relocated the Harvard Law School across the river in Alston. The school's faculty opposed the move with almost complete unanimity (only the librarian was in favor, seeing it as an opportunity to improve the library's physical facilities). Harvard's president Laurence Summers of course had a larger set of concerns, and someone had to convince him that relocating the school was a bad idea. Kagan had worked with Summers at the White House, and the law school's dean appointed her to chair the committee to "examine" the options, reach the foregone conclusion, and report to Summers. She marshaled her forces and her arguments, and Summers chose the other plan. (Harvard had to put its extension plans on hold after the financial crisis of 2008.)

Faculty politics at Harvard had become poisonous in the 1980s, when a *New Yorker* article described it as "Beirut on the Charles." A group of younger left-leaning professors associated with the critical legal studies movement challenged not so much the overtly conservative advocates of law-and-economics, but the more traditionalist heart of the Harvard faculty. Roberto Unger, one of the younger stars, described the traditionalists as resembling a priesthood that had lost its faith but kept its jobs. The traditionalists denied tenure to a feminist scholar, who eventually won a settlement of her sex discrimination charge, and appointment politics sometimes became quite personal. Hiring, especially in constitutional law, became impossible, and Harvard's reputation within the legal academy suffered.

The worst was over by the 1990s, but the experience of the 1980s scarred the faculty. Getting faculty members to pay attention to the law school as an institution had always been fairly difficult, and the difficulties were exacerbated by changes in the legal academy as a whole, where "free agency"—faculty members leaving one school for another for larger financial and reputational rewards—became common. The fights of the 1980s produced a faculty alienated from the school and faculty members alienated from each other. The law school entered a period of institutional stasis, which lasted up to Kagan's appointment as dean.

When Dean Robert Clark announced that he was stepping down, Kagan was the faculty's consensus choice. Summers made some gestures in the direction of doing a real search, reportedly asking the law-and-economics guru and federal court of appeals judge Richard Posner whether he'd be interested in the job (he refused it) before making the inevitable choice.

Kagan became the dean of a large, talented, and dispirited faculty, and worked what one article called a "miracle." The miracle she wrought was getting the law school functioning again. Her first moves involved improving the atmosphere for students. She converted some open space to a volleyball court in the summer and a skating rink in the winter. She provided bagels and coffee for students in the morning. These were cheap, symbolic, and quite effective moves in building a constituency supporting her within the school.

More important, she carried out a faculty decision to shift from a system of having four large sections in the first-year classes to seven. That produced tremendous pressure to expand the faculty. Harvard's faculty was large enough to have twenty-eight people teaching in the first year while continuing to offer a full range of classes to students in their second and third years. It was not large enough to have forty-nine people teaching the first year.

Harvard needed to go on a hiring spree. But "need" and "ability" are not the same. Kagan managed to get her faculty to go along with a slew of appointments through forceful leadership. She stacked the appointments committees with people she could persuade to go along with appointments they might have opposed without her leadership, and made it clear that she did not like it when faculty members disagreed with committee recommendations. As new appointments accumulated, the group of faculty who could be counted as Kagan loyalists grew— from the longtime faculty and, inevitably, from new faculty members who owed their appointments to her.

Of course Kagan didn't have a free hand in picking new faculty members. The residual problems from the 1980s made hiring a political matter, and Kagan was superb at faculty politics. Notably, in public law she tacked right, to overcome suspicion that her Democratic affiliations were simply going to reproduce the politics that had divided the faculty. The law school made three major appointments of conservative public law scholars: Adrian Vermeule, John Manning, and Jack Goldsmith. Goldsmith's appointment roiled the waters a bit, because he had served as head of the Bush administration's Office of Legal Counsel, an office that was associated with the notorious "torture memos," and his role in tempering that office's excesses was not yet fully public when he came to Harvard. Then she tacked left, supporting among others my own appointment to the faculty.

Kagan was something like a shark in the water, always needing to do something new. Her success at the Harvard Law School led her to think, reasonably, that she should be seriously considered as Summers's successor when he was forced out as Harvard's president. But she was too closely associated with Summers for that to happen. Students saw Kagan differently, of course. She was a charismatic figure for them. Her limited wardrobe—the only question each day was what the color of her short jacket was going to be—became an object of gentle humor. Students flocked to the classes she continued to teach, even though they were offered early in the morning so that she could devote the rest of her day to fund-raising and administration. And, again, she showed a deft political touch. Liberal students got a much-expanded office seeking to place them in public interest jobs. On the right, when the Federalist Society held its national student convention at Harvard in 2005, Kagan offered welcoming remarks that became famous. "I love the Federalist Society," she said, to overwhelming applause—whereupon she reminded her audience, "You are *not* my people," this time to laughter.

Kagan left Harvard for the Obama administration at a propitious time for her. The financial crisis hit, and the dean's ability to supply perks became much more limited. The skating rink shut down and the bagels went away, though the volleyball court remained. And resentment of Kagan's strong leadership style had grown, though not to a crisis point.

Kagan's departure for Washington after Barack Obama's election was a foregone conclusion. The only question was what position she'd take, and for how long. Speculation centered on Attorney General and Solicitor General. Presidents hope that their Attorney Generals will form part of the inner cabinet that provides general advice but also will maintain some professional distance. Kagan could do the second, but—because she didn't have a close political relation to Obama—not the first. Naming her Solicitor General would be demographically satisfying as well. Janet Reno had been the first woman Attorney General; Kagan would be the first woman Solicitor General. And, from Kagan's point of view, the political intimacy that comes with being Attorney General probably disqualifies them today from serious consideration for a Supreme Court appointment. Not so the Solicitor General.

Kagan was Solicitor General for just short of a year. She followed the usual practice of arguing about one case in each monthly sitting during which the Court heard oral arguments. Of the six cases she argued, a handful were high profile. Although she had never presented a Supreme Court argument before, to no one's surprise Kagan turned out to be a skilled oral advocate, on a par with the leaders of the specialized Supreme Court bar. She was always prepared, with a close knowledge of the law and precedents.

Kagan argued the high-profile campaign finance case, *Citizens United*. As we'll see later, she took a truly indefensible position. The government's case was supported by a single decision, which later ones had undermined. Kagan didn't agree with the earlier decision's reasoning, but it was all she had to go on. She tried to defend the outcome by reading into the decision things that weren't there, and the Chief Justice went after her with a vengeance. On paper the back-and-forth between Roberts and Kagan looks pretty routine, but by Supreme Court standards it's about as personally pointed as you get.

When John Paul Stevens announced his retirement in Obama's second year, the "own person" preference kicked in. Obama went through the usual process of considering a short list that included Diane Wood and Merrick Garland. Neither had much going for them by 2010. Wood had been a quasi-colleague of Obama's when he taught at the University of Chicago Law School, and her former husband Dennis Hutchinson, one of Obama's closest friends on the Chicago faculty, lobbied heavily for Wood's appointment. That was about it. Concerns about Wood's confirmability also figured in the decision. She had written some forceful opinions in abortion rights cases that were bound to generate intense opposition. Kagan in contrast came from within the administration, and the president's advisers thought correctly that her confirmation would be easy. As Democratic senator Sheldon Whitehouse of Rhode Island put it on the first day of her confirmation hearings, "I don't want to take any suspense out of these proceedings, but things are looking good for your confirmation." The calculation was right. Kagan was confirmed by a vote of 63 to 37, closer than Sotomayor's but wider than Alito's.

The confirmation hearings were routine. She agreed that she could be characterized as a political progressive. But "progressivism" in 2010 wasn't what "liberalism" had been in the 1960s. Bill Clinton had reoriented the Democratic Party, and Kagan's work in the Clinton administration made her comfortable as a Clinton Democrat. As dean at Harvard she had to stay out of active involvement in the primary campaign between Hillary Rodham Clinton and Barack Obama. She might well have been seriously considered for an important position in a Hillary Clinton administration too, although a Clinton administration would have tilted more toward Yale, the Clintons' law school, than Obama's did toward Harvard. Kagan's politics were Bill Clinton's, shifted a bit to the left on her own and through her association with President Obama.

As usual these days, Kagan kept her cards close to her chest, refusing to answer questions about issues that might come before the Court, though she was somewhat more open than Roberts and Sotomayor had been. Kagan's confirmation hearings foreshadowed her likely role on the Supreme Court as leading the opposition to Chief Justice Roberts. Kagan's most important opinion in her first term was a dissent from a Roberts opinion in a case striking down Arizona's system for providing public financing for campaigns. The case is discussed in more detail in chapter 7, but here it's the tone of Kagan's dissent that matters. She referred to the challengers' position, which Roberts and four others accepted, as involving *chutzpah*—the word's second appearance in a justice's opinion. And, responding to Roberts's conclusion that Arizona's system obviously "burdened" people who didn't want to accept public financing, Kagan described the system's burdens in this way: "Pretend you are financing your campaign through private donations. Would you prefer that your opponent receive a guaranteed, upfront payment of $150,000, or that he receive only $50,000, with the possibility—a possibility that you mostly get to control—of collecting another $100,000 somewhere down the road? Me too." The pause implicit before the final words signals contempt.

As the campaign finance opinion showed, Kagan rapidly became one of the Court's most engaging prose stylists. In a quite technical case where the issue was whether "not a" meant "not any one at all" or "not at least one," Kagan did a riff on conversations with a child who says she didn't read a book all summer or didn't read an assigned text, and with a sports fan over whether the New York Mets had a chance of winning the World Series. Just for fun, she threw in a reference to a provision dealing with importing prescription drugs—"(no controversy there!)"—and, demonstrating her skill at appealing to her colleagues, a barely relevant citation to an opinion written by Chief Justice Roberts.

Kagan reportedly expressed some concern a few months later that her words in the campaign finance dissent might have been too sharp. She toned things down only a bit in her second year. Her most important dissent came in a complex case involving the Constitution's guarantee that criminal defendants have a right to confront—cross-examine—the witnesses against them. The case involved a DNA profile developed by a company called Cellmark, and, like a good reporter, Kagan opened her opinion with an anecdote involving a gross error by Cellmark that had been exposed through cross-examination, an anecdote so effective that Justice Alito's prevailing opinion had to devote a footnote to explaining why he thought it irrelevant. As in the campaign finance opinion, she worked out an effective law school style hypothetical to show why Justice Alito's theory of the case didn't make any sense. She asked readers to imagine that "an eyewitness tells a police officer investigating an assault that the perpetrator had an unusual, star-shaped birthmark over his left eye," and then completed the analogy by saying of a DNA profile, "think of it as the quintessential birthmark." Her opinion was filled with colloquialisms—Justice Thomas, who offered his own theory, "would turn the Confrontation Clause into a constitutional geegaw." And her dismissive "Me too" in the campaign finance case found its echo in "Been there, done that" here.

Roberts's questions to Solicitor General Kagan suggested that he understood what she might become, and Kagan's dissent in the campaign finance case suggests that he was right. Her votes would differ from his on major issues but, more important, she would be a major intellectual force. Her response to the Chief Justice's greeting on her arrival at the Supreme Court, "Why only twenty [years]?" was both a prediction and a veiled threat. Depending on who the next additions to the Court's membership were, she might become the Court's intellectual leader—and people might start talking about a Kagan Court instead of the Roberts Court.

WITH SOTOMAYOR and Kagan, the Roberts Court took shape. The four new justices joined five old-timers. Anthony Kennedy was the most central. He had been Ronald Reagan's third choice for the seat he took in 1988. A Californian to his bones, Kennedy was a lawyer and lobbyist in Sacramento, and became an important adviser to Edwin Meese when Reagan was California's governor. Reagan named him to the court of appeals and then, after Robert Bork's nomination was rejected and Douglas Ginsburg's withdrawn, promoted him to the Supreme Court. As his years on the Supreme Court grew, so did Kennedy's sense of his own importance. His rhetoric in opinions and public appearances could be both ponderous and pompous. Often he appeared to be writing for the history books, and of the Roberts Court's senior members he was rather clearly the one most concerned with how the history books would represent him. Kennedy's personal views and his concern for his historical legacy contributed to his position on gay rights—supporting them became something of a signature issue for him, even when doing so required some doctrinal innovation.

Antonin Scalia is generally regarded, though not by me, as the Court's best stylist. He is the master of the sharp one-liner, usually aimed at an opponent on the Court and designed to be picked up by Supreme Court reporters and by his acolytes in the legal academy and the profession. Scalia is self-confident to a fault, often treating lawyers with disdain as they argue positions he disagrees with. Almost from the beginning of his time on the Court, he staked out strong and—at the time—distinctive positions about the proper methods of constitutional and statutory interpretation. But as time went on, his campaigns seem to have failed, or at least gained less ground than he had hoped, and Scalia's writing became increasingly grumpy. In person, he is genial, though sometimes condescending when things don't go exactly his way; but given the deference with which he is received, they almost always do go his way.

Supreme Court justices tend not to be well known to the public. Clarence Thomas is well known, but not for the right reasons. His career on the Supreme Court will always be associated with the allegations of sexual harassment—or something like sexual harassment, even if his actions (if they happened) didn't satisfy the legal standard—made by Anita Hill when he was nominated to the Court. Until the arrival of Justice Alito, Justice Thomas was probably the Court's most conservative member. He is a more faithful proponent of interpreting the Constitution solely by looking to what its words meant when they were put into the Constitution than Justice Scalia. His version of originalism sometimes leads to odd, though defensible positions: dissenting from a Scalia opinion holding that California couldn't prohibit the sale of violent video games to minors without their parents' consent, Thomas relied on an originalist account of children's free expression rights in 1791 (they didn't have any, he concluded). And he has been a completely solid performer in the stock in trade of the Court's work, cases interpreting complex federal statutes.

The Court's older liberals are Ruth Bader Ginsburg and Stephen Breyer, both appointed by Bill Clinton. Ginsburg brought a seemingly frail body, but one with a metaphorically steel backbone, to the Court. She had made a career as the nation's leading legal advocate of women's rights, and has continued to be a strong voice for women on the Court. She is also interested in the technicalities of litigation procedure, her field of specialization as a legal academic. Though sometimes she has been correctly described as the Thurgood Marshall of the women's rights movement, she wasn't a liberal in the Marshall mold. Marshall came out of a Democratic Party shaped by Franklin Roosevelt and

Lyndon Johnson. That wasn't Bill Clinton's Democratic Party, and Justice Ginsburg was a late twentieth-century Democrat, not a New Dealer.

That is even more true of Stephen Breyer. A law professor at Harvard for much of his early career, Breyer went to work for Senator Ted Kennedy as counsel on the Judiciary Committee. He specialized in administrative and regulatory law, and he came to appreciate the importance of compromise and accommodation for getting things done in Congress. President Jimmy Carter nominated him for a position on the court of appeals, and he was so well regarded by both sides in the Judiciary Committee that he was confirmed for the seat after Reagan defeated Carter—an unthinkable outcome today. A technocrat who described himself as a pragmatist, Breyer is impatient with decisions grounded in abstract theory and inattentive to the facts on the ground that Breyer thinks are important.

Looking at the Roberts Court, we see a Court that is diverse along some dimensions, but notably not along others. Three women, one African American, one Hispanic American—the Roberts Court sort of looks like America. The ways in which it doesn't show the contours of the nation's contemporary political terrain.

The Roberts Court has six Catholics and three Jews—and, as arithmetic will tell you, no Protestants. What's most remarkable about this is that no one thinks it's terribly remarkable. University of Chicago law professor Geoffrey Stone tried to gin up some comments about religion when Samuel Alito managed to get the nomination after George W. Bush's process for choosing a nominee broke down. The general response was a shrug. Religion may have been salient in the past, but not now, although perhaps religiosity—some generic religious commitments— still matters. Evangelical Christianity is quite vibrant in the nation, but not at the Supreme Court, although Clarence Thomas probably is best described as an evangelical Catholic. Protestant evangelicals have historically had a strained relation with law, their theology telling them that Christ came to replace law with mercy. Only a Republican president will nominate an evangelical Protestant, and finding one with enough credentials to get through the confirmation process may be difficult. (To be clear, this is a comment on the standards used to measure credentials, not on the ability of many evangelical Protestant lawyers.)

WASPs may matter elsewhere in the nation's political and economic system, though less than in the past. But when you're dealing with as small a number as nine, it's no longer worth noting that WASPs no longer inhabit the Supreme Court.

Then there's the Court's striking lack of regional diversity. You can usually generate at least a chuckle in knowing audiences by observing that residents of Staten Island should be outraged at the fact that it's the only New York borough that isn't represented on the Supreme Court (Kagan from Manhattan, Scalia from Queens, Sotomayor from the Bronx, Ginsburg from Brooklyn). No one on the Roberts Court developed a professional career between the east and west coasts, although one can stretch and say that Clarence Thomas worked for a while in St. Louis. Only Anthony Kennedy is fairly described as something of a westerner, though nothing like the cowgirl Sandra Day O'Connor was.

Historically, presidents tried to achieve some sort of regional balance on the Supreme Court. Richard Nixon looked for southerners to appoint. It mattered to Franklin Roosevelt that people described William O. Douglas and Wiley Rutledge as westerners, even though doing so was something of a stretch.

Nixon wanted to nominate a southerner because his overall political strategy involved shifting southern whites from the Democratic Party to the Republican. That's been accomplished, and presidents don't gain much politically by paying attention to region when they look for Supreme Court nominees. The Court has lost something by losing members from the "fly-over" states, as some people on the coasts refer to the rest of the country. It regularly deals with issues of water law and the rights of Native Americans, important issues in the West about which no one on the Court really knows anything. In a case from Montana, Paul Clement tried to describe how long a river in Montana was by telling the justices that "for the New Yorkers, you know, the East River is 16 miles long, the whole river," to which Justice Sotomayor replied, "But I'm not a Midwesterner, and rivers of more than 200 miles . . ." Montanans would probably be surprised to find that they were regarded as midwesterners. As with religion, the loss of regional diversity shows what politics today looks like.

The Roberts Court is also highly elitist in the educational backgrounds of its members. Eight justices graduated from Harvard and Yale Law Schools, and Ruth Bader Ginsburg started law school at Harvard before transferring to Columbia when her husband got a job in New York. Even other elite law schools such as Chicago and Stanford might feel slighted. I'm hardly in a position to deprecate the value of an elite legal education, but having taught at the University of Wisconsin Law School for eight years I know that lawyers learn different—other—things in less elite schools, and even the best of them tend to follow different career paths. Judge Sidney Thomas's name surfaced toward the end of President Obama's selection process that gave us Justice Kagan. Serving as a student member of the University of Montana's board of regents, Judge Thomas decided to stay, and graduated with honors from his state's only law school before becoming a leading bankruptcy practitioner.* Apparently, though, Judge Thomas couldn't break into the charmed circle of the U.S. equivalent of the *papabile*.

Maybe we can see in the Roberts Court the triumph of the American meritocracy, although again I note the awkwardness of saying so in light of my own academic position and background. Elite educational institutions opened up to merit over the past several generations. The best students at nearly every law school are as good as the best students

---

* A nice quotation from Judge Thomas: "Bankruptcy's *amazing*. . . . It's about life. It's about failure—it's about overcoming failure. It's about dreams dying."

at Harvard and Yale, but the rise of meritocracy means that there are just a lot more really good law students, who make good lawyers, at the elite institutions. Limiting your search for Supreme Court candidates to graduates of the most elite schools simplifies your job, and it's pretty likely that you'll end up with a good—and safe—choice. That's clearly a good thing for the judge-pickers. Whether it's entirely to the Court's good is a different question.

Finally, there's professional background. Over our history Supreme Court justices have come from a mix of professional backgrounds. Many had been judges before their appointment to the Court, but many had been in private practice or in high political office. That mix has basically disappeared from the Court, and now you almost have to be a judge—preferably a federal judge—to get nominated and confirmed. You can massage the backgrounds of the justices: John Roberts was a practitioner before briefly stopping at the court of appeals on his way to the Supreme Court; Anthony Kennedy was a significant lobbyist in California; Elena Kagan wasn't a judge at all, but Solicitor General for a year, and a staffer in the Clinton White House; Clarence Thomas ran a federal agency for several years; Ruth Bader Ginsburg was a public interest lawyer for many years before Jimmy Carter appointed her to the Supreme Court. Yet this is weak tea compared to William Howard Taft, the nation's president before he was appointed to the Supreme Court, or Charles Evans Hughes, who ran for the presidency and served as secretary of state; or Lewis Powell, a private practitioner who had been president of the American Bar Association.

Political experience used to be valuable for Supreme Court justices because they regularly dealt with constitutional and statutory questions about how the law could regulate the way the government worked. We wanted what Justice Robert Jackson (himself a former Solicitor General and Attorney General) called "a workable government," and judges could make it work well, but only, it seemed, if they actually knew something about its operations. Chief Justice Warren Burger may have signaled a shift in perspective when he wrote, in a decision invalidating the legislative veto, a useful technique for Congress to patrol what executive officials do in the modern state: "The choices we discern as having been made in the Constitutional Convention impose burdens on governmental processes that often seem clumsy, inefficient, even unworkable, but those hard choices were consciously made. . . ."

Politics has changed, too. Politicians who tried to make the government work were accommodating sorts, committed to their principles but open to compromise. Today's politicians, emerging from our hyperpartisan and polarized government, are not accommodating. They have their principles and stick to them. That causes enough problems in Congress, with 535 members, many of whom come and go with each election. The problems would be even worse, I suspect, with nine people forced to deal with each other for years on end. Putting people on the Court with political experience in today's environment would mean putting hyperpartisans uninterested in compromise on the Court, which would pretty clearly be a bad thing.

Lawyers who spend their time doing ordinary law are another matter. They know things about the law that judges don't—not only about the law on the ground, but also about deep-rooted concepts in ordinary law that underlie our statutes and the Constitution. Sometimes justices get distracted by the "big" issues of constitutional law and forget that the right way to resolve those issues involves using those concepts from ordinary law (the funeral protest case discussed in chapter 6 is an example of this, I think). Having more judges with backgrounds in real-world practice might be a good idea. Samuel Alito and Sonia Sotomayor, both of whom worked as prosecutors for quite a while, might be the models. They were judges when they were appointed to the Supreme Court, but their real experience had been in ordinary law practice. Getting a career practitioner on the Court could be helpful.

Can we expect the Roberts Court to be reshaped by presidents attentive to these kinds of diversity factors? Probably not.

So: FIVE justices appointed by Republicans, in a political world where the Republican Party had become strikingly more conservative, and four appointed by Democrats, in a political world where the Democratic Party's New Deal liberalism had faded dramatically. The justices were shaped by developments over several political generations. The politics in the Supreme Court's halls would result from how each one understood the political world they came from and inhabited, and from the way they dealt with each other.

CHAPTER 3

The Rookie and
Sophomore Years

Chief Justice Roberts said, "I suspect it's like how people look at their families," referring to the Supreme Court. When the Court's membership changes, "You're bringing in a family member," according to Clarence Thomas. The justices regularly eat lunch together, they occasionally go to public events together, and they sometimes socialize in private. Justices Scalia and Ginsburg have a friendship, nurtured by Justice Ginsburg's late spouse Marty, going back to the time they served on the court of appeals together. Justice Kagan has gone bird-hunting with Justice Scalia. When asked about personal relations on the Court, every justice says that there's never been a harsh word among them.

Despite their sharp ideological differences, none of this should be surprising. A small group of people working on a focused task every day has to get along—at least on the surface. Justice Thomas's analogy to a family is accurate if we keep in mind that many families are slightly dysfunctional. The Supreme Court family consists of a lot of sons- and daughters-in-law, people brought into the family because of one thing, who now have to deal with a lot of people who are there because of something else. Dinners (and lunches) in that sort of family are indeed rather cordial, but a fair amount of passive aggression is always beneath the surface and sometimes bubbles up. And, of course, to say that the justices don't utter harsh words to one another when they meet isn't to say that everything is sweetness and light back in their offices. Most of the Court's work is done in writing—not even through e-mails, but through relatively formal letters sent from one justice to another. Formality promotes good manners, but doesn't always reflect what's going on underneath. His colleagues have said that Chief Justice Roberts runs the Court with "decorum and cordiality," antiseptic words that describe some meals in families whose members aren't all that intimate or even comfortable with each other.

Relations within families always have to adjust when someone new joins, and the new arrivals to the Court have to adjust as well. Justice Sotomayor observed that new justices are "coming into the middle [of] a continuously running conversation." The justices have been arguing and writing about the same issues for years, and often have developed a shorthand, something like the old joke about prisoners who tell their own jokes by shouting out numbers. The punch line of that joke is that a new prisoner calls out "Fifty-four," gets no reaction, and asks why: "You told it wrong," is the answer. For Justice Sotomayor, the justices would be discussing a case in their conference and someone would explain a position that seemed to her "coming out of left field." A colleague "would lean over and say, 'Oh, this has to do with this peccadillo they have about X,Y, Z. . . .'" Eventually the new justice learns the ropes, but it usually takes a while.

The conversation Justice Sotomayor referred to takes on a new shape when a new justice arrives. During Roberts's first months, the Court was hearing cases argued that it had decided to review when Rehnquist and O'Connor were on the Court—when the conversation had been going on for a long time and everyone knew where everyone stood. Justices often decide to grant review with an eye to how the final decision is going to come out. Put two new members in place, and the possible outcomes change. It makes sense to issue cautious and narrow opinions until the "new" Court settles in.

A new chief justice has an additional problem. He is the first among equals, and sometimes it's hard to figure out how to be both first and equal. Chief Justice Burger never did. Chief Justice Rehnquist was famously even-handed, but by the end of his tenure his impatience with extended discussion meant that the justices rarely discussed the cases in detail, conducting all their real business by correspondence.

Chief Justice Roberts slid easily into the role of manager within the Court. He knew his new colleagues professionally, because arguing cases as skillfully as Roberts did requires that you get inside the heads of everyone on the Court. And he knew them personally, at least in the relatively superficial way you get to know people in the cocktail and dinner party circuit in Washington. He loosened the tight reins Rehnquist had placed on discussions, allowing "more back-and-forth, more discussion."

But when Roberts described the justices as umpires, he had more in mind than running the Court smoothly. He repeatedly said that he did have an agenda—just not an ideological one. The Court, he said, had gotten too divided, issuing opinions with too many dissents and, even worse, separate opinions agreeing with the result but offering different reasons. How could lawyers and lower courts know what the law was if the Supreme Court wasn't clear?

The Roberts Court's first two terms gave some hints about whether Roberts would perform as umpire or partisan. The short answer is both.

As HIS first term on the Court ended in June 2006, Roberts gave a commencement speech at Georgetown University. Restating the themes he had struck during his confirmation hearings, he said, "If it is not necessary to decide more to dispose of a case, my view is, it is necessary not to decide more," and he emphasized the value of "broader agreement" among the justices to promote the rule of law. Reports of his talk repeated what had become the conventional story of Roberts's first year: "The Supreme Court has shown a surprising degree of unanimity and consensus since Chief Justice Roberts took over last fall." The Court was "a more harmonious institution than it has been in the past," with "fewer 5–4 decisions, fewer dissenting opinions, and fewer . . . concurrences . . . than in the previous term."

The conventional story focused on ideologically contentious topics —abortion, federalism, campaign finance—that produced narrow and unanimous opinions in cases that had been presented to the Court in ways that invited broad and divided holdings.

The Roberts Court's first abortion decision set the pattern. In 2003, New Hampshire enacted a statute further restricting access to abortions. The statute said that doctors couldn't perform abortions on pregnant young women without notifying their parents and waiting two days. It had three exceptions: for cases in which the parents had already agreed; for cases where the abortion was necessary to prevent the woman's death; and in cases where a judge had held that the woman was mature and that abortion without notification was in her interests. The constitutional law of abortion as of 2003 was complicated. It clearly allowed states to require parental notification, but they couldn't restrict abortions that were "necessary . . . for the preservation of the life or health of the mother." But under New Hampshire's statute a judge couldn't bypass parental notification even when there was a medical emergency threatening the woman's health.

Planned Parenthood said that the statute was unconstitutional because it didn't have a health-based exception. The lower court agreed and entered an order barring the state from enforcing its statute entirely—that is, from requiring parental notification or a judicial bypass in cases not involving medical emergencies. The state's petition for review came to the Court in May 2005, before O'Connor had announced her retirement and while Rehnquist was still Chief Justice. Supported by Solicitor General Paul Clement, the state made two points: its statute was not unconstitutional because its criminal law gave doctors a defense if they performed abortions in cases of medical emergencies; and even if the failure to have an emergency exception was unconstitutional, it should be allowed to require parental notification in non-emergency cases.

In her valedictory opinion on abortion, Justice O'Connor delivered the Court's unanimous opinion on January 18, 2006, two weeks before she finally left the Court. The opinion finessed New Hampshire's defense of its statute, saying accurately but somewhat misleadingly that the state had "conceded" that the lack of a health exception was unconstitutional if it "subjects minors to significant health risks." The state had indeed said that, but it never conceded that the statute did subject minors to such risks in light of the state's criminal law. Having avoided the core constitutional question, Justice O'Connor turned to the easier question of remedy. The lower court had used "the most blunt remedy" instead of one that simply extended the judicial bypass to health emergencies as well as life-threatening ones. This seems a completely sensible result—except that federal courts usually can't rewrite state statutes to extend them, only to limit them. Justice O'Connor's opinion obfuscated this too, referring only to "carefully crafted injunctive relief" against the "few" unconstitutional applications of New Hampshire's statute. But that was enough. The Court had, for the moment, an abortion decision on which all the justices agreed. That couldn't last.

Campaign finance came next. The McCain-Feingold Campaign Finance Reform Act of 2002 prohibited corporations from paying for "electioneering communications," which the statute defined as advertisements "refer[ring] to a candidate" broadcast within thirty days of an election. A group called Wisconsin Right to Life, which received some of its money from corporations, wanted to run campaign ads anyway. It sued the Federal Election Commission, claiming that the McCain-Feingold Act's ban on corporate spending for what it called "grass-roots lobbying" ads—referring to issues and candidates but not expressly asking voters to cast their ballots one way or another—was unconstitutional. Dividing five to four, the Court had upheld the McCain-Feingold Act in 2003. A footnote in the opinion observed, "We uphold all applications of the . . . definition [of electioneering communications]. . . ." The lower court relied on that sentence to reject Wisconsin Right to Life's argument that the First Amendment prohibited applying the ban to the specific ads it wanted to run.

In the jargon, Wisconsin Right to Life in 2006 presented an "as applied" challenge to the statute. Appealing the decision to the Supreme Court, Wisconsin Right to Life said that the 2003 decision didn't resolve all possible "as applied" challenges, and renewed its constitutional claim. The case came to the Court in a technical form that prevented it from simply denying review as it does with most cases, and so the Court set the case for argument even before Roberts and Alito were sworn in.

James Bopp represented Wisconsin Right to Life. He started his career as a small-town lawyer in Indiana and then got involved in the pro-life movement, eventually becoming general counsel to the National Right to Life Committee. The committee and its affiliates like Wisconsin Right to Life supported pro-life candidates, opposed pro-choice ones, and often bumped up against statutes restricting campaign expenditures. So Bopp became something of an expert in campaign finance law as well. Rather than swatting each of the flies buzzing around his clients' heads, Bopp wanted to go after campaign finance law as a whole. His special concern, of course, was spending by and contributions to groups like Wisconsin Right to Life. These groups operated independently of candidates' campaigns but everyone knew that they had candidates they favored and opposed. Bopp believed that, whatever might be said about contributions to candidates themselves, independent spending—and certainly independent spending by ideological groups like his clients—had to be protected by the First Amendment. All they did, after all, was purchase advertisements that stated their positions on the issues that mattered to them, which was precisely what the First Amendment ought to protect. That those ads also benefited or hurt candidates wasn't enough to justify restricting them. For Bopp, every case he argued before the Supreme Court was a chance to get the Court to hold that campaign finance regulations of his clients always violated the First Amendment's free speech guarantees.

Every time he went to the Court, he had several allies. William Rehnquist thought that many campaign finance regulations were entirely constitutional, but the other conservatives thought almost none were. For them, regulating campaign finance was as close to a core violation of free speech as they could imagine. And on most free speech issues Anthony Kennedy could have been a member of the American Civil Liberties Union (which also opposed most campaign finance regulations). The arrival of Roberts and Alito gave the Court a majority with something close to Bopp's view of campaign finance regulations. What they needed was a case giving them the opportunity to say so.

Bopp tried to pitch the *Wisconsin Right to Life* case as that opportunity, but it turned out to be not quite over the plate. The case was argued on January 17 and decided six days later. All the Court said, in a unanimous "per curiam" opinion—that is, by the Court and not by any individual justice—was that the 2003 decision "did not purport to resolve future as-applied challenges." It ducked the merits, finding it unclear whether the lower court had actually rejected Wisconsin Right to Life's constitutional challenge, and sent the case back so that the lower court could decide that question. The case and the issues it presented would be back to the Supreme Court twice—once the next year, and then, spectacularly, in the *Citizens United* case. Both times the Court was sharply divided.

An important anti-discrimination case was the vehicle for another narrow ruling. Tony Goodman was a paraplegic inmate in a Georgia prison, serving time for cocaine possession and aggravated assault— apparently he lurched out of his wheelchair and bashed his girlfriend with a handgun. He claimed that he was confined for all but one hour a day to a tiny cell in which he couldn't turn his wheelchair around, that he couldn't use the toilet or shower without assistance, which was often denied, that he had injured himself in trying to get to the shower or toilet on his own, and that sometimes he had been forced to sit in his own feces and urine when prison officials insisted that he clean his cell himself. All of this, he said, violated the Americans with Disabilities Act (ADA), and he sued for money damages.

George H. W. Bush signed the ADA in 1990, regarding it as one of his signature legislative accomplishments. It's a comprehensive statute, one part of which says that state and local governments can't discriminate in their programs and services against people with disabilities. The statute also allows victims of disability discrimination to recover damages. There's no constitutional controversy over doing that for private businesses. States are different, though, because the Eleventh Amendment has been interpreted to limit Congress's power to use damage payments as a remedy for state and local violations of federal law. (The Eleventh Amendment reads: "The Judicial power of the United States shall not be construed to extend to any suit in law or equity, commenced . . . against one of the United States by Citizens of another State . . . " Since 1890 the Court has construed the amendment to apply to suits against a state by one of its own citizens.) The Court's doctrine is unbearably arcane and largely indefensible, but it became reasonably stable as part of the Rehnquist Court's modest "federalism revolution." Stability didn't mean agreement, though. Nearly every case was decided by the same five-to-four margin, and none of the dissenters appeared to think that the majority's position deserved any serious consideration as new cases arose. Georgia relied on the Eleventh Amendment to protect it against Goodman's claim for damages.

One part of the doctrine involves the Fourteenth Amendment, which gives Congress the power to "enforce" constitutional rights the Constitution protects against violations by state and local governments. The numbers matter here: fourteen is larger than eleven, and the Court has held that the Fourteenth Amendment, adopted seventy years after the Eleventh, overrides it—but only when Congress really is enforcing constitutional rights. And enforcement, the Court said, means that Congress has to identify core constitutional violations and then devise a remedy that is "congruent with and proportional to" those violations.

Here, too, the doctrine is complicated. Discrimination against people with disabilities can be unconstitutional, but—according to the Court—only if it is "irrational." In 2001, the Court held that Congress didn't have enough evidence of irrational employment discrimination by state and local governments to make a damage remedy congruent and proportional.

Goodman's case got the attention of the Department of Justice, which joined his case and his appeal to the Supreme Court. George H. W. Bush had C. Boyden Gray, his former White House counsel, file a statement laying out Bush's reasons for signing the ADA and endorsing Goodman's position. A slew of other interest groups, including the American Bar Association, also weighed in for Goodman. Supported by thirteen other states, Georgia responded by arguing that the Eleventh Amendment barred all ADA damage suits arising out of running prisons.

The Rehnquist Court might have used the Georgia ADA case as a vehicle for a major rethinking of the act's application to the states. Push too hard for that result, and the new justices, not familiar with the terms of the conversation, might bristle. Instead, Justice Scalia took only two paragraphs to reverse the lower courts. Goodman had alleged conditions that amounted to a violation of his rights under the Eighth

Amendment to be free from cruel and unusual punishment, and Georgia conceded the point. So, Goodman's claims under the ADA rested "at least in large part, on conduct that independently violated" his constitutional rights. And Congress certainly had the power to enforce the Fourteenth Amendment by providing a money damage remedy "for actual violations" of constitutional rights. By focusing narrowly on Goodman's allegations that his conditions of confinement violated both the ADA and the Fourteenth Amendment, Justice Scalia was able to get the entire Court behind him.

The Court dealt with a challenge to the military's "Don't ask, don't tell" policy about gays with a broader opinion, but again it was unanimous. Chief Justice Roberts himself marshaled the Court in *FAIR v. Rumsfeld*. The case involved the Solomon Amendment, dealing with recruiting by the U.S. military at universities. Republican representative Gerald Solomon of New York sponsored the amendment because he was outraged by what U.S. law schools had been doing. The Association of American Law Schools (AALS) is a membership organization that requires its members to refrain from discriminating on the usual bases.* Those bases changed in the 1980s and 1990s, when the AALS expanded the list of prohibited grounds of discrimination to include sexual orientation. And the AALS interpreted discrimination to include making law school facilities available to employers who discriminated, whether on the basis of gender and race—historically, serious problems in the legal profession—or on the basis of sexual orientation, more recently seen as equally problematic.

I was involved in applying the AALS's membership policies in the 1990s. The organization had to work hard to get its members to comply with its non-discrimination rules. Some law schools affiliated with religious institutions thought they should be able to discriminate

---

* The AALS isn't an accrediting body, and law schools can grant degrees without being AALS members. But membership is highly valued, in part because the AALS provides services like a recruiting directory; only a handful of schools choose not to seek membership.

in admitting students and hiring faculty on the basis of their religiously grounded objections to homosexuality, as it was then described. Most secular private law schools had no difficulty with the new non-discrimination rules; doing so might reduce their students' access to a handful of jobs in the private sector, but by the time the rules kicked in, few law firms would admit that they discriminated against gays and lesbians. Nor did public law schools have problems with agreeing that they shouldn't discriminate in employment or admissions. The sticking point was military employment. Congress's "Don't ask, don't tell" policy meant that the U.S. military stated openly that it would not hire those it knew to be gay or lesbian. Some public law schools faced a backlash from their state legislators when they tried to bar military recruiters from the law school's employment offices.

Representative Solomon wanted to solve the problem for everyone. The Solomon Amendment went through a number of versions, with law schools figuring out ways to comply with less restrictive versions while still barring military recruiting. Fed up, Solomon dropped the atom bomb. The final amendment said that if any part of a university—law schools—denied military recruiters access equal to that provided other recruiters, the entire university would lose federal funds. A handful of stand-alone law schools were able to thumb their noses, but the pressure on every other school was too great to resist.

I was president of the AALS in 2003, as the litigation was developing. Faculty members at some schools understandably believed that the AALS, having created their problems with its non-discrimination rules, should take the lead in challenging the Solomon Amendment. I argued against doing so, partly because of division with the AALS over the stringency of its interpretation of the non-discrimination policy and partly because I thought the challenge unlikely to succeed. Unable to rely on the AALS to bring a lawsuit, faculty members at a number of law schools formed the Forum for Academic and Institutional Rights (FAIR) as the vehicle for a constitutional challenge to the Solomon Amendment. They argued that his amendment violated the First Amendment's guarantees of free expression and association. In 1977, the Court held unconstitutional a New Hampshire statute requiring that state license plates carry the state motto, "Live Free or Die," because it forced car owners to associate themselves with a statement of belief that some of them rejected. And in 1995 the Court held that the organizers of Boston's St. Patrick's Day Parade had a constitutional right to exclude a group identifying itself as gay Americans of Irish descent from the parade, because doing so interfered with the message the organizers wanted to send through the parade's composition. FAIR argued that having military recruiters on campus sent a message that, as far as the law school was concerned, "Don't ask, don't tell" was an acceptable employment policy, and that they were being forced to accommodate the military's own message that "Don't ask, don't tell" was fine. FAIR also relied on another case rejecting a gay rights claim, where the Court had held that the Boy Scouts of America had a constitutional right of association that protected their decision to bar gays from leadership positions. The Solomon Amendment forced law schools to associate themselves with military recruiters, they said.

All this was complicated by the role of federal funding in the Solomon Amendment. It didn't say that law schools *couldn't* bar military recruiters; all it did was give them a choice—allow military recruiters on campus and your university gets to keep its federal money, bar them and it loses the money. This strategy brings into play one of the most difficult problems in constitutional law today, known in the field as the problem of unconstitutional conditions. The Medicaid part of the Obamacare case presented one version of the problem. Everyone agrees that Congress can tell people who get federal money that they have to comply with some requirements, and everyone agrees that some requirements are unconstitutional. (Imagine a statute saying, "If you want federal money for your astronomy program, you can't teach the Big

Bang theory of the universe's origins.") Drawing the line between the two categories is enormously difficult, and no one has a decent answer.

Chief Justice Roberts solved the problem by avoiding it. Congress, he said, could require law schools to allow military recruiters in, without using the threat of withdrawing federal funds: a "funding condition cannot be unconstitutional if it could be constitutionally imposed directly." So the issue became, would such a requirement violate the First Amendment? The Court unanimously said no. The unanimity resulted partly because FAIR was pushing First Amendment doctrine beyond its previous boundaries—the Solomon Amendment didn't stop the law schools from saying whatever they wanted about the military. Even more, an "unconstitutional conditions" decision might well have implications reaching much further than the First Amendment doctrine needed to uphold the Solomon Amendment as a direct regulation, by allowing the government to tell anyone who took its money what they could or couldn't say. The Court's liberals might well have worried about that possibility, and gave the Chief Justice a unanimous Court to avoid it.

Although the Solomon Amendment didn't stop law schools from saying anything, including putting up signs protesting "Don't ask, don't tell," it did regulate their conduct. Sometimes, though, conduct sends a message. Putting a license plate on your car is conduct, after all. But, Roberts said, the license plate itself said something. The mere fact that military recruiters were on campus was not in itself a message. "There is nothing in this case approaching a Government-mandated pledge or motto that the school must endorse." Whatever messages there were—notices to students that military recruiters would be in the placement office on Friday morning—were "plainly incidental" to the regulation of conduct, and making people send messages incidental to regulation of conduct didn't violate the First Amendment. The St. Patrick's Day case wasn't applicable either, because parades are necessarily about communication, and letting the gay Irish group into the march would have interfered with the organizers' message, but law schools "are not speaking when they host interviews and recruiting receptions." Parades are "inherently expressive"; "recruiting services" are not. And, "Nothing about recruiting suggests that law schools agree with any speech by recruiters." Finally, the Boy Scouts case was different because military recruiters "are not part of the law school." The distinction between insiders—Scout leaders—and outsiders like the recruiters was "crucial."

Roberts ended his opinion with something of a flourish:

> In this case FAIR has attempted to stretch a number of First Amendment doctrines well beyond the sort of activities these doctrines protect. . . . To the extent that the Solomon Amendment incidentally affects expression, the law schools' effort to cast themselves as just like . . . the parade organizers . . . and the Boy Scouts . . . plainly overstates the expressive nature of their activity and the impact of the Solomon Amendment on it, while exaggerating the reach of our First Amendment precedents.

The paragraph is a little clunky, as was some of the analysis in the opinion, but FAIR certainly was pushing the precedents pretty hard, and it's not surprising that even the Court's liberals couldn't see their way to thinking that the gay rights and academic freedom issues rattling around in the case were enough to overcome the national security context.

The Chief Justice may have accomplished his goal of lowering the Court's profile even in cases where he couldn't get his colleagues to agree on a single opinion. The Court's description of the opinions in a voting rights case is the kind of thing the Chief Justice disparaged: "Justice Kennedy announced the judgment of the Court and delivered the opinion of the Court with respect to Parts II-A and III, an opinion with respect to Parts I and IV, in which The Chief Justice and Justice Alito join, an opinion with respect to Parts II-B and II-C, and an opinion with respect to Part II-D, in which Justice Souter and Justice Ginsburg join." But that's not all: "Stevens, J., filed an opinion concurring in part and dissenting in part, in which Breyer, J., joined as to Parts I and II. Souter, J., filed an opinion concurring in part and dissenting in part, in which Ginsburg, J., joined. Breyer, J., filed an opinion concurring in part and dissenting in part." Not to be outdone by their liberal colleagues: "Roberts, C.J., filed an opinion concurring in part, concurring in the judgment in part, and dissenting in part, in which Alito, J., joined. Scalia, J., filed an opinion concurring in the judgment in part and dissenting in part, in which Thomas, J., joined, and in which Roberts, C.J., and Alito, J., joined as to Part III."

What provoked all this? After Republicans won complete control of the Texas legislature in 2003, Congressman Tom DeLay maneuvered to redistrict the state's congressional districts to lock in Republican control of the state's congressional delegation. Protesting DeLay's tactics, Democrats in the state legislature relocated to Oklahoma, hoping that they could deprive the Republicans of a quorum to enact the new district lines. After reams of publicity about the comic opera character of Texas's legislative process, DeLay's plan went through. The congressional delegation changed from seventeen Democrats and fifteen Republicans to twenty-one Republicans and eleven Democrats—which, Justice Kennedy observed, wasn't too big a difference from the Republicans' statewide winning margin of 58 percent to 41 percent (roughly two "extra" seats for the Republicans).

Inevitably, the Democrats went to court. They said that the new districts were a blatant partisan gerrymander, made worse by the fact that the redistricting took place "mid-decade," that is, after an earlier redistricting responding to the increase in Texas congressional seats as a result of the 2000 Census. They also identified several districts where, they argued, the new lines diminished the influence of Hispanic voters in violation of the 1965 Voting Rights Act.

The fractures on the Court resulted from largely ideological divisions among the justices. The Court had dealt with partisan gerrymandering before, and didn't really know what to do about it. Restating what they had said before—part of the "continuing conversation"—Justices Scalia and Thomas thought that the courts shouldn't even consider claims that partisan gerrymandering violated the Constitution. Roberts and Alito took the opportunity to weigh in, with the Chief Justice writing that, though he wasn't about to take a position on partisan gerrymandering's constitutional statute in general, the Texas Democrats hadn't given the Court a usable standard for determining when unconstitutional gerrymandering occurred. Justice Kennedy thought that some day he might come across an unconstitutional partisan gerrymander, but he hadn't done so yet—and even the Texas redistricting wasn't a problem for him because, as he described it, DeLay had simply been retaliating for a couple of decades of Democratic gerrymandering to preserve "blue" Democratic seats in a state that had turned deep red. He did think, though, that one of the new districts violated the Voting Rights Act. The Court's liberals disagreed with much of the discussion of partisan gerrymandering, but agreed with Kennedy about the Voting Rights Act.

The result was that Tom DeLay's partisan gerrymander was upheld by a Court divided on ideological lines. Kennedy's narrative of how the case came about sounds like a description of partisan maneuvers written by a political reporter mildly sympathetic to the unfair treatment Republicans had received at the hands of Texas Democrats. The welter of opinions combined with the fact that the Democrats had won a small part of the case to make it seem as if the umpire had called one ball and one strike. The strike basically ended the game with a Republican win, and the umpires knew what they were doing.

Justice Kennedy played a similar role—seeming to split the difference for the long run while ruling for the conservative position in the case before the Court—in a Clean Water Act case in 2006. Environmental law is one of legal conservatives' bêtes noires. For them it is a bastion of an overreaching scientific and liberal elite, dedicated to pursuing environmental purity at great cost to businesses and ordinary people. One of Roberts's opinions when he was a circuit judge attracted some attention because he expressed skepticism about the constitutionality of what he described as extreme applications of the Endangered Species Act. The constitutional hook was the argument that an endangered species that stayed put in a remote cave or desert couldn't possibly fall within Congress's power to regulate commerce *among* the states. But the Constitution doesn't give legal conservatives many tools for scaling environmental law back, so most of the action occurs in interpreting statutes.

The Clean Water Act of 1972 says that you have to get a permit from the U.S. Army Corps of Engineers if your construction or farming operations discharge pollutants into "waters of the United States," which the act defines as "navigable waters." That term comes from the Constitution, and—despite what you might think—it includes much more than rivers and streams on which you can float a boat. The Corps of Engineers took the position that "navigable waters" includes all wetlands (which are basically permanently water-soaked), "intermittent" streams and their tributaries, and wetlands adjacent to those tributaries even if they were separated from streams and rivers by man-made dikes and barriers. In 1989, John Rapanos started to develop some property, which had about fifty acres of land where the soil was "sometimes saturated," with the nearest largeish body of water at least eleven miles away, although the water on Rapanos's land did eventually drain into Lake Huron. The Corps of Engineers told him that he needed a permit, and when he continued to develop the property, the government filed criminal charges against him. He was convicted in 1995 and sentenced to three years' probation and a fine of $185,000. It took him eleven years to get his case to the Supreme Court.

After argument, the Chief Justice assigned the opinion to Justice Scalia. It took Justice Scalia no more than six sentences of description before he signaled the outcome, when he described the Army Corps of Engineers as "exercis[ing] the discretion of an enlightened despot." Echoing conservative complaints about the burdens environmental law placed on the economy, he then cited a study showing that applicants for permits spent more than two years and a quarter of a million dollars to get one. To Justice Scalia, Rapanos was the victim of "the immense expansion of federal regulation of land use . . . under the Clean Water Act . . . during the past five Presidential administrations"—from Carter through Reagan to George W. Bush. The Corps of Engineers' position, he said, meant that almost "the entire land area of the United States" came under its jurisdiction, including "entire cities and immense arid wastelands."

Justice Scalia tried to use the case to cut back sharply on "the Corps' sweeping assertions of jurisdiction over ephemeral channels and drains." The Clean Water Act covered "*only* those wetlands with a continuous surface connection to bodies that are 'waters of the United States' in their own right," not "[w]etlands with only an intermittent, physically remote hydrological connection" to them. He could get only four votes for his interpretation of the statute's key terms (italics in the original), though. Justice Kennedy jumped ship, to use a phrase (peculiarly appropriate in this case), occasionally cited within the Court when someone who initially supported a position ends up writing separately.

Justice Kennedy said that the Clean Water Act covered everything with a "significant nexus" to navigable waters, and wanted the case sent back to the lower courts to find out whether Rapanos's land had such a nexus. His opinion devoted a lot of space to criticizing Justice Scalia's, and Justice Scalia responded by adding a new section to his opinion, saying that Kennedy was "misreading our prior opinions" and—in a passage filled with eyebrows-raised italics—criticized Kennedy for "ignoring the text of the statute": "Justice Kennedy . . . has devised his new statute all on his own."

Scalia conceded that Kennedy's approach "would disallow some of the Corps' excesses," and that was the case's message to the public. Whether it would affect how the Corps went about its business every day was unclear, but the Roberts Court had sent a muddled signal to the public that the government wasn't exactly playing by fair rules.

THE NARRATIVE of consensus and harmony dramatically oversimplified what had happened during Roberts's first term. High-profile cases were indeed decided on narrow grounds without dissent. The New Hampshire abortion case could have been the vehicle for a further erosion of *Roe v. Wade*, but basically nothing happened. Statistics showing a high rate of agreement within the Court were accurate, but provided only a snapshot. One academic study suggests that disagreement rates go down in the first years after a new Chief Justice takes his seat, then rise, sometimes to even higher levels than before.

The new configurations in the Court's family take shape over a few years, even more so when the Court has to figure out the place of two new members in its family. All the justices want to feel their way forward cautiously: Justice Breyer no less than Justice Scalia had to figure out how to deal with Roberts and Alito both on a personal level and in working out legal arguments that can get their votes. How do you have to phrase your suggestions for changing a sentence or two in a draft opinion? Will they get their backs up if you're too sharp in your criticisms? Will Justice Alito agree with Breyer or Scalia in their approaches to interpreting statutes? The Roberts Court could come into its own only after Roberts and Alito helped set the docket.

Hints of what might come could be found in Roberts's first term. The course the Court took to deciding three other cases, argued after Roberts joined but before Alito took his seat, pointed to what the Roberts Court would look like. When the eight justices hearing the cases voted, they divided evenly. After Alito came on board, the Court split along conservative-liberal lines rejecting the constitutional claims.

In *Hudson v. Michigan*, police officers went to Booker T. Hudson's home with a warrant to search for drugs. As they were required to, they shouted: "Police, search warrant," but then waited only a few seconds before bursting through the door—clearly not enough time for someone to come to the door and open it for them. Everyone agreed that the police violated the Fourth Amendment because they didn't wait long enough. The question in the case was what to do about the constitutional violation. We know from uncountable *Law & Order* episodes that the courts exclude evidence found after the police conduct an unconstitutional search. Conservatives have criticized this exclusionary rule from the beginning, quoting a line from Benjamin Cardozo, one of the nation's greatest judges, asking whether the criminal is to go free "because the constable has blundered." In *Hudson*, Michigan, with the federal Justice Department's support, asked the Court to sharply limit the exclusionary rule. And it did, coming quite close to a broad holding that illegally seized evidence should never be excluded from presentation at a criminal trial if the benefits of presenting the evidence outweigh the costs of excluding it—as they almost always will.

Another case came from Kansas. It was a death penalty case involving a brutal murder of a mother and the death of her nineteen-month-old daughter in a fire set by the defendant as he left the house. The Kansas Supreme Court overturned the conviction because it found that the jury had been given bad instructions about how to decide whether to vote for capital punishment. The issue was quite technical and narrow. According to the U.S. Supreme Court, juries in death penalty cases have to weigh "aggravating" and "mitigating" circumstances. States can require death sentences if juries find that the aggravating circumstances outweigh the mitigating ones. What about the—one hopes rare—cases in which the aggravating and mitigating circumstances are equally balanced? The Kansas Supreme Court said that juries had to be instructed that they weren't required to impose a death sentence then. Notably, the facts in the case make this a largely hypothetical question, because it was quite unlikely, though not impossible, that the jury would have found the circumstances equally balanced. The new majority disagreed with the state court: states could set up their death penalty systems to require the death penalty in these "equally balanced" cases.

The third re-argued case was the most important, because the Court refused to provide constitutional protection for whistle-blowers who complained about misconduct by public employees in the way they should—by telling their supervisors. Richard Ceballos was a deputy district attorney in Los Angeles. He sometimes reviewed the affidavits police officers submitted to get a judge to issue a search warrant. When a defense lawyer told him that the affidavit in his client's case was seriously inaccurate, he investigated and concluded that the defense lawyer was right. He told his supervisors and recommended that they dismiss the case. They didn't; the warrant was upheld; and Ceballos said that his supervisors punished him for doing his job. That violated the First Amendment, he said, because he was making claims about police misconduct, a matter of serious public concern. (As is often true in this kind of employment case, Ceballos's supervisors denied that they were retaliating against him for his complaints, saying they were simply doing ordinary job reassignments in a professional way.)

The Court's precedents about the free speech rights of public employees were complicated. One held that the First Amendment didn't protect someone who complained only about a district attorney's office management, where the mismanagement didn't have any obvious implications outside the office. Another gave some First Amendment protection to a schoolteacher who wrote a letter to the local newspaper complaining about some of the board of education's policies. Ceballos said that his case was more like the second case than the first.

Writing for the now familiar five-justice majority, Justice Kennedy didn't try to place the case in either category. He agreed that the First Amendment protected some "expressions made at work" because "[m]any citizens do much of their talking inside their . . . workplaces." He also agreed that the First Amendment sometimes protected statements dealing with an employee's own work, because often that gave the employee better access to information than an outsider would have. But what did matter was that Ceballos made his statements in a memo to his supervisor: "When public employees make statements pursuant to their official duties, the employees are not speaking as citizens for First Amendment purposes." Apparently Ceballos would have been able to invoke the First Amendment if he had written a letter to the *Los Angeles Times* about the police misconduct, but couldn't invoke it when he did what he was supposed to do and reported it to his supervisor. The four dissenting justices wondered about the Court's sharp distinction between public employees and citizens, observing that many public employees took their jobs *because* they thought that being a public servant was a high form of citizenship.*

The results in the re-argued cases provided better clues to the Roberts Court's initial balance than the more high profile abortion and campaign finance cases.

ROBERTS's SOPHOMORE year was more dramatic than his first, with five-to-four decisions in major cases involving abortion, school integration, and campaign finance. The difference between the terms shows in the length of the opinions: the rookie year abortion decision ran 10 pages, the sophomore year one 59 pages; the rookie year campaign finance decision was 2 pages long, the sophomore year one 89 pages. Justice Kennedy's pivotal position defined the term's work. In each of the major

---

* Justice Souter's dissent also worried about the decision's implications for academic freedom, because professors say things in the classroom and engage in sometimes controversial research as part of their duties. Justice Kennedy's opinion hinted that academic freedom "implicates additional constitutional interests," but didn't explain what those other interests were or how they would affect the Court's "customary employee-speech jurisprudence."

cases the Court repudiated opinions written by Justice O'Connor from which Kennedy had dissented.

The *Wisconsin Right to Life* case came back. The Court had told the lower court to decide whether the organization had a right to broadcast ads opposing the state's senators. The lower court held that it didn't, and now the Court decided that it did. James Bopp argued the case again. This time the Court said that Wisconsin Right to Life had a constitutional right to broadcast ads against the state's senators. Wisconsin Right to Life believed that Senators Russ Feingold and Herbert Kohl were participating in a Democratic plan to stall President George W. Bush's judicial nominations until after the 2004 presidential election, which Democrats hoped would throw Bush out of office. Feingold was running for reelection that year; Kohl was not. Wisconsin Right to Life wanted to run three ads about the filibuster it said was taking place. They would run during the period described in the McCain-Feingold Act. The ads' theme was "Sometimes it's just not fair to delay an important decision." One featured a pastor asking, "Who gives this woman to be married to this man?" with the bride's father replying, "I certainly could. But instead, I'd like to share a few tips on how properly to install drywall." The ads ended: "Contact Senators Feingold and Kohl and tell them to oppose the filibuster."

Bopp agreed that these ads were indeed electioneering communications banned by the McCain-Feingold Act, because they "referred" to Feingold. But, he argued, the act was unconstitutional as applied to the ads. In a 2003 case brought by Republican senator Mitch McConnell of Kentucky, the Court had upheld the McCain-Feingold Act in general over dissents by Justices Scalia, Kennedy, and Thomas (and Rehnquist). Discussing ads similar to Wisconsin Right to Life's, the Court in 2003 distinguished between campaign speech, which it described as "express advocacy" of a candidate's election or defeat, and "issue advocacy" that happened to mention a candidate. The constitutional challenge in

2003 was that the McCain-Feingold's regulations of express advocacy were unconstitutional because they covered too much ground—were "overbroad," in the lawyers' jargon. The Court rejected the challenge because, it said, express advocacy might sometimes corrupt the political process. Winning candidates might be corrupted because they would feel indebted to the ads' sponsors. And the political process might be corrupted in the more metaphorical sense that money would come to play a larger role than it should as people chose candidates to enact good public policy. In 2003, the Court "assume[d]" that the reasons that made it permissible to restrict express advocacy might not apply to "genuine issue ads."

Bopp's problem turned out to be the distinction between campaign ads and issue ads. When the justices talked about the case, Justices Scalia, Kennedy, and Thomas held on to the positions they had taken in 2003. So did Justices Stevens, Souter, Ginsburg, and Breyer. The outcome was in Roberts's and Alito's hands. The Chief Justice decided to try to resolve the case narrowly, partly because of his stated preference for narrow rulings and partly because this was the first time he really had to grapple with the intricacies of the First Amendment and campaign finance law.

He circulated an opinion proposing to hold that the Wisconsin Right to Life ads were genuine issue ads, not campaign ads, and that it was unconstitutional to prohibit issue ads. Roberts drafted his opinion to get votes from the dissenters in the *McConnell* case. He paraphrased a line that Justice Kennedy wrote in 2000. Kennedy wrote that "the tie goes to free expression"; Roberts, "Where the First Amendment is implicated, the tie goes to the speaker, not the censor," adding, in his last paragraph, "We have no occasion to revisit" the *McConnell* case "today." Justice Alito went along, though with a separate opinion saying that if "it turns out" that implementing Roberts's position did "chill[] political speech, we will presumably be asked . . . to reconsider." Roberts's efforts weren't enough. The three dissenters from the *McConnell* case stuck to their guns. So did the four justices who voted to uphold the statute in the *McConnell* case.

Five justices agreed that the First Amendment made it unconstitutional to ban Wisconsin Right to Life's ads, but they had different reasons for that holding. Roberts decided that discretion—a narrow holding—was the better part of valor, stuck in a couple of footnotes criticizing Justice Scalia's dissent, and went with his original position. Maybe, he wrote, campaign ads could place winning candidates in debt, but saying that issue ads could do so was a step too far. "Enough is enough," he wrote. What about corrupting politics through floods of money? Roberts said that the Court had accepted this justification when dealing with campaign ads, but again refused to go any further. "Enough is enough" is good rhetoric, but it's not really much different from a parental "Because I say so."

One issue remained. Were the anti-filibuster ads issue ads that mentioned candidate Feingold, or campaign ads? Roberts said that they were issue ads, because campaign ads had to be "susceptible of no reasonable interpretation other than as an appeal to vote for or against a specific candidate." You *could* listen to the ads and think that you were asked to write letters to Senators Feingold and Kohl about the issue, not asked to vote against Senator Feingold. This is true enough, but anyone with even the smallest feel for politics knew that these "Write Senator *X*" ads were anti-Feingold ads. The desiccated "susceptible of no reasonable interpretation" standard had no connection to the real world of practical politics.

It would be convenient to be able to say that the Roberts Court adopted that standard because not a single member of the Court had ever asked anyone to vote for him or her. That's not right, though. The dissenters were able to see—or hear—the ads as attacks on Senator Feingold, tarted up to get as close to the line between campaign ads and issue ads as Wisconsin Right to Life could go.

In the next election cycle the airwaves were filled with "Write Senator *X*" ads that everyone knew were attack ads, not issue ads. *Saturday Night Live* ran a parody: "Write Senator *X* to tell her to stop telling us to Write Senator *Z* to tell him to stop telling us to write . . ." The experience that Justice Alito wanted to see was not a happy one. And the arbitrary nature of the "enough is enough" argument, if it can even be called an argument, showed that Roberts wasn't really committed to upholding the *McConnell* decision. The time for reconsidering the *McConnell* decision would come in the *Citizens United* case two and a half years later.

THE PATTERN with respect to abortion was the same as with campaign finance: a narrow decision in the rookie year, a broad one—overruling a major abortion rights decision issued seven years before—in the next.

On May 30, 1992, Justice Kennedy stopped by Justice Harry Blackmun's chambers, bringing, he said, "welcome news." The next day Justice Blackmun would receive a draft opinion that would please him, Kennedy said. The case was *Planned Parenthood of Southeastern Pennsylvania v. Casey*, in which pro-choice advocates had gone for broke: Defending a Pennsylvania statute regulating abortions, Planned Parenthood's lawyers decided to try to get the Court to end the constitutional controversy over abortion once and for all. Planned Parenthood said that the case gave the Court a clear choice, between overruling *Roe v. Wade* and reaffirming it fully, and both sides wanted the Court to fish or cut bait.

The opinion Kennedy told Blackmun about did please Blackmun—sort of. It was written and signed by Justices Kennedy, Souter, and O'Connor. The opinion reaffirmed what it called *Roe*'s "core holding," that states could not make it a crime to perform abortions early in a woman's pregnancy—which the justices redefined as before the fetus's "viability," meaning before there was a relatively high probability that the fetus removed from the woman's womb could live on its own.* But, adopting an approach Justice O'Connor had urged for years, it changed the constitutional standard for determining when regulations of abortion were unconstitutional: states could regulate abortions so long as the regulation didn't impose an "undue" burden on women's right to choose. And the "core holding" appeared to continue to make it unconstitutional for states to ban abortions, whether pre- or post-viability, where performing the abortion was necessary to protect the woman's life or health.

Applying the "undue burden" approach to the regulations in *Casey*, the three justices overruled several earlier cases to uphold a twenty-four-hour waiting period between the woman's first visit to the abortion provider and the abortion itself. They struck down a requirement that a married woman notify her husband of the impending abortion or submit a statement that she believed that he (or someone else) would physically assault her if he knew about the abortion. The opinion noted that most married women did tell their husbands, so this requirement applied to a very small segment of women seeking abortions, and most of them faced serious threats of abuse and yet often tried to conceal the problem from everyone else. The notification requirement imposed a substantial burden on a large number of the only women affected by it, and so was unconstitutional.

The notification provision was the first regulation of abortion that Justice Kennedy had ever found unconstitutional. He had come around to the view that *Roe*'s "core holding" was defensible, but thought that states should be allowed to enforce a lot of regulations outside that core.

---

* As a technical matter the Court continued to adhere to the position that states could prohibit post-viability abortions except when such abortions were necessary to preserve a woman's life or health. But the category of "post-viability abortion" without such a necessity is essentially empty: the term describes induced deliveries intended to result in the death of the delivered fetus (or baby or child). Except with respect to some partial-birth abortions, where the doctor believes that inducing delivery would threaten the woman's life or health, no one thinks that this describes anything in the real world.

The decision was an invitation to the pro-life community to shift their strategy from seeking to overrule *Roe* to testing the limits of the "undue burden" test so as to define *Roe*'s core holding as narrowly as possible.

One regulation widely supported by the pro-life community was a ban on what they controversially but effectively called "partial-birth abortions." The term referred to a specific technique for performing abortions. Language itself had become a battleground for the abortion controversy. Pro-life advocates referring to pregnant women seeking abortions as "mothers" and the physicians who performed abortions as "abortionists"; pro-choice advocates said "women" and "doctors." Pro-choice advocates wanted courts to describe the technique by the terms doctors used: dilation and extraction, or intact dilation and evacuation.

By any name, the technique when described sounds pretty gruesome (although, truth be told, it's easy to make almost any major surgical procedure, even the removal of an infected appendix, sound gruesome). Nebraska's ban on partial-birth abortions got to the Court in 2000. It had a feature that mattered to pro-life advocates and to the Court. By the 1990s, everyone involved in the legal controversy over abortion agreed that abortions had to be permitted to save the woman's (or mother's) life, even if the abortions terminated the fetus's (or child's)—as they certainly did. The Court had consistently held that abortions had to be allowed to preserve the woman's health as well. And that continued to be controversial because the Court had insisted that "health" be given a broad definition, to include mental as well as physical health. Pro-life advocates believed that doctors who performed abortions were far too ready to find that continuing a pregnancy posed a threat to the woman's health under the generous definitions the Court insisted on. So their strategy came to include opposition to including health exceptions in new abortion regulations, and Nebraska's statute made an exception only for the woman's life, not her health.

Health exceptions raised another question. Those who thought that health exceptions were constitutionally required agreed that the exception had to come into play when continuing the pregnancy would endanger the woman's health. As techniques of abortion proliferated, they also came to think that the health exception meant that regulations had to allow doctors to use techniques that themselves didn't pose a threat to the woman's health. And at least some abortion providers thought there were medical circumstances where using anything other than a partial-birth abortion would indeed endanger the woman's health.

Justice Breyer wrote an opinion for the Court striking Nebraska's statute down. According to Breyer, the statute imposed an undue burden on women's choice about abortion for several reasons. It purported to deal with only a single technique of performing abortions, which meant that women whose doctors thought that using the technique was safer for the woman could still get an abortion (and so could still terminate the fetus's—or, again, child's—life), using a technique that posed greater risk to the woman. So, Justice Breyer said, the state's ban on partial-birth abortions did little to advance the interest the state asserted in preserving life, except in a handful of cases where the risks of other abortion techniques led women to decide to carry the fetus through to term and regular birth. And then the second constitutional effect came into play. The statute did not have a "health" exception, which meant that the risks women might face by choosing alternative techniques of abortion might be serious ones. That was an undue burden on their choice. And, finally, Nebraska's statute was drafted a little sloppily. Although its target was a specific technique, its terms actually covered more ordinary techniques for performing abortions.

Justice Kennedy dissented. Justices O'Connor and Souter, his co-authors in the *Planned Parenthood v. Casey* opinion, joined Justice Breyer's opinion. They clearly believed it consistent with the "undue burden" standard. Kennedy had a different view. His dissent strongly suggested that he believed that the "undue burden" test would substantially expand the range of permissible abortion regulations. The dissent brimmed with outrage, perhaps because he thought that Souter and O'Connor had betrayed him. It began by describing the partial-birth abortion technique in terms, he said, which would make it clear why "society [was] shocked" by the technique, and he made good on that promise. He summarized the testimony of Dr. Leroy Carhart, a prominent target of Nebraska's pro-life community who challenged Nebraska's statute: "The fetus . . . dies just as a human adult or child would: It bleeds to death as it is torn limb from limb." Describing the techniques should have ended the case, Kennedy wrote: "In light of the description of the D&X procedure, it should go without saying that Nebraska's ban on partial-birth abortion furthers purposes States are entitled to pursue. . . . Nebraska was entitled to find the existence of a consequential moral difference" between gruesome abortion techniques and less gruesome techniques that also ended the fetus's life, apparently because gruesomeness as such has moral weight.

Congress passed versions of a ban on partial-birth abortions in 1996 and 1997, but President Clinton vetoed them. Three years after the Court decided the Kansas case, George W. Bush was in the White House and Republicans held majorities in the House and Senate. This time the president signed a national ban, and Carhart again challenged it. When the case got to the Supreme Court in 2006, Roberts was Chief Justice and, far more important, Justice Alito had replaced Justice O'Connor.

Having written so passionately in 2000, Justice Kennedy was the natural choice to write the new majority's opinion upholding the federal statute.* Of course he had to explain why the federal statute was different from Kansas's. Part of the answer was easy: Congress had

---

* Justice Thomas wrote a separate opinion concurring in the result, saying that Kennedy's opinion "accurately applies current jurisprudence," though he would completely abandon the effort to impose constitutional restrictions on states' ability to regulate abortion. He observed as well that no one had made the federalism argument that Congress didn't have the power under its list of powers to enact the statute.

written the statute a bit more carefully than Kansas had, so it didn't appear to cover abortion techniques other than partial-birth abortions as Kennedy understood them.

The lack of a health exception was a bigger problem. Here Kennedy wrote himself into knots. The federal statute had a list of "findings" Congress made as a preface to the statute's core provisions. The first thing Kennedy mentioned when he started to distinguish the Kansas case was a congressional "finding" that the technique was "a gruesome and inhumane procedure that is never medically necessary." But when he actually got around to writing about the findings, he had to acknowledge that this finding was, as he delicately put it, "factually incorrect." No matter: It was enough that there was "medical disagreement whether the Act's prohibition would ever impose significant health risks on women."

That mattered, Kennedy wrote, because Carhart was challenging the statute on its face. Time enough to deal with the lack of a health exception when some doctor actually presented the courts with a real case in which the doctor said that using the technique was necessary for the woman's health. You might remember the New Hampshire case from the year before, when the Court said that the thing to do when a facial challenge showed that an abortion regulation covered too much was to carve out an exception. You might remember it, but Justice Kennedy apparently didn't. And although Kennedy ended his opinion with the assertion that the statute was "open to a proper as-applied challenge in a discrete case," Justice Ginsburg's dissent shredded that claim by pointing out that, unless the Court did a carve-out, you really can't devise the kind of lawsuit Kennedy imagined. Abortions, especially the ones in which the prohibited technique might be thought necessary for the woman's health, have to be performed quickly. What doctor would risk becoming a federal criminal by performing the abortion and hoping that a court would later agree that it had been medically necessary? And given the difficulties of litigation, how could a woman and her doctor get to court quickly enough to get an order that the ban would be unconstitutional as applied to her condition?

Kennedy's opinion contained an innovation in the rhetoric of the Court's conservatives. Over the decades since *Roe* and especially since the joint opinion reaffirming *Roe*, pro-life advocates had developed an argument that restrictions on abortions were appropriate because women often regretted having had an abortion. Justice Kennedy worked this argument into his opinion. He began by observing that "for many," abortion "is a procedure itself laden with the power to devastate human life." Congress could have thought that the specific type of abortion procedure it banned "implicates additional ethical and moral concerns." Justice Kennedy was sometimes drawn to gauzy sentiments, writing in the joint opinion in *Casey*, for example, "At the heart of liberty is the right to define one's own concept of existence, of meaning, of the universe, and of the mystery of human life." There Kennedy drew Justice Scalia's scorn. Here a similar sentimentality did not: "Respect for human life finds an ultimate expression in the bond of love the mother has for her child." (Note the words "mother" and "child" here as well.) Deciding to have an abortion was "difficult and painful." And then the new pro-life argument: "it seems unexceptionable to conclude some women come to regret their choice to abort the infant life they once created and sustained. Severe depression and loss of esteem can follow." And, fearing that describing the partial-birth abortion technique in detail would increase the risk of depression and loss of esteem, doctors wouldn't describe it clearly enough to put the women in a position to make a fully informed choice.

Kennedy prefaced all this with the statement that the Court couldn't find "reliable data" to measure the phenomenon, which led Justice Ginsburg to criticize the Court for "invok[ing] an antiabortion shibboleth for which it concededly has no reliable evidence." Giving women information would be the right way to deal with the problem, if there was one. The Court's "way of thinking," she wrote, "reflects ancient notions about women's place in the family and under the Constitution—ideas that have long since been discredited."

Justice Ginsburg opened her dissent—which Justices Stevens, Souter, and Breyer joined—by calling the decision "alarming." Justice Kennedy's discussion of "as applied" challenges was a feeble attempt to get around the Kansas decision. His discussion of the moral dimensions of abortion, and of regret and self-esteem, was equally feeble, not so much because those matters might not be built into the constitutional law of abortion but because they really arose from abortion itself, not from the partial-birth abortion technique. In that sense, Justice Ginsburg was right to say that the decision "refuses to take [the Court's precedents] seriously." What mattered was that Justice Kennedy's moral intuitions were that that specific technique was somehow beyond toleration while other techniques—equally fatal to the fetus (or, if one prefers, "the infant life" he referred to)—were acceptable. I should add, of course, that large segments of the American population shared those intuitions, whether or not they fit well together into some reasoned account of choice and life.

Casey said that the Court's abortion decisions called "the contending sides of a national controversy to end their national division by accepting a common mandate." When faced with a regulation of abortion over which they disagreed, neither Justice Kennedy nor Justice Souter managed to heed that call.

ABORTION WAS a test of reliability for Supreme Court nominees from both sides of the spectrum. So was affirmative action. The Roberts Court didn't get an affirmative action case until 2012, but it used a school integration case as its vehicle to lay out the conservative position on the role of race in education. Dissenting from the Court's 1896 decision upholding segregation, Justice John Marshall Harlan wrote, "Our constitution is color-blind." For decades that was what liberals said, while race conservatives believed that governments could take race into account to keep African Americans "in their place," as the phrase was. After the Court held school segregation unconstitutional, race liberals began to argue that overcoming the legacy of segregation meant that governments had to be allowed to pay attention to race: How could you eliminate segregated schools, they asked, if you didn't do so? And, for liberals, the entire society was pervaded by segregation's legacy. They began to support affirmative action programs. As liberals abandoned it, conservatives signed on to the "color-blind" Constitution ideal, for both principled and political reasons. Opposition to affirmative action was part of the Republican strategy for building the party in the South, and for appealing to white "ethnics" who had been part of the liberal coalition but believed that they were losing jobs and other benefits to less qualified African Americans. Color-blindness was a principle easily described as part of the Constitution, and became part of the conservative edifice of constitutional interpretation as well.

Affirmative action wasn't on the Court's docket in 2007, but the Court used two cases involving voluntary programs aimed at integrating schools in Seattle, Washington, and Louisville, Kentucky, to revisit the "color-blind Constitution" ideal. Four justices joined Chief Justice Roberts's opinion finding both programs unconstitutional because they used race as a basis for assigning children to schools, which they said was exactly the vice held unconstitutional in *Brown v. Board of Education*. The opinion's last paragraph said: "Before *Brown*, schoolchildren were told where they could and could not go to school based on the color of their skin. The school districts . . . have not carried the heavy burden of demonstrating that we should allow this once again—even for very different reasons." Justice Blackmun once wrote, "In order to get beyond racism, we must first take account of race." Roberts apparently liked the style but not the substance of Blackmun's sentence, because he ended his opinion: "The way to stop discrimination on the basis of race is to stop discriminating on the basis of race."

Justice Stevens noted how dramatically the landscape had changed by stating his "firm conviction that no Member of the Court that I joined in 1975 would have agreed with today's decision." One of those members, of course, was William Rehnquist. In the 1970s the controversy was over *forced* busing ordered by the courts, not voluntary busing adopted by school boards on their own. Everyone then agreed that achieving integration, even by using methods that paid attention to race, was a policy goal that school boards could set for themselves if they wanted to. In 1973, the Court considered a state statute prohibiting school boards from using busing to achieve integration. With none of the controversy associated with "forced" busing decisions, the Court struck the statute down. Roberts said that that case was different, because the statute barred school boards that had once segregated the schools from trying to overcome segregation's legacy. Seattle had never segregated its schools, and the courts had held that Louisville was in the same position because it had eliminated all traces of prior segregation. For Roberts, taking race into account might be part of a remedy for past discrimination, but it couldn't be a policy for achieving some other end.

Kennedy didn't join the plurality opinion, but wrote a separate concurrence in the result, which as a technical matter defined the law going forward. The message the opinion sent, though, went well beyond what it actually said. Kennedy had a long-standing aversion to affirmative action, which he once wrote was akin to apartheid in South Africa, and in 2003 he vigorously dissented when Justice O'Connor wrote an opinion upholding an affirmative action program at the University of Michigan Law School. To understand why his separate opinion said one thing but communicated another, you have to get pretty deep into the weeds of the case details.

It's easier to describe Seattle's program, which involved the city's ten high schools. Rising ninth graders rank the schools they want to attend. Some schools got more first choices than they have seats. The system used tiebreakers to allocate seats. The first tiebreaker was a preference for students who had a sibling in the school. Race came in with the second tiebreaker. The system as a whole had 41 percent white students, 59 percent in all other racial groups, including African Americans, Asian Americans, and Hispanic Americans. If a school was more than 10 percent out of line with the district's average, the second tiebreaker assigned students who would bring the figure closer to the average; if a school's student body was 60 percent white, non-white students would get a shot at enrollment before whites would.

Louisville's program affected all its public schools. Elementary schools were grouped in clusters by geographical region within the city. Parents of children entering the schools could ask that their children be assigned to a first- or second-choice school within the cluster. The school district had some fuzzy guidelines for deciding whether to assign a child to one of the preferred schools. As the case was presented to the Court, the guidelines tried to keep school enrollments in rough proportion to the district's racial composition as a whole. If a school was at the "extremes" of the guidelines, children "whose race would contribute to the school's racial imbalance [would] not be assigned there."

As a technical matter, Justice Kennedy would have held that the two cities' programs were unconstitutional because they didn't use race clearly enough or in an appropriate way. The Louisville case involved a child entering kindergarten, whose preference for a school within a mile of his home was rejected because his enrollment would contribute to racial imbalance—even though the school had empty seats and the Louisville program wasn't supposed to apply to kindergarteners anyway. Justice Kennedy was bothered by the fact that Louisville "fails to make clear . . . who makes the decisions; what if any oversight is employed; the precise circumstances in which an assignment decision will or will not be made on the basis of race; or how it is determined which of two similarly situated children will be subjected to a given race-based decision." He wrote that there were several "problems . . . evident in Seattle's system," but the only one he described was that the district used the categories "white" and "nonwhite" instead of breaking the latter down into subcategories. He quoted a point made in Roberts's opinion, that a school with 50 percent whites and 50 percent Asian Americans would be balanced, but one with 30 percent Asian Americans, 25 percent African Americans, 25 percent Hispanic Americans, and 20 percent whites—that is, 80 percent non-whites—would be imbalanced. He also agreed with Roberts's point that "the number of students whose assignment depends on express racial classifications is limited." So, Kennedy concluded, neither program did much, and what they did do, they did badly.

You would think that districts would find it easy to redesign their programs to eliminate those problems. The unmentioned "other problems" aside, all Seattle would have to do is create subcategories within the "nonwhite" group, and make race-based assignments when it concluded that, as subdivided, a school was racially imbalanced. But Kennedy's discomfort with race-based decision making took him in a different direction. He criticized Roberts's opinion for "an all-too-unyielding insistence that race cannot be a factor . . . when, in my view, it may be taken into account." Roberts was "profoundly mistaken" if he meant to say that school boards "must accept the status quo of racial isolation in schools" where that isolation didn't result from the boards' own decisions. The "Constitution is color blind" statement was "an aspiration" that "must command our assent." But, "[i]n the real world, it is regrettable to say, it cannot be a universal constitutional principle."

So, what could school boards do? Not, it turned out, fine-tune the Louisville and Seattle programs. Instead, they could use "strategic site selection of new schools; draw[] attendance zones with general recognition of the demographics of neighborhoods; . . . recruit[] students and faculty in a targeted fashion; and track[] enrollments, performance, and other statistics by race." The disconnect between the constitutional defects he found in the two programs and these techniques should be apparent. As Justice Breyer pointed out in his dissent, "Seattle has built one new high school in the last 44 years"—and as he said when he announced his dissent, the city's enrollments were dropping, so "how is that going to work?" And tracking enrollments by race "*reveals* the problem; it does not cure it" (italics in the original).

Roberts and Breyer dueled over "which side is more faithful to the heritage of" *Brown v. Board of Education.* For Roberts, "the position of the plaintiffs in *Brown* was spelled out in their brief and could not have been clearer: '[T]he Fourteenth Amendment prevents states from according differential treatment to American children on the basis of their color or race.' " What, he asked, "do the racial classifications at issue here do, if not accord differential treatment on the basis of race?" And he quoted Robert Carter, who in arguing the case for the NAACP, had said that "no State has any authority . . . to use race as a factor in affording educational opportunities among its citizens." Chief Justice Warren had written that a school board has to "determin[e] admission to the public schools on a nonracial basis." What, Roberts again asked, "do the racial classifications do in these cases, if not determine admission to a public school on a racial basis?"

For Justice Breyer, "*Brown* held out a promise. . . . It was the promise of true racial equality—not as a matter of fine words on paper, but as a matter of everyday life in the Nation's cities and schools." Alluding to the Little Rock school crisis of 1957–58, he said, "attitudes towards race in this Nation have changed dramatically." Parents in Seattle and Louisville "want their children to attend schools with children of different races." They made a "modest request" that the Court not "take from their hands the instruments they have used to rid their schools of racial segregation." The nation had "not yet realized the promise of *Brown*," and Roberts's position "would break that promise." Breyer noted in his oral presentation of his dissent that the dissent was "twice as long as any I have written before," and ended by quoting its final line: "This is a decision that the Court and the Nation will come to regret."

In the duel over *Brown*'s heritage Roberts was careful not to invoke anything the architect of the *Brown* litigation, Thurgood Marshall, had said, although he could have. Marshall's presence on the Court was too recent, and his position on race-related issues too well known, to make that sensible. Justices Souter, Stevens, Scalia, and Kennedy had served with Justice Marshall, and Kennedy provided the fifth vote to overturn Seattle's program. These justices knew Marshall in a way they did not know Robert Carter, and they knew, insofar as anyone could know, what Marshall would have thought about the constitutionality of Seattle's program. He had said enough things at the Court's conferences and had written enough opinions dealing with the related issue of voluntary affirmative action programs to make it clear that he would have found Seattle's program constitutionally permissible (and, in his more expansive moments, perhaps even constitutionally required). Claiming Marshall's authority for the result in the cases would have been an insult to Marshall's memory.

Some of the people who had represented the *Brown* plaintiffs were still alive, though, and they weighed in against Roberts. Robert Carter, by now an elderly federal judge, said, "All that race was used for at that point in time was to deny equal opportunity to black people. It's to stand that argument on its head to use race the way they use it now." Jack Greenberg, another lawyer who worked on *Brown* and later headed the NAACP Legal Defense Fund, said that Roberts's "interpretation" of the plaintiffs' position in *Brown* was "preposterous." The plaintiffs "were concerned with the marginalization and subjugation of black people." And William T. Coleman, Jr., a Republican who had worked on the *Brown* case as a young lawyer and went on to serve in President Gerald Ford's cabinet, called the opinion "dirty pool" and "100 percent wrong."

These cases were low-hanging fruit. All revisited cases decided five to four the other way when Justice O'Connor was on the Court. Justice Kennedy was now the centrist on the Court, and had dissented in the earlier cases. His views hadn't changed; his opinion in the abortion case was little more than a reprinting of his dissent from the Court's prior decision on the same issue. What had changed was the Court's composition.

AN OBSCURE case involving deadlines revealed a technique the Roberts Court would become fond of: When someone tried to hold governments or corporations accountable for their actions, instead of saying that the actions were just fine and completely lawful, the Roberts Court used procedural barriers to thwart the lawsuits at the outset. Keith Bowles was sentenced to life imprisonment for helping some friends beat Ollie Gipson to death. He challenged his conviction on pretty weak constitutional grounds, which the state courts rejected. As the law allowed, he then renewed his challenge in federal court. The trial judge denied his claim too. He now had thirty days to file an appeal, which the trial court could extend by fourteen days. But the trial judge made a mistake. On February 10, 2004, the judge entered a formal order saying that Bowles had to file his appeal by February 27—seventeen days, not fourteen. Bowles filed his appeal on February 26, within the time the judge had given him, but more than fourteen days after the order was entered.

The Supreme Court divided five to four along the usual lines in saying that Bowles's appeal was too late. The underlying legal issue was whether the fourteen-day limit was "jurisdictional," in this setting a lawyers' term. If you don't meet a "non-jurisdictional" deadline, you get a chance to explain why there are good reasons to excuse your failure and strong fairness reasons to let you go ahead with your lawsuit anyway. Jurisdictional deadlines are different: you have to comply with them, come hell or high water, and there's no excusing your failure— even if a judge misleads you about how long you have. The Court had spent several years trying to figure out how to tell when a deadline was jurisdictional or not. Justice Thomas's opinion for the Court held that the fourteen-day deadline was jurisdictional. Surveying the landscape, Justice Thomas divided deadlines into two categories: those written into statutes were jurisdictional, those written into court-developed rules weren't. The fourteen-day deadline was part of a statute, so Bowles was thrown out of court.

Justice Souter's dissent unsurprisingly focused on how unfairly the legal system had treated Bowles. His lawyer did everything he was told to do, and still didn't get a chance to appeal. The best that can be said for the Court's approach is that drawing the line between deadlines in statutes and those found elsewhere defines the strike zone really clearly. And that might help everyone who files a lawsuit: Know the rules, and you know what to do. Still, the dissenters had a point: sometimes there are truly extraordinary circumstances, as when a judge affirmatively misleads someone about a deadline, and the crispness of the rule ought to be relaxed on those rare occasions.

The Court could have chosen a rule with a tiny bit of flexibility, enough to salvage Bowles's case, but instead it preferred a really rigid rule. The Court's choice would almost inevitably disadvantage defendants in criminal cases and ordinary people bringing lawsuits against corporations. Governments and corporations have lawyers who are good enough to know the rules and follow them; ordinary people sometimes sue on their own, and often have lawyers so overburdened that they make small—but in Bowles's case disastrous—mistakes on behalf of their clients.* Exxon's lawyers aren't likely to miss filing deadlines; the lawyer for a gas station operator suing Exxon for terminating her franchise might. By magnifying the mistakes hard-pressed lawyers make,

---

* Bowles's lawyer, Paul Mancino, Jr., was an active criminal defense attorney in Cleveland, in a two-person firm with his son. I should emphasize that Mancino made a "mistake" only because he trusted what the judge's order said and didn't check to see whether the order was consistent with the statutory deadline.

the Court says, in effect, Don't blame us, blame the lawyers. It's an attractive technique for the justices, less so for the rest of us.

The Court also threw Lilly Ledbetter's sex discrimination case out of court on procedural grounds, but the ultimate result was happier, not for Ledbetter but for women claiming sex discrimination. Title VII of the 1964 Civil Rights Act prohibits sex discrimination in employment. Victims claiming discrimination have to file their claims within 180 days "after the alleged unlawful employment practice occurred." It's easy to know when the 180-day period begins when you're fired or passed over for a promotion. Ledbetter's case involved acts of discrimination that were harder to see when they occurred. Ledbetter supervised tiremaking at Goodyear Tire & Rubber Co. from 1979 to 1998. She claimed that at times during that period her direct supervisor gave her bad job ratings because she was a woman; each time her salary was set lower than it should have been if they had treated her fairly. The salary discrepancies accumulated, so that by 1998 she was making $6,000 a year less than the lowest paid supervisor. A jury agreed and awarded her $3.8 million, which the judge reduced, as required by a 1991 statute restricting punitive damages in employment cases, to $360,000.

Justice Alito wrote the Court's opinion saying that Ledbetter filed her claim too late. The employment discrimination "occurred" each year when Goodyear set her salary, so she had to file her claim within six months every year. Justice Alito relied on four prior cases in which the Rehnquist Court had defined "occurred" pretty narrowly, so the decision wasn't a wild departure from precedent. Still, as Justice Ginsburg pointed out in her dissent, Ledbetter's case was different from the precedents. They all involved employment decisions similar to firings, where the precise moment the event occurred was easy for the victim to identify. Ledbetter's claim was different, Justice Ginsburg said, because the discrimination was hidden in the salary-setting decision, something Ledbetter could learn about only as she saw her pay gradually fall behind that of her co-workers: "Small initial discrepancies may not be seen as meet for a federal case, particularly when the employee, trying to succeed in a nontraditional environment, is averse to making waves."

After Justice Alito announced the Court's decision, Justice Ginsburg read her own statement summarizing the dissent. "In our view," she said, "the Court does not comprehend or is indifferent to the insidious way in which women can be victims of pay discriminations." The Court "ignores" "real world employment practices." Justice Ginsburg ended her oral statement by reading the last lines of her opinion: "This is not the first time the Court has ordered a cramped interpretation of Title VII, incompatible with the statute's broad remedial purpose. Once again, the ball is in Congress' court. As in 1991, the Legislature may act to correct this Court's parsimonious reading of Title VII."

Congress responded. Republicans blocked the enactment of a statutory response in April 2008, and Barack Obama made their refusal part of his presidential platform. After his election Congress voted for the Lilly Ledbetter Fair Pay Act in early January, and President Obama signed it, with Ledbetter at his side, on January 29, 2009. It was the first statute he signed into law.

NOT EVERY important decision in Roberts's second year went for the conservatives, because Justice Kennedy sometimes voted against them. He joined Justice Stevens's majority opinion in what people called the Court's global warming case, described in more detail in chapter 5. For now, what matters is that the Court decided that Massachusetts had "standing" to challenge the Bush administration's failure to adopt rules about carbon dioxide emissions from car tailpipes. "Standing" is a legal term that refers to the plaintiff's right to sue based upon the injuries caused by the actions (or inaction) the plaintiff was challenging. According to Justice Stevens, the injury Massachusetts suffered was that global warming would cause sea levels to rise, putting underwater land on Massachusetts's shore. Massachusetts owned some of that land, so global warming would take away its property. Showing his strategic skill, Justice Stevens dropped in a couple of barely relevant quotations from earlier Kennedy opinions.

Kennedy's new role on the Court led him to write the Court's opinion in the 2007 Term's terrorism case, holding that the Military Commissions Act (MCA) of 2006 was unconstitutional because it limited review in the regular federal courts of military commission convictions too substantially. The case was Roberts's first chance to weigh in on terrorism issues; during his rookie year the Court reviewed a terrorism case from the District of Columbia Circuit Court, which meant that he couldn't take part. Roberts and Alito, along with Justice Thomas, joined Justice Scalia's dissent, and the same four justices signed a separate dissent by Roberts. The only problem was that Scalia's fondness for rhetoric led him to include a line that made his opinion inconsistent with Roberts's. Roberts said that there wasn't much difference between the review the majority said the Constitution required and the review provided by the MCA. If that was so, you should expect no more than a handful of cases to come out differently under the MCA standard of review or the one the majority said the Constitution required. And, if *that* was so, it's hard to see that the difference in standards of review would make much difference "on the ground"—maybe the regular courts would overturn one or two more convictions under the majority's standard than under the MCA's. In contrast, Justice Scalia began his opinion with the observation that the majority's decision "will almost certainly cause more Americans to be killed." Maybe so, though not by 2012, because not a single military commission had yet started to hear evidence, much less had a conviction reviewed under the Court's standard. But surely there's a tension between saying that the MCA was constitutional because the standard of review it created was almost the same as the one the Court said the Constitution required, and saying that the Court's standard would cause more American deaths.

THE GLOBAL warming and terrorism cases show that the Roberts Court didn't endorse every policy or constitutional position favored by conservatives outside the Court. Perspective is important, though. The Court before the New Deal overturned the convictions of the Scottsboro defendants. The Warren Court upheld the power of police officers to stop and frisk people on the streets without probable cause to believe that they were about to commit crimes. Yet everyone knows that the Supreme Court in the early 1930s and during Warren's tenure had an identifiable tilt. So too with the Roberts Court in its early years.

The pattern predicted when Roberts took his seat in 2005 had clearly emerged by the end of his sophomore year. Not unanimity and consensus, but continued ideological division, with Justice Kennedy's vote the one that mattered most. He was somewhat more conservative than Justice O'Connor, so the "Kennedy Court" was a bit to the right of the O'Connor (or Rehnquist) Court. His concern for his place in history led him to write separate opinions supporting conservative results, but hinting that on other facts he might come out the other way. Kennedy's opinion in the Seattle school case was doctrinally quite narrow and suggested other ways of achieving integrated schools, though the one thing he singled out—building new schools with an eye to their likely racial composition—was wildly unrealistic in a nation where urban and near-in suburban schools were closing and most population growth occurred in far-out suburbs with little racial diversity. The Seattle case was typical of Kennedy: a conservative result hedged around with qualifications that Kennedy could see as demonstrating his commitment to the principles liberals said they honored.

Chief Justice Roberts was settling in to his role, though with some missteps. He seemed to have a mild case of "quotability-itis"—getting off lines for the sole purpose of seeing them quoted the next day in the newspapers. A little bit of that can go a long way, but getting quotability just right is difficult. Justice Kagan came to think that some of her most quotable lines had been mistakes because they injected a sharpness into her opinions that didn't fit her image of how a Supreme Court justice should present herself to the public—and perhaps because it might damage her ability to lead the Court's liberals in the long run. Roberts's invocation of *Brown v. Board of Education* in the Seattle case was a sheer provocation, not necessary to support the holding and also not something a justice interested in building consensus would have done.

By the end of Roberts's second term, the Court's profile was clear: a "narrowly split Court that leans conservative." As one justice reportedly said, in his first year Roberts "talk[ed] the talk" of compromise and harmony but in his second he wouldn't "walk the walk." That was even before the addition of Justices Sotomayor and Kagan to the Court's family, and the introduction of understated but real conflict between the Chief Justice and Justice Kagan. The "broader agreement" he said he sought eluded him and his colleagues. Roberts was well liked within the Court, and relations among the justices were friendly, but only occasionally could he overcome liberal-conservative divisions, and sometimes he did so by voting with the liberals.

CHAPTER 4

The Court of Public Opinion, the Supreme Court, and Gun Rights

*T*he *Dictionary of Misinformation*, published in 1975, asserted confidently: "Nothing in the Constitution . . . forbids the right of federal or state governments to make any gun-control laws they wish in terms of an individual who is not a member of a 'well-regulated militia.' " In November 1991, Robert Bork (it seems obligatory to write this as Robert Bork!) said that "the National Rifle Association is always arguing that the Second Amendment determines the right to bear arms. But I think it really is the people's right to bear arms in a militia. The NRA thinks that it protects their right to have Teflon coated bullets. But that's not the original understanding." A month later, retired Chief Justice Warren Burger, hardly a flaming liberal, repeated on the *Mac-Neil/Lehrer NewsHour* some ideas he had published two years earlier, though in more heated terms, saying that the National Rifle Association had perpetrated "one of the greatest pieces of fraud" and "misled the American people" into thinking that the Second Amendment had anything to do with an individual's right to own guns outside the militia setting.

In the 1990s Robert Bork was an icon for conservative legal thinkers. Warren Burger was a conventional conservative Republican throughout his career. But by the late 1990s the party had left them both behind, at least on the issue of the Second Amendment. The Republican Party had adopted the NRA's "fraudulent" claim that the Second Amendment protected every individual's right to own guns. Gun rights advocates developed what they cleverly labeled the "Standard Model" of the Second Amendment's original meaning. Their originalism triumphed in 2008 when Justice Antonin Scalia wrote what legal academics accurately describe as the most thoroughly originalist opinion in modern times, striking down the District of Columbia's complete ban on gun possession in the city. How did that happen?

Stories about Supreme Court cases usually begin with something about the characters—the plaintiffs or defendants and their lawyers. I'll get to that, but the story of *District of Columbia v. Heller* begins much earlier than 2002, when Dick Heller and Alan Gura filed their case, and earlier even than 1976, when the District of Columbia's city council adopted the ban. *Heller* really began in 1968, when Congress enacted the Omnibus Crime Control Bill and the Gun Control Act, and Richard Nixon ran for the presidency. Its story included:

- The National Rifle Association, an interest group whose leadership was more radical than its membership
- A lawsuit developed by ideological lawyers loosely associated with the Washington legal networks created in the last quarter of the twentieth century
- Originalism, an approach to constitutional interpretation that caught on because it supported the Republican Party's challenge to liberal Democrats

Importantly, each of these features appeared, in slight variants, in much of the Roberts Court's work, and not just the gun rights litigation.

THE NRA's story is the simplest: a tale of social change and office politics. For most of its first century, the NRA was an organization supporting sport hunting. It sponsored target-shooting competitions and provided its members with low-cost rifles supplied by the Army. It had a small public relations arm, supporting regulations to ensure responsible gun use. Members received a magazine with articles on hunting and advertisements for rifles. An NRA "fact book" published in 1975 stated that the Second Amendment was "of limited practical utility" for ordinary gun control debates.

The rise in crime—and in the fear of crime—in the 1950s and 1960s fueled a change in the NRA's membership. New members were more interested in guns for self-protection, less in rifles for hunting, although the hunting culture of rural America never disappeared from the organization. After expanding its lobbying efforts in Washington, Maxwell Rich, the NRA's executive officer, reconsidered and tried to restore its traditional focus on recreational gun use. Rich's proposal to move the offices from Washington to Colorado produced a revolt among the NRA staff. He responded by firing more than seventy staff members, including the entire lobbying group. Led by chief lobbyist Harlon Carter, they organized a successful counterattack at the NRA's 1977 national convention. After that Carter became the NRA's chief executive, and directed the organization's attention to the new gun rights movement. The Second Amendment became the organization's touchstone.

The NRA remained a membership organization, but like many Washington interest groups, it had a leadership that was more committed to the mission than many of its members were. The NRA wasn't a mere "checkbook" interest group like many in Washington, with members who wrote checks because they supported the group's political activities. People joined the NRA to get its magazine and learn about weaponry, survey the advertisements, and perhaps most important get some of the discounts available only to NRA members. The national office used membership dues to support increasingly intense lobbying.

The leadership wasn't completely out of touch with the membership, of course. Many members agreed with the new focus on Second Amendment rights, although surveys suggested that the Washington lobbyists sometimes opposed gun regulations that many (and sometimes most) members were willing to accept. Those within the NRA who opposed gun regulations, though, tended to be *intensely* against them. The NRA gained a reputation in Washington as an organization politicians shouldn't cross, because the NRA would get them in the next election. It wasn't so much that people who would have voted for a candidate voted against him because of his position on gun control, but rather that the NRA could get people to the polling booth who ordinarily wouldn't have bothered to vote.

The NRA did more than lobby in Washington and mobilize voters outside it. It promoted a new interpretation of the Second Amendment. Its case was simple: what part of "right to keep and bear arms" don't you understand? People had a constitutional right to speak freely, and the Second Amendment was just the same. Prodded by the NRA's increasing activism, and sometimes supported directly or indirectly by the NRA, scholars began to give the argument a more respectable academic form.

The first really important article on the Second Amendment was written by a liberal law professor, Sanford Levinson—though to call him "liberal" may convey a misleading impression. Thoroughly disillusioned with U.S. politics, Levinson—a professional colleague and personal friend of mine—never handled a gun after winning a camp target-shooting medal in his early teens, and was personally uninterested in learning how. He was interested in diagnosing the ills of

American politics, and he turned to history to inform his argument. The Second Amendment, he wrote in 1989, was "embarrassing" to liberals because they were unwilling to treat it as seriously as they did every other constitutional amendment. Properly understood, Levinson argued, the Second Amendment reflected a revolutionary tradition from which liberals drew inspiration in other contexts.

Levinson connected the Second Amendment to the small-r republican tradition, retrieved by historians in the 1970s and by legal academics a decade later (typically, treating as hot news something historians had been discussing for at least a decade). One historian notably called the small-r republicans "men of little faith," who were congenitally suspicious of people who sought to exercise government power. James Madison responded to that lack of faith by designing the U.S. Constitution, which he thought would be organized to keep corruption and overreaching in check even if, as he put it, men were not angels. The small-r republicans were unconvinced. They thought that an alert citizenry was the only real defense against corruption and tyranny. And for them, the word "defense" was not a metaphor but a description. The citizens of a republic needed to be armed against the risk that "their" government would get beyond their control. The Second Amendment was the Constitution's recognition of this aspect of republicanism. (What about the "militia"? In the republican tradition, the word referred to a body of self-organized armed people, not a formal entity run by the government.)

Levinson says that his article has been more widely distributed than any other ever published in the *Yale Law Journal*, and I wouldn't be surprised if it held the all-time record for any law review article. Other scholars filled in the argument, with often excruciating historical detail. The "Standard Model" emerged from this scholarship.

The small-r republican version, though, wasn't entirely suitable for contemporary purposes, so the argument had to be tweaked. The problem was twofold. Both Levinson's version and the more elaborate ones looked pretty bad, as supporters of gun control started to call it the "insurrectionist" interpretation and to associate it with violent right-wing militias in Montana and Michigan. And the military resources available to the national government had grown to the point where the image of stalwart farmers with muskets—or even semi-automatic guns—facing down a national army with laser-guided shoulder missiles was laughable (although gun rights advocates sometimes pointed out that urban guerrillas with small arms could be pretty effective).

The tweaks were obvious: play down concerns about a tyrannical government and play up self-defense. You actually could find a few references to self-defense against criminals (and Indians) in the Founding-era debates about adopting the Second Amendment. More important, you could substitute "ineffective" for "tyrannical" in describing why people needed a right to keep and bear arms. Governments were supposed to protect the people. They could break that deal by tyrannizing them, of course, but also by failing to protect them against marauders. The self-defense version of the Standard Model fit the concerns that drove the NRA's membership to support the Second Amendment, and it became the focus of the Supreme Court's decisions.

As Levinson's example shows, you don't have to be a "gun nut" to accept the Standard Model. *Life* magazine's interview with Robert Bork was paired with one with Laurence Tribe, the liberal counterpart to the conservative Bork. By the turn of the century, Tribe had come around to the Standard Model. The Standard Model has a lot going for it, as matter of ordinary constitutional interpretation. Unfortunately, so did the competition—the traditional view that the Second Amendment deals only with weapons used in a state-organized militia.

LIKE ALMOST all lawsuits, *District of Columbia v. Heller* has many twists and turns. Here I want to highlight only a few parts of the story. I've chosen parts that bring out some of the structures of our constitutional politics within which the Roberts Court operates, and won't deal with many details specific to the gun rights litigation.

The first structural feature involves the role of empathy in the choices movement lawyers make in selecting the plaintiffs in whose name their lawsuits will be brought. We usually think that plaintiffs bring lawsuits. Our personal experience tends to be with automobile accidents or medical care, where someone is hurt, finds a lawyer, and sues. Television ads by entrepreneurial lawyers telling people to call them if they worked with asbestos or used a particular drug show that lawyers sometimes generate lawsuits by identifying a problem and then finding someone to use as a plaintiff. *Heller* was a lawyer-initiated lawsuit, with constitutional entrepreneurs rather than moneymaking ones behind it.

Alan Gura, a young Virginia lawyer with his own law practice, argued *Heller* in the Supreme Court, but the case came about after a lot of discussion among a group of libertarian activists: Gura and Clark Neily as practicing attorneys, Chip Mellor and Robert Levy as financial backers who also were lawyers. Political Washington is full of networks of policy activists—environmentalists, health care specialists, fiscal watchdogs, and hard-line libertarians. People in the networks go to events sponsored by like-minded organizations, chat over the free snacks and lunches, exchange information about what each one is doing, and informally discuss successes and failures to figure out what works and what doesn't. The networks aren't conspiracies in which people plot grand strategies and dictate who should do what tasks. They're more like floating discussion groups.

Neily's full-time job was at the Institute for Justice, a libertarian public interest law firm that worked on cases challenging government regulations—often quite silly ones—that made it hard for small businesses to operate without getting a license. The institute has represented barbers and interior decorators, and mounted a large-scale effort to challenge cities that took houses away from their owners (paying them of course) to promote what the institute's lawyers regarded as fruitless and sometimes corrupt schemes for urban redevelopment. In 2002, Neily suggested that the institute take up gun rights. Mellor, the institute's head, decided that gun rights, though certainly of interest to libertarians, were too far removed from the organization's core interests, but he encouraged Neily to pursue the issue on his own time.

Neily, though, was overburdened by work and family obligations. He needed someone else to do the work, and that meant that he needed someone who could pay a lawyer. Robert Levy was the man. Neily and Levy had been law clerks to the same federal judge when they left law school. Levy had made millions when he sold his high-tech business, and then went to law school to deepen his knowledge and bolster his libertarian beliefs. Levy worked at the libertarian Cato Institute, but he was more interested in supporting libertarian litigation with his money than in actually litigating those cases. Neily asked Levy to put up the money for a gun rights suit against the District of Columbia, and Levy agreed.

They then had to find a lawyer. Stephen Halbrook had been a major figure in developing the Standard Model and had worked with the NRA on some of its gun rights lawsuits. Though not closely linked to the libertarian network, Halbrook happened to practice law in Fairfax, Virginia, just outside Washington. Levy and Neily talked with Halbrook, but Levy objected to paying his standard $400 per hour fee. Levy and Neily then got in touch with Gura, who had been an intern at the Institute of Justice before practicing at a large Washington law firm and then opening his own small practice, where he handled small trademark and copyright cases and occasionally sued police officers for violating the constitutional rights of people they arrested. Gura was perfect: a libertarian lawyer who would take on the case for a much more modest fee.

But, of course, at this point there was no case at all to take on, only an idea for a case. The next step was to find a plaintiff—but not just any plaintiff. The lawyers wanted "sympathetic people everyone could relate to." They combed news stories looking for people in Washington who might have wanted to use a gun for self-protection, then would call to find out whether the person was interested in joining a lawsuit. They wrote op-eds describing their legal theory and inviting people to contact them. They let others in the libertarian network know that they wanted to bring a gun rights suit against the District's ban, so that people with wider contacts might come up with potential plaintiffs.

Eventually, Gura picked six plaintiffs for his lawsuit, which then became their lawsuit. George Lyon's neighbor had been killed in a home invasion. Tom Palmer, a gay man, had brandished his handgun when harassed by gay bashers in San Jose, California, in 1982, before he moved to Washington. Dick Heller worked as a security guard at the Thurgood Marshall Judicial Center. He lived across the street from an abandoned public housing project, which had become a haven for drug users and gangs, and wanted to have a handgun to protect himself at home. Heller was friendly with Dane von Breichenruchardt, who was part of the libertarian network and a friend of Levy's. Finally, there was Shelly Parker, an anti-drug crusader in her Capitol Hill neighborhood, who had been threatened by drug dealers and wanted to follow the advice a District police officer gave her, to get a gun. The case was filed with Parker named first among the plaintiffs.

Levy and Gura wanted "sympathetic people" because, as Levy put it, "the case would unfold in the court of public opinion," so they "needed plaintiffs who would project favorably and be able to communicate with the public and the media." Here the libertarian Levy and Gura implicitly endorsed the role of empathy in constitutional adjudication. They would win in the court of public opinion by having personable plaintiffs tell compelling personal stories. Public support for their cause would translate into judicial support in the real Court.

In the end, the plaintiffs' personal stories really did drop out of the case. People who file constitutional lawsuits have to have "standing," which means that they have to have been injured by the statute they're challenging. Parker, Palmer, and Lyon hadn't even tried to get the District of Columbia to give them a permit for a gun, and lower courts held that they hadn't shown that they were harmed by the ban on gun possession. Without applying for a permit, their lack of weaponry resulted from their choice, not from the city's ban. Dick Heller, though, had applied for a permit and been turned down. That was enough to give him standing.*

But Heller was a gruff older white man, who looked like he might have been sympathetic to the radical-right militias, and who did indeed think that the government was pretty oppressive as in the Standard Model's "insurrectionist" version. He didn't present a good public face for the lawsuit, and he basically was kept out of sight as the case proceeded.

A second structural feature is interest group maneuvering. The NRA "owned" the gun rights issue. It supported lawsuits against federal regulations, relying on statutory interpretation and administrative law, but it avoided the core Second Amendment issue like the plague. It offered many reasons. The Second Amendment applied to the national government, which could be counted on to fight any Second Amendment suit as hard as it could, with all the resources—especially the legal talent in the Department of Justice—available to it. The NRA's resources might outmatch those of cities and states. But it could win suits against cities and states on federal constitutional grounds only after the Supreme Court endorsed the "individual right" interpretation of the Second Amendment itself.† The NRA's leadership found it hard to believe that the courts would strike down many federal regulations even under

---

* Of course, Heller was turned down because the city flatly banned all private gun possession, so it would have been pointless for Parker and the others to have applied for a permit. Gura thought about challenging the lower court's ruling denying Parker standing, but decided it wasn't worth it.

† After the *Heller* litigation was on its way, the NRA did file a lawsuit against Chicago's ban on handgun possession, expecting that it could piggyback on a hoped-for victory by Gura in *Heller*.

that interpretation. The government prosecuted people for possessing guns during drug deals, for example, and no one really thought there was anything wrong with that. Many federal-level regulations were similarly sensible policies. Taking them on would do no good to the NRA's public image.

President George W. Bush was a gun rights supporter, and he eventually made two appointments to the Supreme Court. Gura was pressing his lawsuit before then, though, and the NRA couldn't confidently count the five votes it needed to ensure a victory. It would be a disaster for the organization were the Supreme Court to reject the "individual rights" model. And underneath the surface was probably a concern, impossible to state openly, that winning the Second Amendment argument might actually weaken the NRA by taking away the appeal: "Give us your money because we're the only thing that stands between you and gun confiscation."

The NRA tried to persuade Robert Levy to abandon his plan to find a lawyer to bring the core Second Amendment claim to the Supreme Court. Nelson Lund, holder of a chair at George Mason University Law School endowed by the NRA's foundation, and Charles Cooper, a conservative activist lawyer who had headed the Justice Department's Office of Legal Counsel under President George H. W. Bush, failed in their efforts to get Levy to back down. Levy was more optimistic about Gura's prospects.

Persuasion having failed, the NRA tried to muscle Alan Gura aside. Acting for the NRA, Stephen Halbrook filed a separate lawsuit challenging Washington's ban. Halbrook's complaint did raise the core Second Amendment claim, but surrounded it with several additional issues that would let a court strike the ban down without ruling on that claim. Then Halbrook moved to consolidate the NRA's case with Gura's, saying that they raised overlapping issues, but that the NRA's case was a better vehicle for dealing with all the issues. Courts treat consolidated cases as if they were a single case, which means that one lawyer handles everything—and the NRA hoped that Halbrook rather than Gura would be that lawyer. Gura opposed consolidation, telling the court that the NRA lawsuit wasn't really motivated by the desire to strike the District's gun ban down, but rather "by the [NRA's] improper strategic goals." After denying Halbrook's motion to consolidate, the court dismissed the NRA case, finding that none of the plaintiffs had standing.

The NRA didn't accept defeat easily. Gura lost his case in the trial court because the judge there thought that precedent ran too strongly against it. He filed an appeal to the court of appeals, a station stop on the way to the Supreme Court. Gura's appeal was pending when the NRA appealed the dismissal of its own lawsuit. Because standing was a threshold issue that had to be decided before reaching the merits of the Second Amendment claim, the appeals court decided to deal with Halbrook's case before Gura's. Gura's case came to the fore again when the appeals court agreed that Halbrook's plaintiffs didn't have standing.

Even that didn't end the NRA's attempt to thwart Gura's lawsuit. That lawsuit asked the courts to wipe the District's gun ban off the books. That could be done by legislation, too. The District of Columbia city council wasn't about to repeal its ordinance, but Congress could. The NRA persuaded Utah senator Orrin Hatch to introduce legislation to repeal the ordinance. The NRA was willing to put up with arguments that its actions endangered people in Washington. But it's always easier for Congress to do nothing than to do something, and Hatch's bill languished while the courts considered Gura's appeal.

The final structural feature that the gun rights litigation illuminates is the role of the specialized Supreme Court bar. Gura won in the court of appeals, and the District had to decide whether to go to the Supreme Court. A few of the District's lawyers advised against an appeal. The gun ban wasn't tremendously effective, because District residents could easily buy guns in neighboring Virginia and bring them home. The lawyers suggested that the District revise its ban to allow some people to own guns, after they went through a stringent screening process to get a permit.

The city's young mayor, Adrian Fenty, supported by the city council, decided to appeal anyway. Elected with strong support among the city's white liberals, a group that generally favored strong gun control laws, Fenty believed that his constituents really did want a complete ban, no matter how ineffective it was. His chief attorney Linda Singer got in touch with Alan Morrison, who several years before had left his position in Washington as the chief lawyer for Public Citizen, a liberal public interest group founded by Ralph Nader, to take up a job at Stanford Law School. Morrison had lived in Washington for years, and kept up his contacts with the city, finding the academic life in Palo Alto a little too sedate. His work at Public Citizen made Morrison a member of the specialized Supreme Court bar, and he expected to argue the case if the Supreme Court decided to hear it.

Office politics got in Morrison's way. Peter Nickles, a Fenty family friend and a lawyer with an outsized ego, pushed Singer aside, effectively and then formally taking over her office's work. Nickles had no real Supreme Court experience, but he was confident that he could argue the case well. Others in the city's political circles were less sure, having run into Nickles's sharp elbows on many other issues as well. Facing opposition on many fronts, Nickles decided to retreat on *Heller*. He chose Walter Dellinger to represent the city in the Supreme Court.

Dellinger had been Acting Solicitor General in the Clinton administration—"Acting" only, because North Carolina's conservative Republican senator Jesse Helms blocked his confirmation. Helms believed that Dellinger, himself from North Carolina, was being groomed for a Supreme Court appointment (and he knew that Dellinger had actively opposed him in North Carolina politics). After leaving the Department of Justice, Dellinger developed a large Supreme Court practice, and was at the center of the liberal part of the specialized Supreme Court bar.

Gura faced parallel problems on the other side, including a whispering campaign that he was too inexperienced to handle a major Supreme Court case, even though, as he saw things, he had done pretty well so far. Levy had assured Gura that he would have control of the case no matter how far it went. But Gura was an outsider to the elite Washington bar, and to the circle of lawyers associated with the NRA. The NRA tried to take the case away from him again, generating letters and op-eds pressing Gura to step aside and let a member of the specialized Supreme Court bar argue the case in the Supreme Court.

The NRA had no real leverage, though, and all it could do was coordinate filings by the large number of gun rights groups that wanted to file amicus briefs. Eventually, Heller's side had almost fifty amicus briefs, substantially outnumbering the nineteen filed supporting the District. The NRA wasn't responsible for all the amicus briefs, but it generated more than a few. The most dramatic was a brief filed by a majority of the members of Congress and Dick Cheney, as the Senate's presiding officer. Stephen Halbrook signed the brief. Like the other amicus briefs, Halbrook's added little to Gura's arguments. But the brief gave the NRA the chance to line up support in Congress—or, perhaps, to demonstrate to members of Congress that the NRA still had clout even though it wasn't in charge of *Heller* itself.

THE FEDERAL statutes adopted in 1968 created an extensive system for regulating gun ownership and sales. The NRA tried to block their adoption, but the election-year imperative to do something about crime and the shadows of the assassinations of Martin Luther King, Jr., and Robert F. Kennedy overcame the NRA's lobbying effort. More important for the development of constitutional law, Richard Nixon campaigned on a platform of law and order. What that meant was giving more power to the police, and what *that* meant was criticizing the Supreme Court led by Earl Warren, Nixon's old nemesis from

California politics. For Nixon it wasn't just that the Warren Court was wrong in using the Constitution to require that the police give the *Miranda* warnings, or to require the exclusion from evidence of anything the police seized after they violated the Fourth Amendment. Relying in part on advice from William Rehnquist, a rising star in Republican legal circles, Nixon moved the criticism to a higher level. The Warren Court was wrong, but it was wrong because it was "activist"—a term introduced in 1947 into discussions of the Supreme Court by the liberal public intellectual Arthur Schlesinger, Jr.—and failed to respect the requirements of "judicial restraint." The trope of activism and restraint entered into the wider domain of public conversation about the courts.

Those tropes, though, were incomplete, and Republicans who wanted to develop an alternative to Warren Court activism knew that standing alone, "activism" couldn't be a criticism, because everyone understood that sometimes judges were supposed to be activist: they were supposed to protect freedom of speech—sometimes—against efforts by politicians to shut down their critics; they were supposed to stop racial segregation. You could say that you were against liberal activism, but then all you were doing was saying that your judges ought to be making the decisions, not theirs. Especially after Richard Nixon's four appointments to the Supreme Court, and then Ronald Reagan's, conservative legal activists took that line—basically saying that turnabout was fair play. Some began to advocate for vigorous enforcement of property rights, for example.

Yet simply switching from liberal activism to conservative activism, many conservative legal thinkers agreed, might be a strategy for winning cases but it wasn't a strategy for winning the argument about what the courts should be doing. They needed to shift the ground of the discussion, away from the Court's results to something else. The solution was to say that the Warren Court's decisions were wrong not simply because they were liberal but because Warren and his liberal colleagues weren't using the right *method* for interpreting the Constitution.

The Nixon impeachment proceedings interrupted the development of the Republican argument about constitutional method, but, as it turned out, also gave them the answer they were looking for. Raoul Berger, a quirky, idiosyncratic lawyer (and an accomplished violinist), was an old-line Democrat. The Supreme Court's short-lived rejection of New Deal programs had made a permanent impact on the young Berger, and he held the entirely defensible view that Congress had great constitutional responsibilities that it often discharged quite well. Berger had been working on a book about impeachment when the Watergate affair put presidential impeachment on the front pages. Berger had actually been thinking more about using impeachment against judges, but his book was so timely that he became one of the "go-to" sources during the Nixon impeachment proceedings.

Berger's book on impeachment was a detailed examination of the historical sources of the Constitution's provisions dealing with impeachment. He looked at the English precedents, the discussions of impeachment and its alternatives as the Constitution was drafted and debated, at dictionaries from the Founding era. The term hadn't been put in wide usage then, but Berger's book was originalist to the core. Liberals were happy to adopt Berger's approach as they defended their actions against Nixon.

It turned out Berger really was an originalist, and a liberal from the 1930s rather than the 1960s. His 1975 book's pejorative title told the story: *Government by Judiciary*. Berger used his originalist methods to demonstrate, at least in his own eyes, that the Supreme Court had departed from the Constitution's original design for generations. Now Berger became the object of conservative affection, because he gave them a constitutional *method* to use in attacking the Warren Court. When Ronald Reagan's election put legal conservatives in charge of the Justice Department, Attorney General Edwin Meese tasked the department's lawyers with advancing originalism in their arguments, and Meese himself made many speeches about the new jurisprudence of original intent.

Originalism's defenders had to answer two questions: *Why* should courts use originalism, and *what* exactly was originalism?

Conservatives offered two answers to the *why* question. First, the United States was a constitutional democracy. The "democracy" part meant that today's majorities ought to be able to do pretty much whatever we wanted. If we wanted to protect ourselves from criminals by unleashing the police, we should be able to do it. But, of course, the "constitutional" part meant that we couldn't really do whatever we wanted. Constitutionalism meant that "we" put limits on our choices. We did that when "we" adopted the Constitution.

The scare quotes indicate the problem, which quickly acquired the "dead white men" label. The people who adopted the Constitution were long gone, they were all white, and they were all men. They weren't "we" except in some metaphorical sense, and constitutional theorists tried but usually failed to explain why a metaphorical "we" should keep the real "we" from doing what we wanted.

The other answer was that it takes a theory to beat a theory. As conservatives saw it, the Warren Court was using the language of the Constitution to disguise the justices' liberal policy preferences. To conservatives, liberals were "just making it up" as they went along, and then pretended that they were discovering liberal meanings in the Constitution. Requiring that judges implement the Constitution as it was originally written would keep judges within bounds.

All well and good, but then we have to know exactly what originalism is. And that morphed significantly over the decades before *Heller*, responding to academic criticism of originalism as an academic theory.

These academic distinctions didn't matter to the public. Ordinary people were happy to use the language of original intent. Judges were different. Their law clerks were bright recent law school graduates steeped in academic discussions, and the justices worried at least a bit about their reputations in the legal academy. They didn't want to look foolish for using forms of originalism discredited inside the law schools no matter whether they were vibrant on editorial pages. Originalism transformed itself from being about original "intent" to being about "original public meaning or understanding."

Original "intent" was a problem because it opened up the possibility of "hidden" meanings—things going on in the minds of the Constitution's drafters that weren't publicly disclosed. That possibility had to be rejected if originalism rested on the ground that "we" had placed fetters on ourselves: How could "we" have done so if we didn't know what "we" had done? Another problem was that the Constitution was written and adopted by a bunch of people, and the idea that a collective body—the Constitution's drafters or ratifiers—could have "an" intent was mysterious.

Originalism shifted focus from the drafters to the ratifiers. The Constitution and its amendments are words that get their legal force after the people approve them, so the natural thing was to ask next what the people understood the words to mean. This disposed of the problem of secret meanings, but it introduced a new problem.

You might think that the way to figure out what people understood the words to mean is to find out what they said, openly, they thought the words would do. This got the label "original expected applications": one indication of what the words were understood to mean is what people expected to happen once the words became law. Justice Scalia's position on the death penalty is exemplary. The Fourteenth Amendment says, "No State . . . shall . . . deprive any person of life, liberty, or property, without due process of law." It just can't be that people understood the due process clause to make capital punishment unconstitutional when in the very same sentence it implicitly acknowledged the state's power to deprive people of life (under the right circumstances).

Original expected application may work fine for the death penalty.

It works quite badly for other problems. In 1954, in a case decided the same day as *Brown v. Board of Education*, the Supreme Court relied on the Fifth Amendment's due process clause to hold that Congress couldn't segregate the schools in the District of Columbia. The first Congress approved the Fifth Amendment in 1789. Yet that very Congress tolerated slavery in all sorts of ways. It just can't be that people in 1791 understood the due process clause to make racial segregation unconstitutional. There's a similar problem with gender discrimination and the Fourteenth Amendment. We have plenty of evidence that people in 1868 didn't expect that the Fourteenth Amendment's requirement of "equal protection of the laws" would have any effect on discrimination against women. Feminists of the time objected to the recognition, in another section of that amendment, of the possibility of limiting voting to men. And within five years of the amendment's adoption the Supreme Court held that the Fourteenth Amendment didn't prevent Illinois from saying that women couldn't be lawyers.

You can do some fancy footwork about original expected applications. My favorite is the idea that you can ignore original expected applications when those applications would *uphold* statutes (the three examples I've given), but you have to follow them when they would *invalidate* laws. Conservatives settled on a different answer. Original expected applications provided some information about a provision's meaning, but the meaning could be different from, and sometimes inconsistent with, those applications.

One legal scholar developed a list of the moves originalists made to shore up their theory against intellectual weaknesses. It runs from (a)—"original intent to original meaning"—through (c)—"actual to hypothetical understanding"—all the way up to (h) "the distinction between normative and semantic originalism" (don't ask). At this point originalism—now labeled "original public meaning," which I'm going to call OPM to save space—began to look like a Rube Goldberg machine, and, notably, prominent liberals were willing to sign on to *that* version of originalism. They didn't think it was worth fighting over theories of interpretation when they could do whatever they wanted using the lingo of originalism.

As one law professor put it with a sigh, "Richard Nixon once said that 'we are all Keynesians now,' and constitutional theory is approaching the point where we are [or] will all be originalists. [Conservative] Steve Calabresi is the co-author of [an] article claiming that gender discrimination violates the original understanding of the Fourteenth Amendment. [Liberal] Jack [Balkin] defends the Court's abortion decisions as an originalist reading of the same amendment. [Conservative] Michael McConnell claims that racial segregation was contrary to the original understanding (and so on)." For me, the conservative positions are the most dispiriting. Calabresi and McConnell know that originalism would be discredited in the public's eyes if it meant that the Constitution didn't make segregation and sex discrimination unconstitutional, so they do exactly what they think liberals do—massage the evidence and the theory so that it produces the outcomes they like. By now, originalism has lost whatever conservatives thought they were gaining by resting their objections to liberal decisions on broad grounds of constitutional method.

Still, sometimes you might find a constitutional provision that didn't run up against the problem of original expected applications. Surely, OPM originalism could still work when original expected applications were acceptable in today's society. You could do OPM originalism by looking at the historical materials. Of course, sometimes the Constitution uses technical terms, and sometimes even the words ordinary people might use have special meanings in legal documents. And, equally obvious, not everyone would have thought about what any specific constitutional provision meant. What an OPM originalist has to do is to figure out what a reasonable and reasonably well informed person reading the Constitution's text would have understood the words to mean. There's a risk here, to which some (I think most) OPM originalists have succumbed, that a judge will say to herself, "Well, I have available to me all the information people in 1791 had available to them, so I'm reasonably well informed, and the provision means thus-and-so to me, so it must have meant that to them." But that's bad OPM originalism, and we ought to think about it when it's done well.

Conservatives thought that the Second Amendment was a good candidate for applying OPM originalism. The only possible original expected applications that conceivably could cause a problem were the "bazooka" and "musket" problems liberals raised: the Second Amendment couldn't possibly protect a right for ordinary people to own bazookas even though bazookas are "arms" in some sense, but maybe it meant that people had only the right to own muskets, the sole type of arms available in 1791. Justice Scalia properly dismissed these problems in *Heller* by saying that the word "arms" had the public meaning of "weapons typically used for purposes of self-defense."*

It turned out that the Second Amendment was a good candidate for OPM originalism, but not good enough. *Heller* was a test for conservative originalists' claim that modern originalism's exclusive focus on historical materials would keep judges from advancing their policy views while pretending to interpret the Constitution. Originalism didn't quite fail the test, but it got a grade of C+ or so—pretty much the grade you'd give every other method of constitutional interpretation.

Justice Scalia wrote for the Court's five conservatives, Justices Stevens and Breyer for the liberal dissenters. Justice Breyer's dissent was pragmatic and fact-focused, concluding that, though it wasn't clear that the District's gun ban would do much good, the Court ought to let it try to control violence by controlling guns. In contrast, the Scalia and Stevens opinions were originalist, but the two justices read the

---

* That's not a complete answer; maybe people would typically use machine guns for self-defense if they could buy machine guns as easily as handguns, and it leaves open questions about controls on new weapons technologies that could be adapted for self-defense. It's enough to dispose of the bazooka and muskets problems, though.

historical materials quite differently. The opinions are long and detailed, but their flavor can be captured in a discussion central to the Court's opinion. The Second Amendment has a preamble or preface—"A well regulated Militia, being necessary to the security of a free State"—and what has come to be called its operative clause, "the right of the people to keep and bear Arms, shall not be infringed." The difference between conservatives and liberals turns in large part on how they interpret the relation between the preamble and the operative clause.

Liberals focus on the preamble. For them, it limits the operative clause: people have a right to keep and bear arms only in connection with their membership in a state-organized militia. Judge Bork seems to have had the same view. Today's conservatives see the preamble differently. For them it explains why people wanted to include the Second Amendment in the Constitution, but explanations are not limitations. As Justice Scalia suggested, it's as if the people said, "We've had a longstanding right to keep and bear arms, which we happen to have used when we've served in a militia, and now we want to make sure that we continue to have that right." The right's scope is defined by the long-standing tradition, not by the reference to the militia.

Justice Scalia's opinion parsed the Second Amendment word-by-word, looking at pre–1791 dictionaries, statutes, local constitutions, and more. For the preamble's role, he looks to prevailing legal accounts of statutory interpretation. You can find preambles scattered in the eighteenth-century law books, and treatises of the time tried to explain the relation between preambles and operative provisions. Justice Scalia concluded from his examination of those materials that ordinary, reasonably well informed readers would have understood that the preamble explained the operative clause but didn't limit it. Justice Stevens examined exactly the same materials and concludes that such readers would have understood the preamble as a limitation. This sort of disagreement runs through the two opinions.

I don't want to award the win to either one. For me, the disagreement shows where OPM originalism fails in its ambitions. I've looked at most of the same materials the justices did. My conclusion is that they are something like 60–40 in Justice Scalia's favor. Capturing that sense is tricky, but here's one try: If someone had asked reasonable and reasonably well informed people in 1791 whether the preamble explained or limited the operative clause, about 60 percent of them would have said that it explained but didn't limit, and 40 percent would have said that it limited.

The problem for OPM originalists should be apparent. They want a method that keeps judges from imposing their views in the guise of interpreting the Constitution. Historical inquiry into a provision's original public meaning was supposed to disclose *the* original public meaning. But if you can't find *a* singular, determinate public meaning, you have to add something to OPM originalism to get what you're looking for. And indeed, conservatives have tried.

In a 60–40 situation, you can just go with the 60. But, of course, whether it's 60–40 one way or 60–40 the other is going to be a judgment call, relying on choices about which types of evidence carry more weight (treatises or judicial opinions before 1791), and about what the evidence taken as a whole shows. Policy views are sure to pollute those judgment calls, and you're back in the pickle you started with—judges using the Constitution's language, or, here, their interpretation of the historical evidence, to impose their policy views on a legislature that disagrees with them.

Alternatively, you can punt. Sometimes the OPM is actually going to be overwhelming, as we'll see when we get to the *McDonald* case. When it isn't—in the 60–40 or even 70–30 case—you can say that the courts can't strike the legislation down. That leaves the issue to today's people, promoting the democratic side of democratic constitutionalism.* Of

---

* The academic account of punting distinguishes between constitutional interpretation, which involves OPM, and constitutional construction, a process in which the Constitution's meaning is worked out over time in interactions among the people and their elected

course, that would have led to a different result in *Heller*. Or you can say that you can supplement OPM with other materials—prior judicial decisions, or contemporary views about what the Constitution means. Justice Stevens supplemented the 40 percent side of the case with an ambiguous and barely relevant Supreme Court decision from 1939, coupled with lower court decisions over the succeeding years that had followed the militia-related interpretation of the Second Amendment. Had he wanted to, Justice Scalia could have become a living constitutionalist here, supplementing the 60 percent side with pretty strong evidence that people today think that the Second Amendment protects an individual right to own guns for self-protection and hunting.

Worst of all, you can pretend that a 60–40 case is a 95–5 one, which is what Justice Scalia actually did. His opinion is a lawyer's document, perhaps to no one's surprise. Every piece of historical evidence is marshaled in favor of his case. He dismisses or distinguishes the materials that go into the 40 percent judgment, so that things that you might have thought counted against his interpretation actually count in its favor. Justice Breyer's dissent came up with a 1783 Massachusetts statute prohibiting Boston residents from bringing loaded guns into a house or any other building. Justice Scalia dismissed the evidence: the statute's purpose was "to eliminate the danger to firefighters" posed by gunpowder in burning houses, which "give[s] reason to doubt that colonial Boston authorities would have enforced that general prohibition against someone who temporarily loaded a firearm to confront an intruder." This move's rhetorical effect is clear. The people on the other side—which is to say, his four dissenting colleagues—are either ignoramuses or fools. Justice Scalia has built a reputation on his slashing rhetorical style, but we can wonder whether bringing the rhetorical tools of political talk radio to the Supreme Court is good for it or for the country.

---

representatives, including executive officers like the president. Constitutional construction can look a lot like the living Constitution conservatives deride.

As I've said before, the rhetoric the justices use matters, because how they make the law may be almost as important as the law they make. Justice Scalia ended his opinion in *Heller*: "We are aware of the problem of handgun violence in this country, and we take seriously the concerns raised by the many *amici* who believe that prohibition of handgun ownership is a solution. The Constitution leaves the District of Columbia a variety of tools for combating that problem, including some measures regulating handguns. . . . But the enshrinement of constitutional rights necessarily takes certain policy choices off the table. These include the absolute prohibition of handguns held and used for self-defense in the home." Two weeks earlier, he had opened his dissent in one of the cases arising out of the Bush administration's policy of detaining suspected terrorists at Guantánamo Bay by saying that "today's opinion . . . will almost certainly cause more Americans to be killed. That consequence would be tolerable if necessary to preserve a time-honored legal principle vital to our constitutional Republic." Written as the Court's work on *Heller* was winding up, Justice Scalia's dissent anticipated his conclusion there: the *Heller* decision might "cause more Americans to be killed" by gun violence, but that was "tolerable" because "necessary to preserve a time-honored legal principle," the Second Amendment's decision to "take certain policy choices off the table." But, of course, the Second Amendment didn't take the choices off the table; the Court's interpretation of the Second Amendment did.

Justice Scalia's opinions use a rhetorical trope that the Court's conservatives like. The justices disclaim responsibility for what they are doing: "Don't blame us, blame the Constitution." They wink that they might not *like* what they are doing, but they have to do it. This, even though they are clearly making a choice and then imputing it to the Constitution. Perhaps more subtly than the 95–5 strategy for dealing with a 60–40 problem, disclaiming responsibility may similarly disparage those who disagree. In each of the cases I've quoted, somebody dissented (four people, actually, in three of the cases). Saying that the Constitution *forced* the majority to do what it did implies that the dissenters must have disregarded the Constitution—and their judicial duty. Justice Kennedy's version of the disclaimer strategy may be better, but only because it is transparently self-contradictory: "We are presented with a clear and simple statute to be judged against a pure command of the Constitution. The outcome can be laid at no door but ours."

EXPERIENCED SUPREME Court observers sometimes say that a lawyer with an easy case could stand in front of the justices, recite "Mary Had a Little Lamb," and win his case. Nobody does, but maybe Alan Gura should have when he argued *McDonald v. Chicago.* The Supreme Court had to decide whether the Constitution prevented Chicago from having an absolute ban on handgun possession just like Washington's. Everyone knew that the answer was going to be yes, but not what the Court was going to say. Gura offered a pretty good theory for the result, probably the best one available. Justice Scalia was having none of it. He told Gura that he shouldn't make that argument "unless you are bucking for a place on some law school faculty." The transcript notes "(Laughter.)" "Mary Had a Little Lamb" would have been better, apparently.

To appreciate Gura's problem and Scalia's discomfort we have to go through a fair amount of technical detail. We need the detail to understand exactly how conservative constitutional theory works in practice, which turns out to be pretty much how liberal constitutional theory works. The justices use their general judicial philosophies to reach results they care about *before* they figure out the technical details.

Heller involved the Second Amendment, part of the Bill of Rights. In 1833, the Supreme Court held that the Bill of Rights placed limits on the national government, not on state governments. As a technical matter, the District of Columbia city council is a subdivision of the national government. It exercises the power of the national government to legislate for the nation's seat of government, as specifically laid out in the Constitution. The D.C. city council's power is limited by the Bill of Rights.

State governments (and the cities to which they give some power) are not so limited, at least not directly. Anti-slavery theorists disagreed with the 1833 Supreme Court decision, and thought that the Constitution did—or at least should—limit state governments' power too. The Fourteenth Amendment was adopted in 1868 to write restrictions on state governments into the Constitution. You can find scores of statements from that period saying that the Fourteenth Amendment would put state governments under the same Bill of Rights restrictions the national government had to comply with. From the 1940s on, lawyers referred to this as the "incorporation" of the Bill of Rights into the Fourteenth Amendment. In 1868 the Second Amendment was often singled out as an "incorporated" right, with the Fourteenth Amendment's supporters saying repeatedly that newly freed slaves needed to have the right to own weapons—a right they had of course been denied under slavery—to protect themselves from marauders who wanted to re-create the conditions of slavery. Applying the Second Amendment through the Fourteenth seemed to be the easiest possible case for OPM originalism. This isn't a 60–40 case but more like a 100–0 one, raising none of the theoretical difficulties that surfaced in *Heller*. To OPM originalists, Chicago's ordinances had to comply with the Second Amendment's requirement no less than Washington's did. That's one reason Gura had won his case before walking into the Supreme Court.

The difficulty for the Court's conservatives was that OPM originalism worked in *McDonald* through the wrong part of the Fourteenth Amendment. For our purposes, that amendment has two clauses.* The

---

* There's a third clause that prevents states from denying "the equal protection of the laws," but it wasn't implicated in *McDonald*.

first clause reads, "No State shall make or enforce any law which shall abridge the privileges or immunities of citizens of the United States," and the next, "nor shall any State deprive any person of life, liberty, or property, without due process of law." All the OPM originalist evidence showed that the privileges or immunities clause was originally understood to make the Bill of Rights applicable to the states. People in 1868 regularly quoted an 1823 opinion by Justice Bushrod Washington (George Washington's favorite nephew) dealing with the 1789 Constitution's privileges and immunities clause:

> The inquiry is, what are the privileges and immunities of citizens in the several states? We feel no hesitation in confining these expressions to those privileges and immunities which are, in their nature, fundamental; which belong, of right, to the citizens of all free governments; and which have, at all times, been enjoyed by the citizens of the several states which compose this Union, from the time of their becoming free, independent, and sovereign. What these fundamental principles are, it would perhaps be more tedious than difficult to enumerate. They may, however, be all comprehended under the following general heads: Protection by the government; the enjoyment of life and liberty, with the right to acquire and possess property of every kind, and to pursue and obtain happiness and safety; subject nevertheless to such restraints as the government may justly prescribe for the general good of the whole.*

Keeping weapons for self-defense was precisely the kind of fundamental right to which Washington referred—a right to pursue safety.

The privileges and immunities clause posed two problems for conservatives despite its OPM attractions.

The first was precedent. In 1873, just five years after the amendment's

---

* No one thinks that the shift from "and" in the 1789 Constitution to "or" in the Fourteenth has any effect on the Fourteenth Amendment's meaning.

adoption, the Supreme Court gave the clause an extremely narrow interpretation. Rather than protecting fundamental rights generally, the Court said, it protected only those rights that were distinctive to *national* citizenship, citizenship "of the United States," to use the clause's terms. Those rights were quite limited—a right to diplomatic protection when traveling abroad, for example, and a right to travel through a state on your way to the nation's capital. OPM original-ists typically make some concessions to long-standing precedent, even if the precedent is inconsistent with OPM. They don't object to the government's power to issue dollar bills, for example, despite pretty strong OPM evidence that the founding generation understood the Constitution to limit the national government's powers over currency to gold and silver. And, perhaps conveniently, they rely on precedent in affirmative action cases, where OPM originalism points reasonably strongly (in the 60–40 sense) to the conclusion that affirmative action is consistent with the Fourteenth Amendment's OPM. Justice Scalia called himself a "faint hearted originalist" because of his recognition of precedent's force. More dramatically, he contrasted his originalism with Justice Thomas's, saying in one of his standard talks, "I am a textualist. I am an originalist. I am not a nut." Yet precedent alone wouldn't keep even a fainthearted originalist from using the privileges and immunities clause to strike down Chicago's handgun ban.

The second problem was that the implications of relying on the privileges and immunities clause were quite unclear, and some were unsettling. The Court was flooded with amicus briefs. Legal interest groups and legislators filed them to advertise to their constituents that they were on the right side of the issue, not really to influence the Court. Buried in the pile were some that might have caught the justices' atten-tion. The one filed by the obviously conservative Goldwater Institute urged the Court to overrule the 1873 case and go with the "privileges and immunities" argument. So did another, filed by the perhaps less obviously liberal Constitutional Accountability Center, on behalf of a group of law professors both liberal and conservative.* A justice might fairly wonder about this odd convergence.

And rightly so. The conservatives and liberals who liked the "privileges and immunities" argument did so because the clause was an empty shell into which they could pour their constitutional hopes. The clause protected "fundamental" rights, but Bushrod Washington's statement showed that those rights could be libertarian in a conservative or a liberal sense. The Institute for Justice filed a brief in *McDonald*. The institute is the conservative legal interest group run by William Mellor with Clark Neily of the *Heller* case on the staff, with economic libertarianism its cause. Social liberals took Washington's reference to the "right to pursue happiness" seriously, hoping that judges might use the privileges and immunities clause to guarantee a right to gay marriage.

The Clause did resemble the Second Amendment in one sense. The Supreme Court hadn't said anything substantial about the Second Amendment before *Heller*. The 1873 case meant that the Court hadn't said anything substantial about the privileges and immunities clause either. The blank slate the Court would write on was much smaller in *Heller*, though: future decisions would give more content to the Second Amendment, but the justices could be sure that the content would have something to do with guns and weapons. No one could know what a future Court would say were "fundamental rights." The OPM originalist case for using the privileges and immunities clause in *McDonald* betrayed the impulse that had produced originalism in the first place, the hope that some theory of constitutional interpretation would keep the justices from saying that the Constitution protected rights that they personally believed fundamental. You didn't have to be a "nutty" conservative to find that prospect unsettling.

---

* You might think that briefs "on behalf of" law professors would be true amicus briefs, offered by disinterested scholars to assist the Court. A relatively new phenomenon, such briefs are no less partisan and one-sided than the ones filed by legal interest groups—and the justices know it.

Only Justice Thomas was a consistent OPM originalist in *McDonald*. His four conservative colleagues' faintheartedness led them into a different kind of difficulty. They had to rely on the Fourteenth Amendment's other clause, saying that states couldn't deprive people of liberty without "due process of law." Here they did have precedent on their side, but it was Warren Court precedent that conservatives had long made fun of. Building on a 1937 decision, the Warren Court used the due process clause to "selectively" incorporate Bill of Rights protections into the Fourteenth Amendment. One by one, those protections became applicable to the states because, in the Warren Court's view, they were really important. This approach might seem more attractive to conservatives than the "privileges and immunities" argument, because it was at least tethered to the Bill of Rights: if you couldn't find a supposedly fundamental right in the Bill of Rights, you couldn't protect it simply because *you* thought it was fundamental.

The "selective" part of selective incorporation was a problem, though. No one thought that each and every provision in the Bill of Rights was truly important. The Seventh Amendment guarantees jury trials in civil cases—ordinary car accident cases—where the stakes "exceed twenty dollars." No one thinks that that is a fundamental or even a terribly important right. More significantly, in the nineteenth century the Court held that states did not have to start important criminal proceedings with indictments even though the Fifth Amendment says, "No person shall be held to answer for a capital or infamous crime, unless on a presentment or indictment of a Grand Jury." Again, no one suggests that the Court should retreat from that position.

The due process clause route to incorporation presented textual problems that conservatives had emphasized in the criticism of the Warren Court's "liberal activism." A small one was redundancy: the Fifth Amendment contained its own due process clause. If the same words in the Fourteenth Amendment "incorporated" all the other protections in the Bill of Rights, why did the drafters bother to spell out those other protections in the rest of the Bill of Rights?

Another textual problem comes from the word "process." Some Bill of Rights protections do deal with process—the grand jury clause, for example. Others deal with substantive rights. The First Amendment's guarantees of free speech and press aren't really about process. Nor, of course, is the Second Amendment as a vehicle for a right of self-defense, unless you do some fancy footwork and treat the amendment as guaranteeing a process—armed resistance—against a potentially tyrannical government. Conservatives were fond of quoting the liberal scholar John Hart Ely, who derided the use of the due process clause to protect substantive rights. To Ely, the phrase "substantive due process" was self-contradictory, something like "green pastel redness."

Even worse, the due process clause was the liberals' foundation for the fundamental right to privacy and the right to choice with respect to abortion. Using the due process clause, liberals had done exactly what Justice Scalia and other conservatives feared the privileges and immunities clause would do. Incorporating the Second Amendment via the due process clause amounted to a vindication of liberal constitutional theory.

No matter. Justice Thomas grabbed one horn of the dilemma by being a consistent OPM originalist who invoked the privileges and immunities clause. Justice Alito wrote for his other conservative colleagues and grabbed the other horn, relying on precedent and the due process clause to selectively incorporate the Second Amendment into the Fourteenth.

For conservatives no less than for liberals, results mattered more than theory.

HELLER AND *McDonald* settled almost nothing—no news to scholars of constitutional law, who know that individual decisions almost never settle things, but perhaps dismaying to the public. Indeed, as a matter of pure form *McDonald* didn't even decide whether Chicago's handgun ban was unconstitutional. The Court sent the case back to the lower court to make the inevitable ruling against the city. Even *Heller* didn't resolve much. We now know that cities can't completely ban the possession of handguns for self-defense purposes in the home. That holding can have narrow or broad readings. Emphasize the home and governments can still prohibit gun possession—concealed or open—on the streets. What about in your front yard? I can see arguments going both ways, although I'm sure that courts would hold that the right recognized in *Heller* extends at least to the yard in a scenario suggested by Clint Eastwood's *Gran Torino*, in which a person takes a gun from his house and brandishes it in his front yard to scare off marauders.

Emphasize self-defense and maybe governments have to allow gun possession on the streets—and the possession of other, less lethal weapons useful for self-defense. We've already seen scholarly articles asking whether sharp-bladed knives are "arms" covered by the Second Amendment, a question about which most NRA members probably have no views whatever. I'm particularly fond of the case claiming that banning the possession of nunchakus—or, more seriously, Mace and other self-protection sprays—violates the *Heller* right because nunchakus are useful for self-defense.

Heller doesn't really tell us whether the right it protects is a small one, dealing with self-protection in the home using weapons commonly available for self-defense, or a big one, dealing with the right to bear arms generally, with possession in the home just an example of the right. And determining whether it's big or small affects how lower courts will apply *Heller*. If it's a small right, state legislatures and city councils can adopt any remotely reasonable regulation of gun possession outside the home. If it's a larger right, lower courts will have to decide whether the right is like the First Amendment. Legislatures *can* regulate the right to speak and publish, but they have to have really good reasons for doing so, and their regulations have to do a really good job of promoting those reasons. In connection with the Second Amendment, the jargon is: strict scrutiny, compelling state interest, and narrow tailoring—terms we'll sometimes see again in this book. Not all constitutional rights are like the First Amendment, though, and sometimes you can have a right that the government can regulate for decent though not "compelling" reasons. Here the jargon is: intermediate scrutiny. As things have shaken out, so far the lower courts invalidated only one important gun regulation other than complete bans like Washington's and Chicago's— Illinois's complete ban on carrying guns outside the home.

More: some forms of speech, like obscenity and fraudulent statements, fall outside the First Amendment, and some weapons might fall outside the Second Amendment, but lower courts will have to decide why. The Supreme Court has suggested two lines of argument: speech might not be covered if it doesn't have anything to do with the reasons we have for protecting speech, or it might not be covered if as a historical matter legislatures have always regulated it (like obscenity). These two approaches—functional and historical—might come into play in Second Amendment litigation too.

Heller makes the problem even worse. Every constitutional decision leaves issues undecided. Sometimes the justices get snarky about that. Justice Breyer criticized the *Heller* majority for "throw[ing] into doubt the constitutionality of gun laws throughout the United States," because the decision opened up so many questions without indicating, except in the most general terms, how to answer them. Justice Stevens added the words "Do not accept the summary you have just heard" to his oral announcement of his dissent, referring specifically to the Court's treatment of precedent but perhaps applicable to the opinion as a whole. Justice Scalia responded, in effect, "Give me a break. This is the first case dealing with the Second Amendment. You can't expect us to answer all the questions you might have about the decision's scope right now. We and the lower courts will work that out in the future."

Yet almost exactly a year earlier, Justice Scalia had joined a dissent by Chief Justice Roberts listing forty questions the Court had left unresolved—"a few uncertainties that quickly come to mind"—when it held that a judge had to sit out a case involving a person who had just recently contributed a large amount to the judge's election campaign. In 2008, the Chief Justice and Justice Scalia seem to have thought that "[t]he Court's inability to formulate a 'judicially discernible and manageable standard' strongly counsels against the recognition of a novel constitutional right," and they weren't ready to say, "Let's try this out and see how lower courts work out the problems over the next few years." Perhaps it's no surprise that Justice Breyer was on the other side of that case too.

Maybe, though, *Heller* differs from the judicial disqualification case. Justice Scalia did say that many regulations might be justified historically. Scalia introduced the possibility of historical justifications after establishing to the majority's satisfaction that the Second Amendment protected an individual right. But, he wrote, "Although we do not undertake an exhaustive historical analysis today of the full scope of the Second Amendment, nothing in our opinion should be taken to cast doubt on longstanding prohibitions on the possession of firearms by felons and the mentally ill, or laws forbidding the carrying of firearms in sensitive places such as schools and government buildings, or laws imposing conditions and qualifications on the commercial sale of arms." Inserting this passage to secure Justice Kennedy's vote, Justice Scalia sought to allay concern that *Heller* would sweep quite broadly.

Scalia said that the regulations he listed were "only . . . examples." Academic commentators were quick to raise questions. There's the "Martha Stewart problem": she's a convicted felon, barred by federal law from possessing a handgun in any of her homes to protect herself, yet it's hard to see why she shouldn't be allowed to have a gun. There's the "reformed felon problem": why should someone who committed a violent felony thirty years ago and has lived a life pure as the driven snow since be barred from having a handgun to protect himself—particularly if he lives in less protected surroundings than Martha Stewart does? There's the "misdemeanor problem": federal law makes it a crime for a person convicted of a misdemeanor crime of domestic violence from owning a handgun. Is such a person enough like a felon to be covered by the rationale for keeping guns out of the hands of felons? There's the "employee problem": federal law makes it a crime for an employee of someone who's been convicted of a felony to have a gun as part of her employment. What about the security guard at an apartment building owned by Martha Stewart? And what about the "sensitive places" exception? Why would the core of *Heller*'s analysis focus on the utility of guns for self-defense *in the home* if the exception is limited to "sensitive places"? So, maybe *Heller* means that the Constitution doesn't allow states to prohibit carrying guns on the public streets. And, if a capitol building or a courthouse is a sensitive place, what about a national park?

The listed regulations were only "presumptively" permissible. How can we find out when the regulations actually are permissible? There are two possibilities: the functional and historical approaches I mentioned in describing the "small" and "large" Second Amendment after *Heller*.

A functional approach would ask whether the reasons for the well-established regulations extend to newer ones. Does a gun in Martha Stewart's hands, or in the hands of the reformed felon, pose the same kind of threat to the public that a gun in the hands of a violent felon does? That's a sensible question, but it might not be the one the Court in *Heller* thought judges should ask. After all, Justice Breyer's dissent was thoroughly functionalist, and Justice Scalia derided that dissent for giving judges too much power. The problem, such as it is, of judicial power doesn't go away when the courts think functionally about whether a specific regulation is permissible.

So perhaps we should take the historical approach and ask whether the long-standing exemplary prohibitions are similar to—or maybe whether they are descendants of—prohibitions that were widely understood to be permissible in 1791 or 1868. In deciding *Heller*, the justices were able to rely on a generation or more of scholarship on the question of interpreting the Second Amendment to protect an individual right or a militia-related right. There's almost no relevant scholarship on the historical pedigree of the "longstanding prohibitions" Justice Scalia listed, not to mention the others not on his list. Without that sort of scholarship to rely on, lower court judges are almost certain to do a terrible job using the historical approach. Worse, some of the most common prohibitions, such as the federal ban on gun possession by people convicted of domestic violence misdemeanors or in national parks, were adopted within the past half century—hardly "long-standing," although you can massage them to make them "like" traditional restrictions on gun possession by felons or at public fairs.

Beyond that, the historical approach is going to produce some quite peculiar analyses. It's one thing for courts to deal with the original understanding of the Second Amendment. It's going to be another— much less attractive, I think—for them to try to figure out what people in 1791 understood the Statute of Northampton to mean. For those of you who aren't intimately familiar with the Statute of Northampton, adopted in England in 1328, the statute provides that "no man great nor small, of what condition soever he be . . . be so hardy to come before the King's justices, or other of the King's ministers doing their office, with force and arms, nor bring no force in affray of the peace, nor to go nor ride armed by night nor by day, in fairs, markets, nor in the presence of the justices or other ministers, nor in no part elsewhere. . . . " You can see the glimmerings of the "sensitive places" exception here, but the statute seems to sweep more broadly, apparently prohibiting weapons possession anywhere large numbers of people might gather ("fairs" and "markets"). Maybe it provides the historical basis for upholding a ban on having guns on the public streets generally. Maybe, though, people in 1791 understood the Statute of Northampton more narrowly. One source written in 1716, for example, says that "no wearing of arms is within the meaning of this statute, unless it be accompanied with such circumstances as are apt to terrify the people; from whence it seems clearly to follow, that persons of quality are in no danger of offending against this statute by wearing common weapons, or having their usual number of attendants with them for the ornament or defence." I have no view on what people in 1791 thought the Statute of Northampton meant. I'm sure, though, that having judges discourse on its meaning, and the treatise's discussion of "persons of quality," is going to be unedifying.

Heller does indeed represent the triumph of originalism, the culmination of the long conservative campaign to shift the ground of constitutional discourse. But the triumph may be bittersweet. The originalism in *Heller* and *McDonald* may be unsatisfactory in the cases themselves. In *Heller*, Justices Scalia and Stevens fought on originalist turf. The very fact of real and defensible disagreement about the original understanding undermined the conservative claim that only originalism stood between us and willful judges using constitutional methods as the cloak for their policy preferences.

DEMOCRATS MIGHT have hoped that *Heller* and *McDonald* would take the gun control issue off the table of national politics. The NRA's campaign against all forms of gun control had capitalized on the argument that *any* form of gun control would put the nation on the slippery slope down to complete gun confiscation. The Supreme Court's decisions should have taken that argument away from the NRA, leaving the way open for the kinds of gun control that Democrats had sometimes advocated—most notably, improving the system for identifying people who bought guns at gun shows from unregistered dealers.

As the discussion of gun safety and gun control after the Newtown school shootings showed, it didn't work out that way. Republicans had become committed not merely to the argument that the Constitution prohibited the government from banning guns but to the proposition that it was generally a good thing for law-abiding citizens to own guns. When they could, they enacted laws *eliminating* existing restrictions on guns. The Republican-controlled legislature in Wisconsin, for example, passed a law allowing people to carry their guns into the state capitol— one of the "sensitive places" the Court's decision in *Heller* said could be protected against guns. Political movements like the gun rights movement may bring cases to the Supreme Court, and their advocacy can make previously "fraudulent" arguments plausible and even correct. The gun-rights movement's effectiveness in legislatures suggests that political movements may be more important on the ground than they are in the Supreme Court—and that the academic shouting around the issue of originalism is a sideshow.

CHAPTER 5

Business Stooge or Umpire?
Business Cases in the Roberts
Court

"**B**USINESS REIGNS SUPREME," proclaimed *The Washington Post* at the end of John Roberts's second term. The story quoted Robin Conrad, the litigation director for the U.S. Chamber of Commerce. "In case after case, the court this term understood the business community's need for clarity and predictability in the law." The next day, Supreme Court correspondent Tony Mauro's story was headlined "HIGH COURT REVEALS A MIND FOR BUSINESS." That theme began to pervade year-end roundups of the Supreme Court's work. A year later, the law professor and legal journalist Jeff Rosen profiled business litigators Robin Conrad and Theodore Olson in the Sunday magazine section of the *New York Times*, in a story entitled "Supreme Court, Inc." Rosen noted that the Chamber of Commerce "filed briefs in 15 cases and its side won in 13 of them," and pointed out that the Roberts Court had "heard seven antitrust cases in its first two terms—and all of them were decided in favor of the corporate defendants." In 2010 the theme was the same: "JUSTICES OFFER RECEPTIVE EAR TO BUSINESS INTERESTS" was the headline for a story by the *Times*'s Adam Liptak.

Academics weighed in with the same message. The political scientist Lee Epstein, Judge Richard Posner, and the legal economist William Landes offered a statistical analysis concluding that "liberal" decisions on economic matters dropped from 54 percent for the last five years of the Rehnquist Court to 38 percent under Chief Justice Roberts. Part of the reason was that the Roberts Court decided to review liberal decisions from lower courts at a slightly higher rate than the Rehnquist Court did: "Should this trend continue, and should the Roberts Court reverse a higher fraction, of these liberal lower court decisions," Epstein and her co-authors wrote, "it might be reasonable to conclude that the current Court is distinctly favorable toward business interests." Looking at individual judges, they found that four of the ten most conservative justices on business issues from 1953 to 2010 were on the Roberts Court—Alito, Roberts, Thomas, and Scalia. An overview of the 2011–12 term found that the Court had "a strong pro-business slant with business interests receiving fifty out of fifty-two potential votes."

Not surprisingly, liberal interest groups piled on. Writing for a publication of the American Constitution Society, the public interest litigator Alan Morrison said that "Corporate America" had been "Saved by the Supreme Court." Neal Weare, a litigator at the Center for Constitutional Accountability, which describes itself as a think tank "dedicated to fulfilling the progressive promise of our Constitution's text and history," compiled a position paper with the title "U.S. Chamber Quietly Completes Undefeated 7–0 Term: Success versus Solicitor General's Office Unprecedented." According to Weare, "the Chamber has prevailed in 68 percent of its cases before the Roberts Court," up from 56 percent during William Rehnquist's service as Chief Justice and from 43 percent during Warren Burger's. Chief Justice Roberts and Justice Alito were "the Chamber's strongest champions," voting for its positions 84 percent and 92 percent of the time in cases that divided the Court five to four or five to three. And the number of close cases increased under Roberts to 28 percent, compared to the Rehnquist Court's 18 percent.

Conservatives didn't buy it. Responding to Rosen's article, law professor Eric Posner (Richard Posner's son) called some of Rosen's numbers "meaningless." The Chamber of Commerce got more of its cases before the Court, Posner suggested, because it was good at selecting candidates for review. More broadly, Posner pointed out that some cases pitted one business against another, and that sometimes consumers benefited when businesses won their cases. The conservative-leaning law professor Jonathan Adler examined the Roberts Court's environmental law cases and concluded that, as of 2009, there was "no evidence of a 'pro-business' bias." Ramesh Ponnuru upped the ante: "Supreme Court Isn't Pro-Business, But Should Be," he wrote in 2011. He cited losses by corporations in a case dealing with global warming and, pointedly, one of the few decisions in which the Chamber of Commerce was itself the plaintiff—a challenge to one aspect of Arizona's laws limiting business's ability to hire undocumented workers, a challenge that the Chamber lost. Raw statistics couldn't capture the difference between important and unimportant cases, and for Ponnuru, business was losing the important cases while piling up "good" numbers in trivial ones. At most, the pro-business decisions were "holding actions," postponing but not eliminating the possibility of imposing large damages on businesses. By 2012 the exasperated title of one article by Stephen Richer in Forbes.com, "The Alleged Pro-Business Bias of the Supreme Court . . . Sigh . . . ," captures the conservative view.

Richer listed the "business stooge" articles—Rosen and Liptak in the *New York Times* (presumptively "liberal"), liberal publisher Katrina vanden Heuvel, and the liberal interest group Alliance for Justice—as well as the "not so fast on those accusations" ones, from the Federalist Society, Ilya Somin and Ilya Shapiro, both libertarian-leaning commentators, Eric Posner, Ponnuru, and Jonathan Adler. The arguments divided along partisan lines. Liberals want to be able to describe the Roberts Court as pro-business and conservatives want to describe it as neutral. The division mirrors what Roberts said during his confirmation hearings. He referred to "someone" who had asked him, "Are you going to be on the side of the little guy?" Roberts's response: "If the Constitution says that the little guy should win, the little guy's going to win in court before me. But if the Constitution says that the big guy should win, well, then the big guy's going to win, because my obligation is to the Constitution."

In most cases involving business interests, the problem of determining bias is even more complicated, because most of the cases involve statutes, not the Constitution. Even if the Supreme Court rules in favor of businesses in these cases by a wide margin, that doesn't show that the Court is biased: maybe the justices are simply the faithful agents of a pro-business Congress. Rosen noted that the Court was "surprisingly united in cases affecting business interests," with twenty-two of the thirty cases he analyzed "decided unanimously, or with only one or two dissenting votes." As Rosen's critics pointed out, that statistic can't tell us much about the Court's pro-business bias. Maybe the Court was unanimous because the cases were easy ones in which it was pretty clear what Congress meant. (Sometimes a justice will go along with a result he or she disagrees with because the case isn't all that important and it's not worth writing a dissent. Even so, this sort of faux unanimity won't support a claim that pro-business bias is important, because the fact that the case isn't important is built in to the unanimity.) Worse for the "pro-business" meme, the politics and law of the Supreme Court's business cases are more complicated than the politics and law of its cases on abortion and affirmative action. Here are two important examples.

The Roberts Court took a number of cases involving patent law. Populist Democrats used to try to keep the scope of patents narrow. They thought that patents gave people monopolies (mostly true), and that monopolies were bad for consumers (mostly true, too). The high-tech revolution changed how patents fit into the political system, as suggested by the common observation that Democrats get a lot of political contributions from people in high-tech industries. The new view of patents is that they encourage creativity. The image of the inventor in the garage behind the house isn't entirely accurate, but it captures the idea that patents are good for a certain class of small businesses. Once something is invented, though, it has to be exploited. Getting a patented item to market helps consumers—the little guys—but can be done effectively only by big businesses. Patent cases sometimes set small entrepreneurs against big businesses, but it's usually quite unclear whether consumers will win or lose if a patent is invalidated. It's easy to imagine a case in which liberals vote to uphold a patent because they think that consumers as little guys are going to gain a lot from being able to buy the new device, and conservatives vote to uphold it because they like the big businesses that typically are the ones who get the patented item to the larger market. Really, the "becauses" in that sentence are superfluous. No one knows enough about the effects of patent law on innovation and marketing to be sure who's going to benefit from decisions making it easier or harder to get valid patents. In general, the justices are simply going to try to build the best—that is, the most legally defensible—body of patent law they can.

The Roberts Court has also been interested in cases involving a doctrine known as "preemption." Though complicated in the details, its basic structure is straightforward. Suppose Congress passes a statute regulating labeling on prescription drugs, which says that some things—risks associated with taking the medication, for example—have to be placed on the labels and that other things, such as claims about all the ailments the drug is good for, can't. The statute also sets up a system of penalties for manufacturers who don't label their drugs properly. Every state also has laws dealing with prescription drugs, and some may address what could and could not go on labels. Even after the national statute comes into effect, there will be state laws saying that manufacturers (generally, not just drugmakers) have to pay damages to people who are injured as a result of the manufacturers' negligence or other misconduct.

Preemption doctrine deals with the interaction between national statutes and state laws. Sometimes Congress wants every manufacturer to comply with the same set of rules all over the country. Maybe it wants drug labels to be uniform, for example. Then the national statute is said to preempt state laws. Preemption might occur even if the state law might be seen as bolstering Congress's efforts. A Texas law adding something to a drug label might give consumers more information, which is what labeling is all about, but it would also force manufacturers to develop a special label for drugs sold in Texas, adding to the costs of the labeling system.

Sometimes, Congress is willing to let different states add things to its own system of regulation. Maybe Congress would let Texas consumers sue drug manufacturers for negligently misleading them, even though the national statute makes manufacturers liable only if they willfully mislead consumers. Then the national statute doesn't preempt the state one.

Businesses that operate all over the nation like statutes that preempt state law. For one thing, they can direct their lobbying efforts at Congress or national regulators like the Food and Drug Administration, rather than having to set up lobbying efforts in every state. Even if Congress ends up creating a somewhat more stringent system of regulation than some libertarian-leaning state would, it might be cheaper for businesses that operate on a national scale to comply with one set of slightly restrictive national rules than to comply with fifty sets of rules (and that could be true even if every one of those fifty sets was less restrictive than the national set). Of course, if preemption gives big businesses an advantage, it might put the mom-and-pop stores that operate only locally at a disadvantage. Here, too, lobbying matters. The mom-and-pop businesses can lobby in their state legislatures, but might find it hard to set up a national lobbying organization in Washington. They might operate on small profit margins, and be able to afford to take some time and money to go to the state capitol, but not dues to the National Federation of Independent Businesses equivalent to what big businesses can pay to the Chamber of Commerce or the National Association of Manufacturers.

So, one component of the politics of preemption is big business versus small business, and it's not clear how liberals and conservatives divide on that line. Yet, where the justices find preemption, they give Congress more power; when they find no preemption, they give it less. We know, or think we know, that today's conservatives are small government people who like to see more power in state governments and less in Congress. Conservatives who like federalism, then, should be *against* preemption, and liberals who like congressional power should be for it. Indeed, we can see some of that happening, because Justice Thomas is quite skeptical about claims that a national statute preempts state law. However, the politics of preemption means that being in favor of state power—liking federalism, as conservatives are said to do— means being against big business, which conservatives are also said to do. It's hard to have it both ways. George W. Bush's administration conducted a sustained campaign to expand federal preemption. That told us what kind of conservatism the administration was committed to—more pro–big business than pro–states' rights. Judicial conservatives do have an agenda, developed over decades, but preemption wasn't a real agenda item. The justices see the cases one by one; they view the preemption issues as connected to specific statutes, not part of some larger program. That's why the voting lineups sometimes seem odd. It's probably best to see preemption cases as ones in which the justices' individual views about what the law really means determine the outcomes.

The politics of preemption have another dimension, which extends to other cases. In 2009 the Supreme Court decided *Wyeth v. Levine*, a typical modern preemption case. Diana Levine had severe migraine headaches. Her doctor prescribed a nausea drug, Phenergan, made by the "Big Pharma" company Wyeth. The drug's label said that it should be administered by injection into a muscle or, sometimes, into a vein by using a drip. The doctor's assistant injected the drug with a different method called IV push, but apparently missed the vein so that it came into contact with arterial blood. The result was a disaster. Phenergan and arterial blood combine to produce gangrene, and Ms. Levine had to have her arm amputated. The prosthetic replacement arm was all right, but she could no longer pursue her main career, as a musician and music teacher. She sued her doctor for malpractice and Wyeth for not including a warning on the drug label against using the IV push method. The claim against Wyeth was that its action was a tort under Vermont law. The doctor settled with Ms. Levine, but Wyeth resisted the lawsuit, arguing that its label complied with the federal drug laws, which, it said, preempted state tort law.

Diana Levine was a victim of a medical disaster suing Big Pharma, a classic "little guy" versus big business case. Her lawyer specialized in medical malpractice—a trial lawyer of a special sort. Plaintiff-side trial lawyers are strong supporters of the Democratic Party. The reason is partly historical and partly structural. Trace the history of this group of lawyers back, and you find their predecessors representing workers seeking compensation for injuries they suffered in the workplace. The lawyers practiced on their own or in small firms. Many shared the ethnic backgrounds of their clients, because the clients found the lawyers within their own communities. The corporations they sued were represented by lawyers in large law firms, many of which were—at the time—part of the Protestant establishment. Eventually, the trial lawyers expanded their interest from workers' compensation to general civil litigation on behalf of "little guys." Medical malpractice was a big part of their work; later a related plaintiffs' trial bar developed for litigation by shareholders against corporate management, and for consumers against manufacturers.

Plaintiff-side trial lawyers get rich when they win their cases, because they are paid contingency fees, calculated as a percentage of the plaintiffs' recovery. The fees are zero if the plaintiffs lose, which makes these lawyers very careful in selecting cases like Levine's, where the pull of empathy is likely to lead to large damage awards. The jury in Levine's case awarded her about $7 million in damages, and standard contingency fee rates would have transferred about $2 million of that to her lawyers. The financial stakes get bigger when the plaintiffs' lawyers are able to structure their cases as class actions on behalf of a large number of victims. Even if each victim suffers only a small amount, put millions of them into a class action and you end up with large liabilities—and large attorneys' fees.

Successful trial lawyers can get quite rich, but when they do, they tend to remain Democrats. Meanwhile, big businesses heavily lobbied the Republican Party to change the laws to make it harder for plaintiffs to win—and for plaintiff-side trial lawyers to get big contingency fees. Republicans all over the country supported medical malpractice reforms that place limits on awards for emotional distress and on attorneys' fee awards. Congress adopted the Securities Litigation Uniform Standards Act in 1998, over President Clinton's veto, to make it harder for shareholders to win their cases against corporate managers who, the shareholders claimed, had behaved very badly. The Class Action Fairness Act, which tries to limit the number of successful class actions, rattled around in Congress as part of the Republican reform agenda for about a decade before the Republican-controlled Congress enacted it in 2005. These Republican efforts can be understood as part of a project sometimes referred to as "defunding the left," where "the left" here refers to the trial lawyers who support the Democratic Party.

Again, though, this merely complicates the politics of preemption at the Supreme Court. Defunding the left means ruling against people like Diana Levine, but finding that her malpractice lawsuit is preempted by the federal Food and Drug Act means supporting national power against the states. What's a conservative—or, for that matter, a liberal—to do? The precise legal issue in Levine's case was this: Did the federal statute regulating labeling of prescription drugs preempt state laws dealing with the information drugmakers have to put on their labels? The Food and Drug Administration had approved the labels Wyeth put on Phenergan, but Vermont's judges held that they weren't enough because they didn't specifically warn about the dangers of using the IV push method of injecting it. Wyeth said that complying with the federal labeling requirements was enough, and any additional requirements imposed by state tort law were preempted either because the state law was an "obstacle" to accomplishing the federal law's purposes, or because federal law prohibited it from adding warnings that the FDA hadn't approved. The majority rejected both arguments. The federal law allowed changes to labels pending later approval by the FDA, Justice Stevens said, and added that the warnings wouldn't interfere with Congress's user-protective goals.

The lineup in Levine's case was this: for Levine, Justices Stevens, Ginsburg, Breyer, and Souter—liberals all, but of course favoring state power over national power here—and Justices Kennedy and Thomas; for Wyeth, Chief Justice Roberts and Justices Scalia and Alito. Maybe Justice Kennedy's vote can be accounted for by treating him as a waffler, but surely not Justice Thomas's. Other preemption cases produce lineups that don't fit the "little guy"/liberals versus "big business"/conservative narrative at all well. It certainly looks as if politics or "Supreme Court, Inc." isn't going to tell us much about how the cases come out. Maybe the law does.

Two years later, another case involving warnings on labels came to the Court. Gladys Mensing got tardive dyskinesia, a disease that affects the nerves controlling muscles used to walk, eat, and talk. At seventy-six Mensing could no longer live on her own. People found it hard to understand her when she talked, and she stopped shopping for herself and stopped going to church. Her nerves were damaged because, starting in 2001, she took a drug called metoproclamide. That drug was a generic version of a patented drug, Reglan, which had been approved for use in treating stomach problems in 1980.

After the patent expired, generic producers began to make the drug, and by 2001 it was available only in generic versions. When Reglan went on the market, the FDA approved its labels, which recited the risks known in 1980 associated with taking it. Reglan's producer knew that there was some risk that taking the drug for long periods could cause tardive dyskinesia, and so it included a mild warning on the label, and strengthened this a bit as evidence of the seriousness of the risk accumulated. Under the federal drug statutes, the labels on generic drugs have to be identical to those on the patented versions, so the labels on the generic drug Ms. Mensing took didn't have strong warnings about tardive dyskinesia. (In 2009 the FDA required such a warning, but that was too late for Ms. Mensing.)

Gladys Mensing sued the generic's maker, PLIVA. The lawsuit relied on a state law requiring that all drugs warn of known risks, asserting that PLIVA knew or should have known that long-term use of the generic drug had a high risk of causing tardive dyskinesia, and failed to include an appropriate warning on its labels. Like Wyeth, PLIVA said that federal law preempted state law. Wyeth lost, but PLIVA won. The difference? Federal law allowed Wyeth to change its labels even without FDA approval, but it barred generic manufacturers from doing so—the labels on generic drugs had to track the labels the FDA approved to the letter. So it was impossible for PLIVA to provide the warning state law required, and preemption law holds that you don't have to comply with state law if federal law makes it impossible for you to do so.

The lineup in Mensing's case was conservative versus liberal. Still, fitting the decision into the "pro-business" narrative is messy. You have to say that the Roberts Court was pro–small business (PLIVA) but anti–Big Pharma (Wyeth). But it seems a stretch.

The contrast between Levine's case and Mensing's is reproduced in a pair of cases involving car safety. The first one was decided by the Rehnquist Court in 2000. It involved Alexis Geier, a seventeen-year-old who lost control of her 1987 model Honda Accord and slammed into a tree in Washington, D.C. She was wearing a seat-and-shoulder belt, but her car didn't have an airbag. The accident smashed her face, leading to more than a dozen surgical repairs. Geier and her parents sued Honda. Relying on the ordinary law of accidents as it applied in Washington, D.C., their suit claimed the company had been negligent in failing to put airbags in the car. Honda's lawyers pointed out that federal car safety laws didn't require 1987 model cars to have airbags, and argued this meant that federal law preempted the negligence claim. The Geiers' lawyers replied that the federal statute had a "savings" clause, which said that "compliance with" federal regulations didn't preempt the Geiers' negligence claim. Dividing five to four the Court ruled against the Geiers, saying that, properly interpreted, the federal car safety rules affirmatively authorized carmakers to choose to provide or omit airbags for 1987 models. Stating that the ordinary law of accidents that imposed liability for making one rather than the other choice would interfere with Congress's policy, Justice Breyer wrote the Court's opinion, and Justice Thomas was among the dissenters. Maybe this shows that Justice Breyer is a technocrat who supports whatever federal agencies do, and Justice Thomas a defender of states' rights.

The Roberts Court version of the case makes any simple story impossible. This time the accident involved Thanh Williamson, who was sitting in the rear middle seat of her family's Mazda minivan when another car drove head-on into the minivan. She was wearing the lap belt Mazda provided for the rear middle seat, but it wasn't enough to protect her, and she died in the collision. Her family sued Mazda for negligently failing to use a stronger lap-and-shoulder belt for that seat. Mazda invoked the same preemption doctrine that Honda had used, but Mazda lost. Justice Breyer wrote this opinion, too. The difference between the cases, he said, was that Congress didn't express any view about what kinds of seat belts should be used in rear seats. Allowing states to tell carmakers what to do, through their tort law, didn't interfere with any choice Congress itself had made. The decision was unanimous, although Justices Thomas and Sotomayor wrote separate opinions. (Justice Kagan was recused because the United States, through the Solicitor General's Office, filed a brief in the case supporting Williamson, and Kagan had participated in the filing.)

At this point one has to abandon any effort to impose a "pro-business/pro-consumer" story on the car safety cases. Indeed, I can't imagine a plausible story about the outcomes that invokes anything but the justices' views about what the law actually requires. They were calling the balls and strikes as they saw them.

THE "BIG" cases are another part of the picture. Businesses might win five or ten minor cases but still come out behind if they lose one really important case. It's one thing to get the Court to say that Big Pharma doesn't have to pay its detailers overtime wages (as we'll see in chapter 6), but something quite different when the Court upholds Obamacare. Business seemed to be the loser when, in what is known as the global warming case, the Court held that the Environmental Protection Agency had to adopt rules regulating carbon dioxide emissions from automobile tailpipes, and business victories in less important environmental cases pale in significance, according to Jonathan Adler. Ramesh Ponnuru pointed to that case and to a case the Chamber of Commerce litigated and lost in the Supreme Court as big ones that went against business. Looked at closely, the outcomes suggest a more mixed verdict.

The Chamber of Commerce's case involved the response Arizona's

Republicans orchestrated to what they described as a crisis caused by the federal government's failure to secure the borders against illegal immigration from Mexico. In one Arizona case Justice Scalia asked the Court to empathize with Arizona's plight by understanding "the very human realities" that led to Arizona's statute: "Its citizens feel themselves under siege by large numbers of illegal immigrants who invade their property, strain their social services, and even place their lives in jeopardy. Federal officials have been unable to remedy the problem, and indeed have recently shown that they are unwilling to do so"—the last comment a slam at the Obama administration's decision to refrain from deporting young people who were brought to the country illegally by their parents and thereafter led entirely conventional lives.

Arizona's Republican-controlled legislature worked up several laws dealing with illegal immigration. A law adopted in 2007 got to the Supreme Court four years later, with another that attracted greater national attention arriving in 2012. The 2007 law told the state's employers that they would lose their licenses to operate their business if they hired undocumented workers. (This is another area of law where the very terms we use have political overtones: illegal aliens, unlawful immigrants, unauthorized aliens, undocumented workers—the same group, but described differently.) Of course, such workers play a large role in Arizona's economy, and the Chamber of Commerce stood behind the businesses that hired those workers. It relied on the Immigration Reform and Control Act (IRCA), which Congress passed in 1978 in one of its spasmodic efforts to deal with immigration issues. One provision makes it a federal crime for anyone to hire "unauthorized aliens," knowing that the workers are unauthorized. Responding to business worries about having to comply with both the detailed national requirements associated with this provision and possible state laws on the same subject, Congress added a provision preempting state laws "imposing civil or criminal sanctions (other than through licensing and similar laws)" on employers who hired unauthorized aliens. The provision illustrates the business interest in complying with a single national rule.

The Chamber of Commerce took the position that the federal statute preempted Arizona's law. Justices Breyer, Ginsburg, and Sotomayor agreed (Justice Kagan was recused because she had been involved in the litigation as Solicitor General). The Court's conservatives ruled against the chamber, holding that Arizona's law fit within the parenthetical exception for "licensing laws." They relied mostly on the ordinary meaning of the word "license," and indeed Justice Breyer had to engage in some linguistic contortions to explain why a law that enforced the ban on employing undocumented workers by denying businesses their licenses wasn't a "licensing" law.

The details of the competing arguments don't matter here. Is this, as Ponnuru says, a case showing that the Court isn't "pro-business"? The conservatives and liberals divided, with the liberals taking what Ponnuru would describe as the pro-business position. There's an obvious alternative explanation: for the justices, the case wasn't a business case at all, but an immigration case. The Court's Republicans followed the party line (pre–November 2012), and so did the Democrats.

That explanation falls apart though when we take into account the 2012 case involving Arizona's other restrictions—making it a state crime to fail to comply with national alien registration requirements and another crime for an undocumented alien to seek work in Arizona, and, most controversially, authorizing police to arrest undocumented aliens and demand to see their papers. Justices Scalia, Thomas, and Alito dissented from a decision written by Justice Kennedy and joined by Chief Justice Roberts, which found that national law preempted the most important and controversial provisions in Arizona's law. You can come up with fancy explanations for Kennedy's and Roberts's votes—they were being "statesmen," they understood better than the leadership of the Republican Party that the party's long-term interests would be served by tempering its anti-immigrant stance. But what was almost certainly going on was that Kennedy and Roberts actually thought that the law of preemption, fairly applied, led to the conclusions they drew.

The global warming case involved the federal Clean Air Act, one of the nation's signature environmental laws (enacted in 1963 and given real teeth in 1970, when major amendments were signed by President Richard Nixon). The act now says that the Environmental Protection Agency has to set standards for the emission of "any air pollutant agent" from cars that "cause[s] . . . air pollution which may reasonably be anticipated to endanger public health or welfare." As the global warming issue came to increasing public attention, pressure built on the EPA to regulate the emission from carbon dioxide from car tailpipes. The theory was that carbon dioxide was an air pollutant, and that tailpipe emissions contributed to global warming, which endangered public health and welfare. The EPA dawdled in developing standards for tailpipe emissions, and during George W. Bush's administration a coalition of states and public interest groups sued to force it to do so.

The EPA had reasons for sitting on its hands. Some were political: the Republican Party had become increasingly skeptical about the very idea of global warming, even more skeptical about the idea that human activity was causing global warming, and strongly opposed to expensive regulations that, in the Republican view, dealt with a threat that probably didn't exist. Some of the EPA's reasons, though, were policy-based: experts in global warming policy tend to think that regulating tailpipe emissions is a terrible way to reduce global warming. They agree that something has to be done to reduce the carbon (dioxide) footprint of all our activities, but they tend to think that direct regulation of emissions isn't going to do much. Experts prefer either some sort of carbon tax or what's known as a "cap and trade" system, which lets producers figure out ways to make money by reducing their emissions. The best justification for including a requirement to set emissions standards is that the looming threat that standards will actually go into effect will prod Congress into adopting a better solution.

Politics and policy pushed the EPA into offering its legal reasons for not regulating tailpipe emissions. First, it said that carbon dioxide wasn't an "air pollutant agent" under the Clean Air Act. Its argument focused on the word "agent." It wasn't enough that carbon dioxide played a part in a chain of chemical reactions leading to global warming. To be an "agent," carbon dioxide had to pollute the air itself. The EPA seems to have decided to define air pollution agents as gases that make you sick when you inhale them. Second, and more important, the EPA said that setting standards for tailpipe emissions interfered with the government's ability to develop a more comprehensive strategy for addressing climate change, a strategy that had many policy dimensions and, importantly, involved complex negotiations with other countries, including China, rapidly becoming a major source of carbon dioxide in the air because of its heavy use of coal to support the energy demands of its expanding economy.

The Supreme Court rejected the EPA's position, with Justice Stevens writing an opinion for five justices; the dissenters were Chief Justice Roberts and Justices Scalia, Thomas, and Alito. For the majority, the Clean Air Act gave "air pollutant" an extremely broad definition, and sharply limited the reasons the EPA could give for not regulating air pollutants. Complexity and foreign policy weren't among the permissible reasons.

The global warming decision looks like a win for liberals and environmentalists and a big defeat for the car industry and for business more generally. Bush's EPA continued to drag its heels and didn't actually do anything before the 2008 elections, but President Obama's EPA administrator eventually issued proposed regulations for tailpipe emissions. Though some states went to court to challenge those rules, a lower court upheld them in 2012. Still, no one really expects the standards to take effect—ever. On every side of the issue, people know that a policy of imposing standards on emissions from car tailpipes is a bad one. Eventually, people knowledgeable about climate change think, Congress and the president will come up with a comprehensive and better climate change policy. The business loss in the Supreme Court will be washed away when that policy is enacted. Business might not like the comprehensive policy, but it's going to be better for business than emissions standards. The Supreme Court's decision might have some modest effect in making it easier to enact a comprehensive policy; the threat that a bad policy might actually be implemented might have some political effects. But from a business point of view, losing the global warming case in the Supreme Court was no more than a loss in a minor skirmish far away from the larger battlefield.

THE PREEMPTION cases and the global warming case show that in some cases "business" losses aren't really losses for business. Similarly, unanimous or near-unanimous cases might show the Court doing the pro-business work Congress wants it to do. The cases might tell us something about Congress, but not about the Roberts Court. Sometimes, though, the decisions pit liberals against conservatives, and do shed light on the Roberts Court's approach to business.

The *Ledbetter* case described in chapter 3 captures the Roberts Court's way of being pro-business: the use of procedural rules that favor the big guys. The conservatives shut down cases against big business; the liberals want them to go forward. The conservatives don't actually deny that the plaintiffs were screwed by big business. They simply make it impossible for plaintiffs to bring cases that would impose liability on businesses for their violations of law, because plaintiffs won't be able to find lawyers willing to take their cases for contingency fees that they might never see, and will be small even if they win their cases. Defenders of the conservatives can say that the justices weren't ruling for or against business as such; they were just making sure that plaintiffs follow the rules.

The best way to defeat trial lawyers is to keep them from telling persuasive stories to juries. Procedural rules are a good way to do that. In two high-stakes procedural cases, the Roberts Court set up large obstacles to getting cases heard on the merits.

Here's the story trial lawyer Kirk Hulett told: Vincent and Liza Concepcion wanted new cell phones. They saw an advertisement from Cingular Wireless saying that they could get "free" phones when they signed a two-year contract. They signed the contract and got the phones. They later realized that they had paid Cingular (which AT&T later acquired) the sales tax on the phones, so, they said, the phones weren't really free. AT&T's assertion that they were, they maintained, amounted to consumer fraud under California law. There's little doubt that the Concepcions didn't come to this understanding all by themselves. Trial lawyers fish for cases, looking at advertisements, reading newspapers and specialized trial lawyer publications for ideas about promising cases and then going out to find potential plaintiffs. Eventually the Concepcions connected up with Hulett's law firm, a prominent plaintiff-side trial firm specializing in "securities, business tort, and consumer class and individual actions."

Hulett's firm filed a class action lawsuit on behalf of everyone who got the "free" phones and paid the sales tax. The suit had to get over a big hurdle. As many consumer contracts do today, the AT&T service contract had a provision requiring that all disputes between buyers and AT&T go through arbitration rather than an ordinary trial in civil court. Arbitration proceedings are less formal than civil trials and can reach results more quickly. If you lose an arbitration case, you can appeal to the ordinary civil courts, but those courts' power to review arbitrations is quite limited—they can reverse arbitrators' decisions only if the arbitrators made really serious mistakes, not merely because they were wrong (in the judge's eyes).

Many consumer advocates believe that arbitration is skewed in favor of businesses like AT&T. They think that the awards arbitrators give to consumers who win their cases are smaller than the awards juries give, and consumers win less often anyway. Plaintiff-side trial lawyers hate arbitration, of course. It directs potentially lucrative cases away from them into a system in which they usually have a much smaller role—and from which they cannot make nearly as much money.

Over the past several decades, the Supreme Court has increasingly upheld contract provisions substituting arbitration for civil trials, relying on an old statute, the Federal Arbitration Act (FAA), adopted in 1925. For about sixty years the Supreme Court construed the FAA narrowly, but that changed starting with some decisions by the Burger Court. By the time Roberts became Chief Justice, there were few contract-based claims outside the FAA's reach.

Trial lawyers are nothing if not ingenious. They developed a way of using arbitration as a reasonably good substitute for fee-generating civil trials. The technique was classwide arbitration. Class actions are now familiar to most of us. They have deep origins in old procedural rules, but the modern version took off from some revisions in the rules dealing with class actions in the 1960s, an era of consumer activism. The idea is simple. People like the Concepcions suffer quite small financial injuries individually—between $17 and $30 in sales tax. It's never going to be worth it for them to file a lawsuit to recover that tiny amount. But put them in a group—a "class"—of everyone who paid the sales tax, and the damages mount to the point where the class action might be worth pursuing by lawyers relying on contingency fees. The class action then becomes a way of ensuring that businesses don't get away with big profits through practices that hurt each consumer only a little bit.

Classwide arbitration has some of the same advantages, especially in cases where the injuries are purely financial. In the 1990s, trial lawyers began to bring classwide arbitrations. Businesses figured this out pretty quickly, though, and wrote provisions into their consumer contracts saying not only that complaints had to be pursued through arbitration, but that no classwide arbitration was allowed, only individual arbitrations.

The trial lawyers had one more arrow in their quiver. The FAA says that arbitration agreements are "valid . . . and enforceable, save upon such grounds as exist . . . for the revocation of any contract." You can revoke any contract if one side forces the other to sign, for example, and an arbitration clause isn't enforceable if it's obtained by force. The trial lawyers looked around for a "ground" for revoking contracts that might be applicable to provisions prohibiting classwide arbitration, and they thought they had found one in a doctrine known as "unconscionability." An unconscionable contract is one that the courts find really, really unfair. The doctrine of unconscionability flourished briefly during the consumer-friendly 1960s and 1970s and still lingers on in states like California. Consumer contracts such as the Concepcions' have many of the characteristics courts have identified as suggesting that degree of unfairness. Those contracts are offered on a take-it-or-leave-it basis: nobody expects the Concepcions to haggle with AT&T over some provision hidden in the fine print of the multi-page contract. Indeed, and this is another characteristic, no one really expects them even to read the contract, much less understand all its provisions.

The California Supreme Court agreed that contacts containing provisions barring class action arbitrations were unconscionable. That made the entire contract void, and liberated Hulett to file an ordinary class action for consumer fraud in the civil courts. AT&T objected, of course, and took the case to the Supreme Court.

Expressing a view of class actions widespread in the business community, AT&T's lawyer Andrew Pincus called *Concepcion* "a classic abuse of the class action procedure," a "sleazy" effort "to extract a quick settlement in a meritless case." A member of the elite Supreme Court bar, Pincus was no slouch as a storyteller either. He pointed out that the sales slip the Concepcions got clearly showed that they had been charged the sales tax. Even more, California's tax laws meant that AT&T had to charge the sales tax, even if they were giving away the phones. AT&T didn't make any money by collecting the taxes (although Pincus didn't point out that some people might have signed up with AT&T rather than Verizon because they thought they were getting completely free phones). Pincus emphasized that the arbitration provisions weren't unfair, stressing that AT&T's arbitration provision said that the company would pay $7,500 to any consumer who received from the arbitrator more than AT&T offered in settlement—and double the winner's attorneys' fees.

The Supreme Court agreed that the FAA preempted the application of California's version of unconscionability doctrine. It wasn't exactly that California had singled out class action waivers of arbitration for special treatment, although some of the rhetoric in Justice Scalia's opinion for the five conservatives suggests that the majority was concerned about that. Rather, Justice Scalia wrote, preemption doctrine says that state laws that interfere with the effectiveness of federal statutes like the FAA are preempted. And, he said, California's rule did interfere with the FAA's goal of providing "streamlined proceedings." Class actions in arbitration would inevitably bring lawyers into what should be informal proceedings, and the lawyers would inevitably slow things down.

Justice Breyer's dissent focused on what he and the three other liberals saw as the majority's excessive claims about how classwide arbitrations would interfere with arbitration's attractive features. He concluded by raising the banner of federalism: "Federalism is as much a question of deeds as words. . . . We do not honor federalist principles in their breach" by stopping California from enforcing its own distinctive version of unconscionability doctrine.

The Supreme Court addressed class actions more directly in what everyone appears to be compelled to describe as the largest class action ever, an employment discrimination suit against Wal-Mart (the largest private employer in the United States) that involved a class of somewhere in the neighborhood of a million plaintiffs, filed in the name of Betty Dukes and a handful of other female workers..

Journalistic convention, playing into the hands of trial lawyers, requires that reporting on important Supreme Court cases humanize them by telling the stories of the individual whose name is attached to the case. That convention makes doctrinal sense in class actions, because the rules regulating class actions say that the named party has to present claims that are "typical" of those in the class. Betty Dukes had been working as a salesperson for twenty years before Wal-Mart hired her. After a month there, she told her manager that she wanted to work her way up the ranks. The manager told her to wait until three months had passed. After that she got a tiny raise, and nothing more. According to Dukes, the store had no regular system for announcing open positions or any career paths laid out. Everything seemed to be in the hands of the store's manager, who repeatedly denied Dukes's requests for greater responsibility and promotion—and filled job openings with male employees. Five years after she started working at Wal-Mart, she was demoted from "Customer Service Manager" to cashier. She thought it was because she had been receiving counseling for returning late from breaks, but she also observed that nothing happened to men who did the same thing. Eventually, she found out that men with experience similar to hers were making substantially more money than she was. In 2001, Dukes and five other female Wal-Mart employees, represented by a prominent class action law firm, filed a class action against Wal-Mart itself, alleging that its practice of leaving promotion decisions in the hands of local managers and its general corporate culture predictably led to discrimination against women.

The case ambled along for eleven years before the Supreme Court decided to throw it out. Jeffrey Toobin reported a common view that "some things are simply beyond the abilities of our federal courts. And cases with a million plaintiffs are among them." The sheer size of the case may have motivated the Court's decision, but the doctrine it announced had strong implications for smaller and more conventional class actions.

The class action rules require that members of the class present a question of law or fact "common" to them all. Dukes's lawyers argued that the common question was this: Despite its stated policy against gender discrimination, Wal-Mart had a corporate culture pervading the entire company down to the store level; that culture implicitly encouraged gender discrimination in promotion; store managers who made specific decisions about promotion exercised their discretion in ways consistent with the corporate culture without being expressly directed to do so; Wal-Mart should therefore be liable for each employment decision made by its local managers. At the oral argument, Justices Scalia and Kennedy thought the argument self-contradictory. Kennedy asked Joseph Sellers, representing Dukes, to explain "what is the unlawful policy that Wal-Mart has adopted." The complaint "faces in two directions. Number one, you said that this is a culture where . . . the headquarters knows everything that's going on. Then in the next breath, you say, well, now these supervisors have too much discretion." For Justice Scalia, Sellers was "whipsaw[ing]" him: "On the one hand, you say the problem is that they were utterly subjective, and on the other hand you say there is a strong corporate culture that guides all of this."

The concerns Justices Kennedy and Scalia expressed were about the underlying theory of liability—the merits of Dukes's claim. Justice Scalia's view of the merits was reasonably clear: "Left to their own devices most managers in any corporation—and surely most managers in a corporation that forbids sex discrimination—would select sex-neutral, performance-based criteria for hiring and promotion." As the case had reached them, though, it involved only a procedural argument over whether the case could be pursued as a class action. Justice Scalia had to translate his concerns about the merits into a ruling about procedure.

He did, by saying that the case didn't have the "glue" showing that the questions of law and fact were "common" to all members of the case. "Without some glue holding the alleged *reasons* for all those decisions together, it will be impossible to say that examination of all the class members' claims for relief will produce a common answer to the crucial question *why was I disfavored*" (italics in the original). Dukes's lawyers had presented an expert who presented some statistical evidence suggesting that Wal-Mart had a general corporate culture of some sort. Wal-Mart's lawyers strongly disputed the value of the expert's testimony, and Justice Scalia's opinion seemed skeptical as well. The only real corporate policy Dukes had been able to establish was the policy of allowing local managers to make discretionary decisions, and that, Justice Scalia wrote, "is a policy *against having* uniform employment policies." Without such uniformity, there couldn't be "commonality." Some managers might discriminate on the basis of gender, others wouldn't, so "demonstrating the invalidity of one manager's use of discretion will do nothing to demonstrate the invalidity of another's."

Justice Ginsburg, who prides herself on her background as a scholar of procedural rules, wrote the dissent. She noted that "managers, like all humankind, may be prey to biases of which they are unaware." Statistical evidence can tease out this sort of bias. More important, she pointed out that every decision about hiring or promoting an individual will be dissimilar to every other such decision along some dimension— training, experience in the store, personality. She took the majority to be saying that dissimilarity was enough to prevent a class action against discretionary decisions from going forward to a decision on the merits, at least without substantial evidence of some other common source for the statistical showing.

Justice Ginsburg's dissent accurately called the majority's procedural approach "far-reaching." Plaintiffs use class actions to sue employers, prisons, schools, and other large institutions. Sometimes those institutions have stated policies that violate federal statutes or the Constitution. Often, though, the stated policies say one thing and actual practice shows another. Whenever a low-level manager or official deviates from the stated policy, the defendant institution can say that the manager was exercising discretion improperly, and that other instances involve dissimilar facts—different enough to defeat the class action and to relegate each individual plaintiff to his or her own lawsuit. Courts have to decide to let cases go ahead as class actions near the start of the litigation, which means that plaintiffs haven't had a chance to rummage though the defendants' records to find smoking guns (e-mails showing managers disparaging women workers because they were women, for example) or even guns with slightly warm barrels. They have to do more preliminary investigation now, which is expensive and can't provide any assurance that the judge will let a class action go forward. And, because the stakes in these individual cases are relatively small, potential plaintiffs may find it difficult to get a lawyer to take on their cases.

As the Supreme Court considered her case, Betty Dukes became a spokesperson for the cause. When the Court ruled against her, Dukes, who continued to work at her local Wal-Mart as a greeter making $35,000 a year, called the decision "devastat[ing]" for civil rights law. The Court took her case "to give corporate America a huge advantage over everyday American citizens." The lawyers for Dukes and others in the original class action began to restructure the cases, breaking them down into smaller class actions on behalf of workers in individual states and specific stores. Of course, those suits were more expensive to pursue and less threatening to Wal-Mart's national management. Dukes took some comfort in the fact that Wal-Mart did have some women in higher managerial positions, and that job openings were now posted at the store.

THE STRUCTURE in the Arizona immigration case and the global warming case is exactly the same. The cases deal with national laws that happen to have some effects on businesses. But what businesses care about is the larger regulatory environment, not the specific provisions the Supreme Court deals with. I've used the term "comprehensive" in discussing both cases, because that's the language policy makers use. We're going to have comprehensive policies dealing with immigration and climate change. When we do, those two Supreme Court cases will fade from business's concern. Small businesses in Arizona might have some problems in hiring workers for a few years, until Congress sorts things out in a comprehensive immigration statute. Carmakers are unlikely ever to have to do anything to comply with the EPA's proposed tailpipe emissions standards, which a comprehensive climate change policy will displace. Most minor skirmishes fade away, although occasionally they determine the battle's outcome. Still, it's important to keep the larger battlefield in mind when thinking about whether the Supreme Court is pro-business, anti-business, or simply doing its job interpreting the statutes as the cases come before it.

The "procedural" cases about arbitration and class actions are a different matter. Carmakers are only one sector of the business community. The procedural cases help all businesses that deal with lots of consumers and have lots of employees. Knowledgeable businesspeople would surely throw the global warming case over the side as long as they were guaranteed wins in the procedural cases.

The Roberts Court's overall balance sheet in business cases fits the "pro-business" view of the Court reasonably well, even after we take into account all the qualifications I've discussed. *Concepcion* and *Wal-Mart* are just part of the overall picture. Many academics who study the Roberts Court's procedural rulings have concluded that those decisions have pro-business, anti-consumer effects. Nothing's guaranteed in the law, of course; entrepreneurial public officials, including ambitious state attorneys general, can take up the consumer cause after discouraged trial lawyers leave the scene. The important point is that the procedural cases show that we can't determine whether the Roberts Court has a pro-business tilt simply by toting up the wins and losses. We have to pay attention to the rules the Court has set down to guide litigation in the cases that don't ever get to the Court. Those rules seem to be pretty clearly pro-business. Big business should be quite happy with the work the Roberts Court has been doing for them so far.

CHAPTER 6

Sticks and Stones, Lies
and Insults

If the First Amendment had a Facebook page, many people seem to think, the Roberts Court would "like" it. Kenneth Starr, now president of Baylor University, reportedly called the Roberts Court "the most free speech court in history." And we've become accustomed to thinking that liberals "like" the First Amendment too—the American Civil Liberties Union (ACLU) and all that. So, you might think the Roberts Court couldn't be a conservative Court.

The story's more complicated, though. Liberals don't like the Court's campaign finance decisions, although the ACLU does. And if you count up the decisions, the Roberts Court rejects more free speech claims than it accepts, and actually accepts fewer free speech claims than the Burger or Rehnquist Courts did. Statistics don't distinguish between important cases and minor ones, so we have to look more closely. With the important exception of cases involving advertising and similar business activities that happen to fall under the First Amendment, politics doesn't explain much. A desire for simple rules does.

Sometimes judges say that they prefer rules over vaguer "standards" because rules keep them from making things up—from saying that the law just happens to be what they favor for policy reasons. That's why the Roberts Court's attraction to rules for free speech law is connected, loosely, to its originalism. But sometimes the Roberts Court goes for standards instead of rules. When Chief Justice Roberts wrote an opinion for the conservative majority adopting a general standard for excluding illegally seized evidence at criminal trial, Justice Breyer in dissent advocated "a clear line."

The preference for rules depends on circumstances, and, I think, on the temperament of individual judges. It's roughly associated with political conservatism, but conservatives don't always like rules instead of standards and liberals sometimes do.

Xavier Alvarez was a liar. After being elected to the board of directors of a water district board in California, Alvarez introduced himself at the board's first public meeting. Perhaps to enhance his credibility, or maybe for no good reason, Alvarez said, "I'm a retired marine of 25 years. I retired in the year 2001. Back in 1987, I was awarded the Congressional Medal of Honor. I got wounded many times by the same guy. I'm still around." His statements about his military service and the Medal of Honor were false. Type "living recipients of Congressional Medal of Honor" into your Web browser and you find an alphabetical list. It doesn't have Alvarez's name on it.

You might be surprised to learn that lots of people lie about getting military awards. Sometimes they're defendants in criminal cases trying to get sympathy from a judge or a jury. Sometimes they think that making the claim will help them raise money for themselves or, in Rick Strandlof's case, for a charity he formed to raise money for Iraq War veterans, though in the end some donors wondered whether he'd actually used the money to send care packages to Iraq. Justice Alito offered an astonishing list of such claims in Alvarez's case: "When the Library of Congress compiled oral histories for its Veterans History Project, 24 of the 49 individuals who identified themselves as Medal of Honor winners had not actually received that award"; in 2003, "more than 600 Virginia residents falsely claimed to have won the Medal of Honor." (As of summer 2012 there were eighty-one living recipients of the Medal of Honor.) Inevitably, these days, there's more than one Web site devoted to identifying people who lie about their military service. One's called "StolenValor.com."

"Stolen Valor" is also the name Congress gave to a statute it enacted in 2005, the Stolen Valor Act. It's been a crime for almost a century to wear some military decorations without authorization. As lies about military service proliferated, Congress decided that the problem needed stronger medicine. The Stolen Valor Act makes it a federal crime to claim falsely that you've received a military award, and makes it a felony to lie about receiving the Medal of Honor. Congress's justification: lies about receiving military awards tarnish the value of the awards given to people who actually deserved them. The lies end up dishonoring those whom the nation sought to honor.

Alvarez pleaded guilty to violating the Stolen Valor Act, but reserved his right to challenge its constitutionality under the First Amendment's protection of freedom of speech. The Supreme Court agreed with him that the Stolen Valor Act was unconstitutional. The Court was fractured. Justice Kennedy wrote an opinion for himself, Chief Justice Roberts, and Justices Ginsburg and Sotomayor. Justice Breyer agreed that the statute was unconstitutional, as did Justice Kagan, but they had a different theory to explain why. Justices Thomas and Scalia joined Justice Alito in dissent.

Note the alignment. In many First Amendment cases the justices don't line up according to the dominant "conservative versus liberal" narrative. You need some doctrinal background to understand *United States v. Alvarez*. In 1942, the Supreme Court issued a unanimous opinion upholding the conviction of a Jehovah's Witness for using "offensive" words in a public place. During a proselytizing campaign by Jehovah's Witnesses in Rochester, New Hampshire, a police officer tried to move Walter Chaplinsky off the sidewalk. Chaplinsky responded by shouting at the officer, "You are a God damned racketeer" and "a damned Fascist and the whole government of Rochester are Fascists." In a decision that almost certainly would be different today, the Supreme Court said that Chaplinsky's words fell into a category—"fighting words"—that had never been covered by the First Amendment. Justice Frank Murphy, probably the Court's member most devoted to civil liberties, wrote:

> There are certain well defined and narrowly limited classes of speech, the prevention and punishment of which have never been thought to raise any Constitutional problem. These include the lewd and obscene, the profane, the libelous, and the insulting or "fighting" words—those which, by their very utterance, inflict injury or tend to incite an immediate breach of the peace. It has been well observed that such utterances are no essential part of any exposition of ideas, and are of such slight social value as a step to truth that any benefit that may be derived from them is clearly outweighed by the social interest in order and morality.

The government defended the Stolen Valor Act on the entirely sensible ground that lies—deliberate falsehoods told by someone who *knows* they are false—shouldn't be covered by the First Amendment either. In Justice Murphy's words, lies are no essential part of any exposition of ideas, and they have almost no social value as a step to truth or, indeed, as anything else.

The government faced two problems. Only two years earlier, the Court had held unconstitutional a federal statute making it a crime to make and distribute movies showing gross examples of animal abuse.

The statute was aimed at so-called crush videos, a genre catering to people whose sexual fetish involves watching women in high-heeled shoes crush helpless animals. The case before the Court didn't involve a crush video, though; the video showed a quite violent fight between pit bulls, of the sort that led to Michael Vick's conviction for animal abuse. Finding the statute unconstitutional, Chief Justice Roberts wrote that the Court had upheld Chaplinsky's conviction because fighting words, and the other categories the Court had listed, historically were not covered by the First Amendment, but not because fighting words and the like didn't have significant social value. Maybe, the Chief Justice wrote, there might be some additional categories that had similarly not been regarded as covered by the First Amendment, but crush videos weren't part of any such category. Determining whether speech of a particular sort had significant social value would involve the courts in a balancing process that was outside their proper role. Only Justice Alito—devoted to his family dog—dissented.

In *Alvarez*, the government had to show that as a matter of history, the First Amendment didn't cover lies. Of course there are lots of cases where lies are covered: perjury (a false statement made to a court), lying to government agents, lies used to get people to buy things that don't do what their sellers say they do. Alvarez's lawyers pointed out that all these cases involved lies plus something else—an attempt to get some real gains from telling the lies. But, they said, Alvarez told a simple lie, for no obvious purpose. So, the government had to show that lies *as such* had never been treated as covered by the First Amendment.

That's a doctrinal problem, and a serious one for the government. Its other difficulty was even more serious. It involved the rhetoric associated with the case. People lie all the time. To use examples that came up repeatedly in the case: kids lie to their parents about where they were after curfew; spouses lie to each other about whether one is having an extramarital affair. In popular culture, an "ordinary" lie is at the heart

of *Mad Men*, where Don Draper lies about who he is.* Alvarez's lawyers
and those who supported his constitutional claim told the Court that it
would be terrible were legislatures to have the power to make it a crime
to tell an ordinary lie.

The government wasn't able to overcome the doctrinal and rhetorical
hurdles. Justice Kennedy devoted several pages to showing that lies as
such weren't a historically recognized category of speech not covered by
the First Amendment. The rhetorical problem surfaced in his discussion
of the Stolen Valor Act's "adverse" effect on speech. He said, accurately,
that the act "would apply . . . to personal, whispered conversations
within a home," though I wonder how the government would find out
about such statements or why it would bother to prosecute someone for
making them. More important was Justice Kennedy's argument that

> Permitting the government to decree this speech to be a criminal
> offense, whether shouted from the rooftops or made in a barely audi-
> ble whisper, would endorse government authority to compile a list of
> subjects about which false statements are punishable. That governmen-
> tal power has no clear limiting principle. Our constitutional tradition
> stands against the idea that we need Oceana's Ministry of Truth. Were
> this law to be sustained, there could be an endless list of subjects the
> National Government or the States could single out.

Pretty clearly in the background here were laws around the world
making it a crime to deny that the Holocaust occurred, or to assert that
Turkey committed genocide in Armenia—and maybe even the possibility of a statute in the United States making it a crime to deny (or assert)
that human activity causes global warming. Yet the limiting principle
supporting the government's position on the Stolen Valor Act is pretty

---

* Although Draper refrains from perpetuating the lie when doing so would be necessary to
get a government contract.

clear. The government wasn't contending that legislatures had the power to make false statements a crime. It was saying that legislatures ought to have the power to decide that some lies—false statements made by people who know that the statements are false—are socially harmful. Lies are different from merely false statements. Holocaust deniers typically don't believe that the Holocaust did occur yet go around saying that it didn't. There is a better defense of Justice Kennedy's position, one suggested in Justice Breyer's separate opinion: that prosecutors and juries will mistakenly conclude that someone made a false statement knowing that it was false (told a lie), when the person actually believed it to be true, or that prosecutors and juries will only go after liars who are also political outliers.*

This doesn't deal with the rhetorical problem posed by white lies or Don Draper. Justice Kennedy's rhetoric, though, is revealing. He doesn't consider the fact that Congress and state legislatures have lots of things on their minds. Of course there are "moral panics," when legislators gin up public excitement about some imagined social evil and then legislate against it, but as the Web site I mentioned earlier shows, a surprisingly large number of people do falsely claim to have won military honors. The Stolen Valor Act doesn't seem to me a response to an imaginary problem or one whose importance Congress exaggerated for political gain.

Once Justice Kennedy and his colleagues decided that the First Amendment covered lies as such, the existing doctrinal framework kicked in. The government had to show that the Stolen Valor Act promoted a "compelling interest" in a way that was "necessary to achieve" that interest. The interest in protecting the honor associated with the Congressional Medal of Honor was compelling, but, according to Justice Kennedy, the government hadn't shown that criminalizing lies

---

* An example of the first concern might be Senator Mark Kirk's statement that he had received a military award, when in fact he was a leading member of a group that had received the award; Rick Strandlof, an anti-war activist, might be an example of the second.

about receiving the medal was necessary to do so. It had "no evidence" that "the public's general perception of military awards is diluted" by lies such as Alvarez's. And, with checking someone's claims so easy, the government could rely on public inquiry and obloquy to expose these lies. Justice Kennedy relied on a core First Amendment dogma: "The remedy for speech that is false is speech that is true."

Justice Breyer took a slightly more narrow approach. He thought that the government had failed to satisfy, not the high standard Justice Kennedy proposed, but a slightly easier one, of "intermediate scrutiny." The difference didn't matter in *Alvarez* because Justice Breyer agreed that the connection between the Stolen Valor Act and protecting the honor associated with the Medal of Honor was too weak. But, Justice Breyer thought, it might matter in connection with things like some aspects of trademark law and election law, where some states have made it a crime to lie about an opponent—again, to disseminate a statement that you *know* to be false.

The Court's three most conservative members dissented. Justice Alito's strongest point focused on the judgments Justices Kennedy and Breyer made about Congress's ability to protect the honor associated with military awards by something other than the Stolen Valor Act. Deciding what techniques work better and worse, Justice Alito argued, was basically a legislative task, not a judicial one. Justice Kennedy's arguments show that the Roberts Court considers itself a body equal to the legislature in assessing whether something is a social problem worth addressing. If five justices think that it isn't, they'll find something in the Constitution to explain why Congress made a mistake.

IF XAVIER Alvarez is merely a troubled man, Fred Phelps is a despicable one. Phelps founded the Westboro Baptist Church in 1955. He describes his beliefs as "Primitive Baptist," and his church, headquartered in Topeka, Kansas, isn't affiliated with any of the major Baptist organizations. Starting in the 1990s, Phelps, then in his sixties, dragged homosexuality into his theology. Members of the Westboro Baptist Church—around forty in number, most of them members of Phelps's family—believe that the deaths of U.S. soldiers in combat express God's judgment that the United States has become sinful because of its toleration of homosexuality. They travel around the country to demonstrate near soldiers' funerals, at which they display signs such as "THANK GOD FOR DEAD SOLDIERS," "FAGS DOOM NATIONS," and "YOU'RE GOING TO HELL." Phelps, two of his daughters, and four grandchildren held one such demonstration just before the burial of Matthew Snyder, a Marine who had been killed in Iraq. They displayed their signs at a place where they were entitled to be, about 1,000 feet from the church where the funeral was held.* Snyder's father sued Phelps and his daughters for the tort of intentional infliction of emotional distress (IIED for short). He had seen only the tops of the signs but not the content as he drove to the funeral, but learned of what they said when he saw a television news broadcast about the demonstration. Instructed that liability required that it find that the Westboro Church members "intentionally or recklessly engaged in extreme and outrageous conduct that caused [Snyder] to suffer severe emotional distress," the jury returned a multi-million-dollar judgment against the church members. A lower court vacated the judgment, finding that it violated the First Amendment, and the Snyders appealed to the Supreme Court.

The Court had dealt with the IIED tort before. The pornographic magazine *Hustler* ran a series of parody ads describing in graphic and offensive detail the "first time" public figures had had intercourse. The ad about the conservative Christian minister Jerry Falwell said that his first time had been a drunken incestuous encounter with his mother. Falwell—not his mother—sued *Hustler* for IIED. In 1988, the Supreme

---

* After the demonstration at Matthew Snyder's funeral, Maryland enacted a law prohibiting demonstrations within 100 feet of funerals. The Westboro church members' demonstration wouldn't have been unlawful under that statute.

Court held that the First Amendment barred recovery for the intentional infliction of emotional distress on a public figure such as Falwell.

Margie Phelps, one of Fred's daughters, argued the case for the family, and despite some observers' skepticism about the ability of someone so closely associated with the church to do an effective job, performed at least as well as the average first-timer at the Court. The Court ruled in Phelps's favor, with only Justice Alito dissenting, though Margie Phelps's performance almost certainly had little to do with the outcome. The Court expressed sympathy for the Snyders: "Westboro's choice to convey its views in conjunction with Matthew Snyder's funeral made the expression of those views particularly hurtful to many, especially to Matthew's father. The record makes clear that the applicable legal term—'emotional distress'—fails to capture fully the anguish Westboro's choice added to Mr. Snyder's already incalculable grief." Even so, it extended the *Falwell* rule to cover actions filed by private figures, where the speech was "of public . . . concern, as determined by all the circumstances of the case."

Justice Alito's dissent captured the outrage many people feel about Fred Phelps's behavior. He had engaged in a "vicious verbal assault," a "malevolent verbal attack" on someone who simply wanted "to bury his son in peace." Phelps's technique of demonstrating at funerals reflected a cynical strategy: "the media is irresistibly drawn to the sight of persons who are visibly in grief. The more outrageous the funeral protest, the more publicity the Westboro Baptist Church is able to obtain." Alito ended his dissent: "In order to have a society in which public issues can be openly and vigorously debated, it is not necessary to allow the brutalization of innocent victims. . . ." Justice Alito's point—that "society" shouldn't sacrifice "innocent victims" just because we want open debate—seems exactly right.

VERMONT REQUIRES pharmacists to keep records of the prescriptions written by physicians, classified by the doctors' names. It barred the pharmacists from selling lists showing the number of prescriptions for each drug written by each physician, even though the lists did not identify the patients involved. To understand why, it helps to understand how prescription drugs are marketed. Drug manufacturers—"Big Pharma," to use the disparaging term—employ two techniques. They market directly to consumers, with advertisements on television and in newspapers that proclaim the benefits of their products (and, because of FDA requirements, also describe side effects). But, of course, ordinary consumers can't just go to their pharmacy and say, "I saw an ad for Levitra, and I'd like to buy ten pills to try it out." Levitra, Cymbalta, and all the other medications advertised on TV are available only by prescriptions written by doctors. So the drug manufacturers urge consumers to ask their doctors about getting a prescription for Levitra or Cymbalta.

That's where the manufacturers' second marketing technique comes in. They send employees, known as "detailers," around to doctors. The detailers are to prescription drugs what racetrack touts are to horses: they tell the doctors all the advantages to be gained by prescribing the specific medication they're pushing—a term whose resonances with drug addiction aren't inaccurate. Maybe more important, they urge doctors to prescribe medications still covered by patents rather than the cheaper generic versions of similar drugs, telling the doctors that they have a new, improved, and newly patented version of the drug that's now gone generic. Of course, the drug manufacturers make more money on the patented medications than the generic companies do on theirs.

That's where Vermont became concerned. The state had to pay for a good chunk of the cost of medications, especially through Medicaid. Believing that doctors were prescribing too many in-patent medications and not enough generic ones, they wanted to change the doctors' habits. The ban on buying lists of prescriptions from pharmacists was part of that effort. With the lists, drug manufacturers could identify which doctors weren't prescribing "enough" of their products and which were prescribing "too many" generics. Their detailers could then target those doctors for persuasion. By making it more difficult for detailers to identify possible targets for their sales efforts, the ban on selling information for use by drug manufacturers would help control medical costs. Given Vermont's goal of controlling medical costs, it limited the ban on selling prescription lists to sales for marketing uses, and didn't stop the pharmacists from selling the lists to those who intended to use them for research.

The Supreme Court held Vermont's statute unconstitutional, with Justice Sotomayor joining the four Republican appointees. As usual, to understand the competing positions you have to know something about First Amendment doctrine. As with *Alvarez*, we go back to the 1940s.

Law professor Tom Gerety describes F. J. Chrestensen as "the P. T. Barnum" of the early 1940s. Seeing war clouds gathering, as Winston Churchill later put it, Chrestensen also saw a business opportunity. He bought a decommissioned Navy submarine for the then enormous amount of $2 million (more than $32 million today). He planned to open it for tours, charging adults 25 cents and children 15 cents. New York City's police commissioner Lewis Valentine denied him a permit to dock the submarine in New York harbor at the south of the island, citing concerns about sanitation. Chrestensen wasn't put off. He went to state officials and got permission to dock the submarine on the East River, at a pier owned by the state. Valentine wasn't put off either. He told Chrestensen that he couldn't hand out fliers advertising the attraction, citing concerns about littering when people discarded the handouts. The back-and-forth continued. Chrestensen printed a sample flier, advertising the submarine on one side and protesting the city's harassment on the other. Valentine said, "No go." Chrestensen then went to court. Eventually the Supreme Court ruled unanimously against Chrestensen, saying that the First Amendment didn't limit the government's power to regulate "purely commercial advertising."

Skip ahead about thirty years. In 1971 Virginia convicted Jeffrey

Bigelow, the editor of an alternative weekly newspaper in Charlottesville, for publishing an advertisement for abortion services in New York (presumably targeted at students at the University of Virginia), where providing such services was legal. The case reached the Supreme Court in 1975, after the Court had struck down all the nation's restrictive abortion laws. Justice Harry Blackmun, the author of *Roe v. Wade*, wrote the Court's opinion, saying that it was unconstitutional to prohibit advertising about the availability of a legally available product.

Bigelow was the first Supreme Court decision giving First Amendment protection to a commercial advertisement. It might have been a sport because of its relation to *Roe v. Wade*; indeed, the Court tried to jawbone the Virginia Supreme Court initially by sending the case back to it after *Roe v. Wade*, apparently thinking that the state court might void Bigelow's conviction on abortion-related grounds (it didn't).

Sometimes doctrine takes on a life of its own. Ralph Nader and other consumer advocates had already begun to think of using the First Amendment to challenge a host of restrictions on price advertising, and *Bigelow* gave them the doctrine they needed. They focused first on widespread bans on advertising of prices for prescription drugs, which they believed kept prices artificially high. The bans favored the neighborhood pharmacy against large commercial pharmacies. If consumers didn't know that they could save money by driving to Walgreens, they would fill their prescriptions at the pharmacy in their doctor's building, wasting their money. A year after *Bigelow*, Justice Blackmun wrote the Court's opinion striking down Virginia's ban on drug price advertising, writing that the consumer's "interest in the free flow of commercial information" might well be "as keen, if not keener by far, than his interest in the day's most urgent political debate."

That line liberated commercial speech doctrine. The Court acknowledged that governments could regulate commercial advertising more readily than political debate. A state could ban false or misleading commercial advertising, something it almost certainly couldn't do when political debate was involved. (How many political advertisements have you seen in which one or the other side makes claims that are false or misleading? Somewhere around 100 percent, I'd guess.)

The business community saw the new doctrine as an opportunity to get rid of regulations that, as they believed (probably correctly), typically tried to protect small businesses from competition. The doctrine developed rapidly. The Court settled on a doctrinal formulation when it struck down a regulation developed by New York's utility regulators responding to the nation's energy crisis by banning advertisements that "promoted" electricity use. According to the Court, governments could regulate commercial speech only with rules that "directly advanced" the government's interest, and the rules had to be necessary: "If the governmental interest could be served as well by a more limited restriction on commercial speech, the excessive restrictions cannot survive." Lawyers described this as "intermediate" scrutiny for regulations of commercial advertising—more stringent than none at all, but less demanding than the tight standards ("strict scrutiny") for regulating political speech.*

By the turn of the millennium, intermediate scrutiny looked in practice a lot like strict scrutiny. The Court upheld a handful of regulations of commercial advertising, but struck down many more. And, prodded by Justice Thomas, the justices began to question whether commercial advertising should be treated differently from political speech. Their structure was, "Maybe there aren't any constitutionally significant distinctions between commercial advertising and political speech, in which case the regulation we're considering would certainly be unconstitutional, but even if there are differences and we apply intermediate scrutiny, this regulation doesn't satisfy the test we've developed in the electricity advertising case."

Overall, the First Amendment had, peculiarly, become a mechanism

---

* The justices use the term "intermediate" in commercial speech cases, but refrain from using the term "strict" as a contrast, for internal doctrinal reasons that aren't worth describing in detail here.

for protecting marketplace competition against government regulations aimed at protecting some businesses from competition. That might well be a worthy goal, though what the First Amendment has to do with marketplace competition was obscure for most of the nation's history. The Court had tried to use the Constitution to protect competition before, using the Constitution's due process clauses. It gave up the attempt during the New Deal. The modern Court's commercial speech doctrine revives the effort under a different constitutional guise.

That's where things stood when Vermont's prescription data-mining case got to the Court. In an opinion by Justice Kennedy, the Court held that Vermont's ban violated the First Amendment because it regulated speech—the dissemination of information lawfully acquired by pharmacists—in a way that discriminated on the basis of both content and speaker. The regulation "disfavors marketing, that is, speech with a particular content" and "disfavors specific speakers, namely pharmaceutical manufacturers." As had become the custom, Justice Kennedy observed that "the outcome is the same whether a special commercial speech inquiry or a stricter form of judicial scrutiny is applied." Because the regulation allowed researchers and journalists—an "almost limitless audience," in the Court's words—access to physician-related information, the regulation did little to protect physicians' privacy. Doctors who didn't like to discuss their prescription practices with detailers could simply refuse to meet with them. Nor was the connection between cost control and the regulation close enough. According to Justice Kennedy, under the regulation costs are controlled because detailers can't present doctors with accurate information that might lead them to prescribe more expensive drugs, perhaps mistakenly. But "[t]hose who seek to censor or burden free expression often assert that disfavored speech has adverse effects."

Justice Breyer in dissent characterized the regulation differently. For him, it was "inextricably related to a lawful governmental effort to regulate a commercial enterprise." Such regulations were almost inevitably content- and speaker-based. As to content, regulated businesses engage in many forms of communication—commercial advertisements, advertisements on public policy proposals of interest to the businesses, securities disclosures—but regulators will select only some of those, on the basis of their content, for regulation. And as to speaker-based regulations, regulators might identify a specific subset of an industry where problems are especially severe and impose requirements on manufacturers in that subset without imposing similar regulations on others in the same industry.

Justice Kennedy's opinion made much of the fact that everyone *but* pharmaceutical manufacturers could use physician-identified prescription information. Indeed, if we make a list of all the possible users of such information—pharmaceutical manufacturers, university researchers, journalists, any interested citizen—the statute does exclude only one group from using the information. The relevant question, though, was not the length of the list of possible users but the likelihood that any potential user would be interested in identifying specific physicians. The pharmaceutical manufacturers of course were interested in doing so. An occasional journalist might think it important to use a doctor's name to bring to life some story about prescription practices, but it is hardly clear that university researchers, or anyone else, would think the name important. In practical terms, the regulation covered the vast bulk of those who might actually use the information. And it would do a reasonably good job—the kind of job the nominal test for commercial speech demands—of promoting the government's permissible regulatory goal of protecting physician privacy.

The prescription data-mining case offered the Court a choice: characterize the regulation as involving "speech proposing a commercial transaction," or as involving "speech inextricably related to a lawful governmental effort to regulate a commercial enterprise." What was the basis for Justice Kennedy's choice? Largely, that taking "intermediate scrutiny" seriously or applying Justice Breyer's approach would, as Chief

Justice Roberts put it in the crush video case, amount to adopting a a "free-floating" test. As in *Snyder v. Phelps*, the Court appears to prefer simplicity in rules for its own sake—or for reasons that it doesn't spell out in detail.

I COULD go on, dealing for example with the Court's decision that California couldn't bar sales of violent video games to minors. These three cases, though, are a decent sample of what the Roberts Court thinks about free speech. There are quite a few moving parts in what the Court is doing. Some of them may ultimately be rooted in the playground response to taunts: "Sticks and stones may break my bones, but words can never hurt me." Sometimes the Court appears to agree, but it's wrong. Words can hurt—or, at least, sometimes legislatures should be allowed to decide that words hurt even if the justices don't think so.

Let's begin with some rhetorical tropes we find in the Court's opinions. In the crush video case, Chief Justice Roberts rejected balancing because "[t]he First Amendment itself reflects a judgment by the American people that the benefits of its restrictions on the Government outweigh its costs." Responding to the argument that the Court's commercial speech cases were basically aimed at promoting economic efficiency, and quoting one of the most celebrated statements of Justice Oliver Wendell Holmes, made in 1905, Justice Kennedy echoed the thought in the prescription data-mining case: "The Constitution 'does not enact Mr. Herbert Spencer's Social Statics.' It does enact the First Amendment." The justices obviously think that this trope is effective rhetoric, and maybe it is. But it's pretty clearly analytically indefensible. The issue in each of the cases is *what* the First Amendment protects —what judgment the American people had made about the kind of speech the government had tried to regulate. The rhetorical trope says that if something is protected by the First Amendment, the Court doesn't engage in balancing but simply strikes the statute down because it violates the First Amendment. Well, sure, but so what?

"The American people" and "we" appear in a different rhetorical trope. In *Alvarez*, Justice Kennedy wrote: "The Nation well knows that one of the costs of the First Amendment is that it protects the speech we detest as well as the speech we embrace." More revealing is Chief Justice Roberts's version, at the conclusion of his opinion in *Snyder v. Phelps*:

> Speech is powerful. It can stir people to action, move them to tears of both joy and sorrow, and—as it did here—inflict great pain. On the facts before us, we cannot react to that pain by punishing the speaker. As a Nation we have chosen a different course—to protect even hurtful speech on public issues to ensure that we do not stifle public debate. That choice requires that we shield Westboro from tort liability for its picketing in this case.

The words with which Justice Alito concluded his dissent got the point: the Snyders might wonder why they have to suffer to benefit the rest of us. Often, maybe very often, the public gets the benefits of expression *and* bears a substantial portion of its costs. Ordinary street demonstrations, for example, disrupt traffic and make it more difficult for merchants to conduct their usual business. Speech critical of government policies increases the chance that some people will violate the law or precipitate violence. In *Snyder*, though, the "we" who "have chosen a different course" do not suffer the pain inflicted on the Snyders, though we might benefit from the church members' speech on a matter of public concern.

The Court's rhetoric, effective to some readers, conceals important analytical issues.

First, there's the press itself. Basically, the justices can be sure that major newspapers and commentators are going to have good things to say about them when they report, "The Supreme Court upheld a First

Amendment claim today." And First Amendment decisions, one study of television news suggests, are the most reported of all the Court's decisions.

Maybe the praise will be slow in coming if the case is *Citizens United* or some other campaign finance decision, but otherwise the press understandably likes the First Amendment. Editorial writers worry that allowing any regulation of speech might encourage politicians to go after them. For reasons different from the justices', the press wants a simple, almost "anything goes" First Amendment.

Here are some of the editorials on the cases I've discussed:

- The *New York Times* on the crush video case—"Disgusting But Not Illegal." According to the editorial, "Almost no one would say depictions of animals being crushed or mutilated are worthwhile. . . . [But] the First Amendment is a remarkably fragile institution that does not need more exceptions carved out from its meaning. . . . [A]nimal cruelty videos may be repugnant to many, but America's legal tradition keeps them from being illegal."
- The *New York Times* on the funeral protest case—"Even Hurtful Speech." The Court's "narrow ruling . . . provided an admirable reminder of how broad the protection of free speech is under the Constitution's First Amendment. . . . In the kind of incisive language he is capable of when he cares about the legal principle at stake, Chief Justice Roberts described the effects of words wielded as weapons against individuals, while arguing that even deeply flawed ideas must be defended because they are part of the public debate on which this country depends."
- *The Washington Post* on the same case—"The Right to Even Ugly Free Speech." "In upholding the rights of the members of Westboro Baptist, the Supreme Court . . . rightly embraced one of this country's most cherished principles. Speech cannot be quashed or punished simply because it is hateful or expresses an aberrant point of view."

- *The Washington Post* on the Stolen Valor Act decision—"a commendable reinforcement of the First Amendment and its sanctity." "As reprehensible as statements like Mr. Alvarez's may be, the court was correct: Criminalizing certain types of speech is not the answer." Alvarez's lies "deserve rebuke for insulting those who serve and their families. . . . It's just best that such discipline come from the public, not the law, and that the freedoms for which real Marines fight continue to be treated as sacred."

All this is pretty much standard fare for newspapers, which are sanctimonious about the First Amendment's sanctity. For that reason—and because they know that they are sometimes irresponsible themselves—editorialists don't give much priority to the fact that words can indeed hurt. Against the *Times*'s defense of "even deeply flawed ideas," a skeptic might point out that a jury found that the Phelpses did what they did for the very purpose of hurting the Snyders, not to play a part in "public debate." One might even say that the Chief Justice himself wielded words as weapons against the Snyder family, telling them that they must put up with their pain because that's good for the rest of us. Against *The Washington Post*'s editorial on the same case, the skeptic might point out that there's a real difference between being "hateful" and being "hurtful." And against the *Post*'s distinction between a rebuke "from the public" and one from "the law," we might wonder where the *Post* thought the law came from other than from the public acting through its representatives in Congress.

The press doesn't always approve decisions finding that the government violated the First Amendment, even if we put campaign finance cases to one side. The *Post* criticized the Court's decision to bar California from preventing young people from buying violent video games, which the paper thought was a "reasonable limitation" on minors' access to extremely violent games. The editorialists thought that minors' access to materials could be regulated in ways that adults' access couldn't be. Here the skeptic might think that selective empathy could be at work; the editorialists might be worrying that their kids would be able to get their hands on violent video games, so the regulation affected them personally. They couldn't imagine wanting to hurt an animal or wanting to watch an animal being hurt, so allowing crush videos wasn't going to affect them at all.

The basic point, though, is clear: overall, a justice is going to get more praise than criticism from newspapers and commentators for upholding a First Amendment claim, no matter what the claim is. And justices being people, they'd rather get praise than criticism.

From a lawyer's perspective, there's a reason rooted in the way we think about law itself for the Court's approach, deeper than concern for getting good press notices. The Roberts Court likes rules with sharp edges—a well-defined strike zone. And free speech doctrine has developed some rules. The clearest and most important is that governments can't regulate political speech without a really good justification—the "strict scrutiny" approach. The Court developed that rule after decades of experience taught it the lesson that leaving things fuzzy—allowing "intermediate scrutiny"—was a really bad idea.

The experience was simple, though it took time for the Court to learn the lesson. Like the rest of us, government officials don't like to be criticized. But unlike the rest of us, they can do something about it. They can use their power to suppress their critics. What they say is that they're not really worried about the criticism as such, but about the bad effects the criticism will have: criticize an ongoing war, and the government will have a harder time recruiting soldiers; say that the government's a reverse Robin Hood, taking from the poor and giving to the rich, and the poor are going to start taking things back. And, truth be told, speech *does* increase the risk that these things will happen. It's just that officials typically exaggerate the risk. And as Justice Oliver Wendell Holmes once memorably wrote, the government

throws "poor and puny anonymities" in prison because they've criticized a government policy.

What the Court learned was that *everyone* exaggerates the risk posed
by speech critical of government policy: political speech. Legislatures
enact statutes that aren't really needed; prosecutors charge puny and
poor anonymities; juries affected by the heightened political passions of
the moment convict them; lower court judges throw the book at them;
and appeals court judges uphold the convictions. Eventually the Court
figured out that the only way to keep things under control was to tell
everyone that they can't go after political speech unless they have a
really good reason—a "compelling state interest" is the way the Court
puts it—backed up by strong evidence and "narrowly tailored" so that
the statute does no more than is needed to advance that interest.

All this is quite sensible. But we have to understand the underlying
structure. Speech does increase the risk that harm will occur, but sometimes people exaggerate the risk pretty seriously, and we can understand
the systematic reasons for the exaggeration—political self-protection in
the case of political speech. We guard against systematic exaggerations
by adopting hard-edged rules. In short, we use rules for reasons.

Now, back to the Roberts Court cases. Are there good reasons to
think that legislatures, prosecutors, and juries systematically exaggerate the harm caused by animal cruelty videos, lies, data mining, and
deliberate attempts to hurt people by targeting them with cruel signs
that drag in some public issue? I'm pretty skeptical, and certainly the
justices haven't offered any reasons of the right sort. Justice Kennedy
in *Alvarez* waved his hands in the right direction in the Stolen Valor
case, where he worried that telling legislatures that they could make
it a crime to tell a lie might lead them to compile a list of prohibited
falsehoods, but as we've seen, that hardly seems likely. He didn't
give a systematic reason for that fear, one rooted in the way politics
actually works.

The early commercial advertising cases do hint at the right kind of reason. We used to have a lot of neighborhood pharmacies, which meant that there were a lot of pharmacists who voted. They organized as an interest group to protect their turf by getting Virginia's legislature to ban price advertising, reducing the ability of Walgreens and other chains to compete against them. Some regulations of speech result from the capture of government power by narrow interest groups, and maybe we should use hard-edged rules to guard against that possibility.

Maybe so, although critics early on pointed out that using the First Amendment to protect market competition seemed rather removed from the dramatic struggles over political speech that had produced the First Amendment. But even if the interest group capture story makes sense, it's not true across the board. Sure, animal welfare groups, and maybe even animal rights fanatics, might have been behind the ban on crush videos, but they aren't interest groups of the right sort. They're not really out to benefit themselves financially, although of course the leaders and staff members of animal rights interest groups do need to get things done to explain why people should give the organizations money to pay their salaries, as neighborhood pharmacists might be. They just think that crush videos are really bad, and they got Congress to agree. And, of course, the quintessential interest group, "Big Pharma," lost a legislative fight against prescription data mining. That's just ordinary politics at work, and we shouldn't deploy the big guns of the First Amendment on the side of people who had a fair chance of winning a legislative fight but happened to lose it.

The interest group story doesn't work well to explain the Roberts Court's approach to free speech issues. What does explain it, I think, is a preference for simple rules. It treats bans on animal crush videos and prescription data mining as the same because both involve regulation of speech because of its content. That's certainly simper than having one rule for animal crush videos and another for data mining, though simplicity may be its only virtue. Chief Justice Roberts described the government's advocacy of a balancing test to determine whether the

First Amendment barred Congress from banning crush videos as "star-tling and dangerous." Although he didn't elaborate, his Court's cases make it clear that the justices are attracted to hard-edged rules because they think that such rules keep *them* from making the kinds of mistakes that they've found in our history of suppressing political speech.

There are real benefits from having simple rules in a complex world, to use a phrase popularized in legal circles by the law professor Rich-ard Epstein, but of course there are costs too. The hard-edged rules guard against exaggerating harm, but they also prevent the regulation of speech that really does cause actual harm. And, probably worse, the Court may think that its rules are simple enough, but they aren't. So we get the costs of using simple rules without many of the benefits.

The funeral protest case is a good illustration of the Court's pref-erence for simple rules. The Court chose the "matters of public con-cern" rule because the jury instructions were too complicated. A rule that precludes recovery for statements on matters of public concern is certainly simpler than one allowing recovery under some rather lim-ited circumstances. Yet, why would a rule allowing the imposition of liability for statements on matters of public concern made for the very purpose of inflicting emotional harm (and succeeding in that purpose) "stifle public debate" in a manner inconsistent with the choices "we" have made in the First Amendment? As in the Stolen Valor case, here too the majority seems to have forgotten that deliberate intention is part of the offense.

Maybe the "public concern" rule is simpler than the instructions the jury got in *Snyder v. Phelps*, though I have my doubts. Yet the Roberts Court really isn't committed to a First Amendment of simple rules. Even in the Roberts Court, First Amendment doctrine is actually quite complicated. When you have a complicated overall structure, it's hard to justify refusing to make one subdoctrine slightly more complicated on the ground that you really really want doctrine to be simple.

The majority in the cases I've described says that regulation of speech because of its content has to survive strict scrutiny. But that's not true. Consider again the *Ceballos* case decided in 2006, Chief Justice Roberts's freshman year. There the Court said that the First Amendment wasn't violated when an assistant prosecutor was fired after reporting to his supervisors that the police had violated the Constitution—a regulation of speech because of its content—because it was speech made by a public employee as part of the employee's job. So already we have a complication in free speech doctrine: the government can't regulate speech because of its content when it's dealing with citizens generally, but it can when it's dealing with its employees. Even that rule isn't as simple as it could be: courts are going to have to decide whether some speech was part of the job, or was outside the job.

Then there's *Morse v. Frederick*. Joe Frederick moved to join his father in Juneau, Alaska, in 2000. He was something of a smart-alecky kid, who didn't fit in to the new environment. The Olympic Torch Relay ran through Juneau on its way to Salt Lake City in 2002. School authorities decided to let their students out of school to view the torch passing.[*] On a lark, to show that he didn't take anything very seriously, Joe and some friends stood on the roadside holding up a banner, "BONG HITS 4 JESUS." Joe later said that the banner didn't really mean anything, and the IM-speak and the mix of capital and small letters doesn't make a lot of sense. Deborah Morse, the school's principal, thought otherwise. For her, the banner advocated drug use. She suspended Frederick from school for five—later increased to ten—days.

Frederick got a lower court to hold that his suspension was clearly unconstitutional. With the support of the Bush administration and organizations of public school officials, Morse appealed to the Supreme Court. Her lawyer was Kenneth Starr, then most recently prominent as the special prosecutor in the investigation of Bill Clinton. The school

---

[*] They described this as an official school activity; Frederick and his supporters thought the students were basically being dismissed from school early.

officials supporting Morse asked for an extremely broad ruling, that
schools could punish students for speech during school time that was
inconsistent with the schools' self-defined educational mission. That in
turn set off fire alarms in Christian Right circles. They already had run
up against principals who tried to discipline students for congregating
in the halls or outside the school, during school time, for prayer sessions.
Some of them came into the case on Frederick's side. The Rutherford
Institute and the Alliance Defense Fund, both Christian Right litigation groups, found themselves on the same side as the pro–gay rights
Lambda Legal Defense Fund, which had their own problems with
schools trying to shut down gay-supportive activities.

Starr quickly understood at oral argument that the broad position
he had staked out wasn't going to fly. The amicus briefs pretty clearly
unsettled even the Court's conservatives. Chief Justice Roberts wrote
the Court's opinion. Calling the words on the banner "cryptic" and
reworking that observation to make the point that to some viewers, "it
probably means nothing at all," the Chief Justice said that the principal's interpretation that they advocated drug use was reasonable. That
was enough to decide the case. The school could restrict student speech
reasonably understood to be "promoting illegal drug use."

Justice Alito's concurring opinion drove home the point that the case
should be seen as a drugs-in-schools case, not a speech-in-schools one,
saying that the Court's decision went to "the far reaches of what the
First Amendment permits." Echoing the concerns in the amicus briefs,
Justice Alito cautioned against allowing schools to regulate speech that
was inconsistent with their self-defined educational missions. Picking up on conservative criticisms of political correctness, Justice Alito
observed that "some public schools have defined their educational missions as including the inculcation of whatever political and social views
are held by" school officials and teachers.

So now we have an even more complicated First Amendment. Governments can regulate speech because of its content in schools, at least if

the speech is "reasonably" understood to advocate drug use. And, notably, this is a regulation of ordinary citizens, not government employees.

As the late-night TV ads say, "But wait, there's more." In 1996, Congress made it a crime to provide "material support" to terrorist groups, and defined "material support" to include "training." The material support statute is clearly constitutional for most sensible applications—sending terrorist groups money, buying weapons for them, training them how to make improvised explosive devices. Ralph Fertig had contacts with a Kurdish liberation group the State Department designated a terrorist organization. Fertig founded a seat-of-the-pants organization he called the Humanitarian Law Project that operated out of a small office in an undistinguished building on a Los Angeles shopping street. He worried that an aggressive prosecutor might go after him for providing material support by providing training for the Kurdish group in dispute resolution and international law. With the help of the Center for Constitutional Rights, a left-oriented public interest law group, and David Cole, a civil liberties lawyer who teaches at Georgetown Law Center, Fertig, the Humanitarian Law Project, and several Americans who wanted to advise the Tamil Tigers of Sri Lanka, another group that the State Department designated a terrorist organization, began a legal challenge to the material support statute, filing suit in 1997.

The challenge dragged on for over a decade before it reached the Supreme Court. The lower courts repeatedly accepted Cole's argument that terms like "training" were unconstitutionally vague. Twice Congress modified the statute, attempting and failing, in the courts' view, to tighten up the definition. The lower court said that the current statutory definitions—"training" was "teaching designed to impart a specific skill" and "expert advice" was "advice derived from scientific, technical or other specialized knowledge"—were still too vague. By 2009 the government had had enough and appealed to the Supreme Court.

By then the Tamil insurgency had ended with the extermination of the remaining Tamil Tigers and their supporters. Fertig continued to want to give the Kurds technical assistance. He said that he and his group would give them training in peaceful methods of dispute resolution, so that they could negotiate with their adversaries, and training about using international law to petition various international organizations for relief, pretty clearly meaning humanitarian relief such as food and medicine. The Humanitarian Law Project's central claim was that making it a crime for its supporters to do that violated their First Amendment rights.

Chief Justice Roberts disagreed. He forthrightly characterized the material support statute's ban on training and expert advice as a regulation of speech because of its content, rejecting some weaselly efforts by Solicitor General Kagan to describe the ban in other terms. So, the ban had to promote a compelling or very strong government interest—easy enough: fighting terrorism to protect national security certainly is such an interest. It also had to be "necessary to further that interest." The Chief Justice wrote that it was. Referring to "findings" Congress had made, and relying heavily on a detailed affidavit from a State Department official, Roberts wrote that "support" in pretty much any form "helps lend legitimacy to foreign terrorist groups— legitimacy that makes it easier for those groups to persist, to recruit members, and to raise funds." It also created foreign policy problems, "undermining cooperative efforts between nations to prevent terrorist attacks." Turkey was the target of Kurdish terrorist activities; it "would react sharply to Americans furnishing material support" to those groups, and "would hardly be mollified by the explanation that the support was meant only to further those groups' 'legitimate' activities," of which, from Turkey's point of view, there weren't any. Going beyond what the affidavit said, the Chief Justice argued as well that teaching the Kurds how to negotiate might allow them to drag out peace negotiations while they gathered strength, and that teaching them how to seek relief from international organizations might end up getting them money for food and allowing them to use their other funds to buy more weapons.

In saying that the views of Congress and the State Department were "entitled to deference" about "factual inferences" (though not an "abdication of the judicial role"), Chief Justice Roberts basically shrugged his shoulders and said, "Congress and the president have told us that providing technical assistance that terrorist groups ask for makes it easier for them to carry out violent acts. Who are we, mere Supreme Court justices, to tell them that they're wrong?" Fair enough. As the Chief Justice put it, the Court couldn't insist on hard evidence, a "dangerous requirement," because "in this context, conclusions must often be based on informed judgment rather than concrete evidence." Still, you could say the same thing about judgments underlying Vermont's ban on prescription data mining: Vermont's legislature tells us that preventing prescription data mining will help keep medical costs under control. Who are the judges to tell them they're wrong? There are complicated factual inferences at issue there, too.

Of course, maybe there's a special "national security" exception to the usual way the Court applies its rule about regulating speech because of its content. Chief Justice Roberts did say that "in this area perhaps more than any other, the Legislature's superior capacity for weighing competing interests" mattered. Then, though, we could say, "Well, if you're going to make an exception for national security, you're already making the system of rules more complicated. Why not make an exception for lies too?"

Another possibility is that the justices themselves think that national security is more important than controlling medical costs. But that is simply substituting their policy judgments for the legislature's. And remember that experience in the executive branch was important in President Bush's choice of John Roberts and Samuel Alito for the Court. For them, the home team might be the national security bureaucracy in the executive branch.

There is a final, truly depressing possibility. Maybe the justices forgot the lesson of experience that generated the strict rules in the first place—that everyone exaggerates the risks speech poses to national security. They may have forgotten that "everyone" means everyone, including the justices of the Supreme Court.

In light of the complexity of First Amendment doctrine, it's not a good argument that you don't want to tweak a particular rule to make it a little bit more complicated. Instead of looking to Richard Epstein, the Court might look to Albert Einstein, who reportedly said, "Everything should be made as simple as possible, but not simpler." First Amendment law should be as simple as possible, but not simpler.

Finally, there's the big enchilada: tobacco advertising. As we've seen, the usual ideological alignments get scrambled a bit in First Amendment cases. Not always, though. The lines between conservatives and liberals are as firm in commercial speech cases as they are anywhere else.

Indeed, they seem to be even firmer. A year after the prescription data-mining decision, the Court decided another case involving pharmaceutical companies' detailers. The issue was whether they were "outside salesmen" under the Fair Labor Standards Act. If they were, the employers didn't have to pay overtime wages. The issue is an ordinary one of statutory interpretation and administrative law. Remarkably (to me), the Court divided in exactly the same way that it had in the data-mining case, with the conservatives ruling in favor of Big Pharma and the liberals dissenting on behalf of the detailers.

Tobacco regulation presents a similar picture. Efforts to regulate tobacco advertising go back a long way, to a 1971 statute banning cigarette ads from television. David Kessler, Bill Clinton's commissioner of the Food and Drug Administration, was an anti-smoking activist because of smoking's public health effects. In 1996 Kessler, with Clinton's strong support, proposed a comprehensive set of regulations aimed at sharply reducing the appeal of ads for tobacco. The nation's tobacco companies immediately went to court. Four years later, the Supreme

Court ruled that Congress hadn't given the FDA the power to regulate tobacco advertising—a decision based on administrative law, not constitutional law. The lineup was conservative versus liberal.

Meanwhile, Massachusetts had adopted regulations of tobacco advertising modeled on the FDA regulations. Again the tobacco companies challenged the regulations, this time relying in part on the First Amendment. Again they won in the Supreme Court. And again the Court divided along conservative-liberal lines.

Congress enacted a statute in 2009 requiring that the warnings on cigarette packages cover 50 percent of their front and back, and expressly giving the FDA the authority to develop regulations of tobacco advertising. The FDA moved quickly (by the standards of most administrative agencies), promulgating stringent regulations in 2011. The FDA told tobacco companies that their advertisements couldn't use color, and the black-and-white had to be devoted only to text (no pictures, even in black-and-white, of Joe Camel or the Marlboro Man). It also required that cigarette packages carry one of several pictures, delicately described as "graphic images," showing in disgusting detail some of the medical consequences of smoking, including blackened lungs and tracheostomies.

The tobacco companies are exercising their right to go to the Supreme Court with their First Amendment challenge to the 2009 statute and the FDA's regulations. Of course we can't know in advance how the justices will rule, but we do know what doctrine they will apply. In March 2013 Attorney General Holder decided not to ask the Supreme Court to overturn a lower court's decision striking down the regulations. Instead he asked the FDA to develop a better record to support the regulations. The regulations will eventually get to the Supreme Court.

As the prescription data-mining case shows, the justices seem to be moving pretty quickly toward finding that commercial advertising that isn't false or misleading is fully protected by the First Amendment. And, it seems, they're inclined to define "misleading" pretty narrowly. They'll ask whether color photographs are inevitably misleading, for example. Further, as one lower court has held, they might say that the disgusting pictures are themselves misleading, suggesting mistakenly that everyone who smokes will end up with a tracheostomy. Of course the tobacco companies need only five justices on their side. The Court's commercial advertising decisions suggest—though they don't guarantee—that five will indeed accept their arguments.

To cap it off: in 2012 the Court, dividing basically along political lines, held that the First Amendment imposed stringent restrictions on how unions could raise money for political activities from workers who were required by law to pay dues. Calling the existing rules that required workers who didn't want to support those activities to say so—to "opt out"—a constitutional "anomaly," Justice Alito and his conservative colleagues almost explicitly invited anti-union litigators to bring the next case, in which they might well hold that unions had to set up a system in which everyone had to "opt in" to a fund for political activities.*

A recent academic study finds a relationship between what the authors describe as the political tilt of speech that the government tries to regulate and the political tilt of individual justices: liberal justices protect liberal speech but aren't bothered by regulation of conservative speech, and the other way around for conservative justices. The match isn't perfect, but the association seems to be there. There's an old story about buying milk. It comes from the nineteenth century, so you have to imagine how milk was sold then. A buyer complained that the seller had diluted the milk with water. When asked whether he'd seen the seller pour water into the can, the buyer said, "No, but the fish swimming in it was circumstantial evidence." We can't see politics operating in the Court's free speech decisions, but there's circumstantial evidence that it does.

---

* Chapter 7 discusses the different treatment the Court gives to shareholders who object to the use of corporate funds as political contributions.

CHAPTER 7

Citizens United and Campaign Finance

After the Roberts Court held in the 2010 case of *Citizens United v. Federal Election Commission* that corporations could use their money to pay for political advertisements as long as those advertisements were "independent" of candidates' campaigns, liberals feared that corporate money would flood the airwaves with ads supporting conservatives, swamping liberals' efforts to get their voices heard. The money did rush in, with the 2012 presidential campaign costing more than $5 billion. Some of that was indeed from corporations. But President Obama's reelection suggests that liberal fears about *Citizens United* were overstated.

Misunderstandings of *Citizens United* abound. That's because trying to understand campaign finance law is a lot like trying to understand the tax laws. Like the tax code, campaign finance law is incredibly intricate, with loopholes, provisions trying to close loopholes, and creative lawyers opening new ones. The financial stakes in tax law are big, which means that rich people hire good lawyers to help them pay as little as they can. The political (and financial) stakes in campaign finance law are big too, so rich people hire lawyers for exactly the same reasons. But even more, sometimes understanding campaign finance law *is* understanding the tax laws.

The Koch brothers became the evil twins of campaign finance—at least to Democrats—largely as a result of the Supreme Court's decision. They are rich, and they own corporations. *Citizens United* lets them make contributions from their corporations' treasuries. But they didn't need *Citizens United* to let them do that. Tax law already permitted it. Koch Industries is the nation's second biggest private corporation. Its Georgia-Pacific company makes Dixie cups and Brawny towels, and it owns oil pipelines and refineries. The word "private" in the description of Koch Industries matters. According to one IRS source, Koch Industries is a "Subchapter S" corporation.* Instead of paying corporate taxes on their income, then sending the rest on to shareholders as a dividend on which the shareholders also have to pay individual income tax, Subchapter S corporations let the shareholders avoid the corporate level tax and pay only the individual tax. The result is that there's no difference whatever between a contribution to a campaign by one of the Koch brothers and a contribution by Koch Industries. *Citizens United* didn't even cut down on the number of checks the Koch brothers had to write, because Koch Industries sent them a check that went into their personal accounts, and they wrote checks from those accounts.

According to supporters of campaign finance laws, *Citizens United* opened the checkbooks of big corporations for spending on political campaigns, mostly to support conservatives who do corporations' bidding. The Koch brothers became the poster children for demonizing corporate spending in politics—and the Roberts Court.

---

* The IRS isn't supposed to give the public information about the tax situation of any specific individuals, but a Treasury official blurted the information out after the Koch brothers drew publicity, in what seems to have been an attempt to deflect attention from the IRS.

Citizens United did have something to do with the Koch brothers' contributions to support conservative candidates, but not because it said that corporations were people. Before *Citizens United*, the lawyers for the Koch brothers had to tell them that they might be in legal trouble if they didn't limit their contributions for ads advocating the election of a named candidate; after it, they knew that they faced no legal risks at all. *Citizens United* gave the Koch brothers and other very rich people constitutional permission to spend as much as they wanted on campaigns, as long as they funneled the money through "independent" organizations. That's what's worth thinking about; not whether corporations are people.

DAVID BOSSIE was Inspector Javert to Bill Clinton's Jean Valjean. He pursued fringe anti-Clinton conspiracy theories during the 1990s, eventually winding up on the staff of Republican representative Dan Burton of Indiana. Bossie's aggressive tactics—to give them a mild characterization—helped discredit the Republican investigations, and House Speaker Newt Gingrich pressured Burton to remove Bossie from his staff. In 2008 Bossie headed a conservative organization, Citizens United, which described itself as "dedicated to restoring our government to citizens' control," mostly by producing video documentaries. Some are inspirational invocations of conservative Republican themes—*Ronald Reagan: Rendezvous with Destiny, hosted by Newt and Callista Gingrich*—and others attacks on Democrats—*Hype: The Obama Effect*.

During the 2008 campaign for the Democratic nomination, Citizens United produced a documentary, *Hillary: The Movie*, which the Supreme Court described antiseptically as "an extended criticism of Senator Clinton's character and her fitness for the office of the Presidency." It was an attack video of the sort we have unfortunately become accustomed to, and would have gone unremarked after the nomination fight ended—except that Citizens United used the video not only to challenge Senator Clinton but to challenge the entire federal regime of campaign finance regulation.

Congress adopted the first modern comprehensive set of campaign finance regulations in the 1970s in response to disclosures during the Watergate investigations about how President Nixon's campaign raised money. The Federal Election Campaign Finance Act of 1971 regulated contributions and expenditures. It limited how much anybody could contribute directly to a candidate's campaign and to the candidate's political party. And, to prevent people from evading the limits, the statute limited how much you could give to an organization that coordinated its advertising with the candidate's. It also limited how much candidates could spend and, again to avoid evasion, sharply limited how much individuals could spend to support (or oppose) a clearly identified candidate. The McCain-Feingold Bipartisan Campaign Reform Act of 2002 worked within the same framework but tightened the regulations a bit.

The ABCs of First Amendment campaign finance law are these.

"Money is speech." Not literally, of course, and non-lawyers who take it literally often think that it shows why the law is an ass. "Money is speech" means that the First Amendment has something to say about the constitutionality of regulations of the use of money in connection with speech. That has to be right. Nobody would think that the First Amendment had nothing to say about a state law that prevented newspapers from buying newsprint even though that's "just" regulating money.

More seriously, suppose many of my friends think that Ron Paul would be a terrific president. Of course they could stand on street corners and shout their support for Paul to passersby. They might think that standing on street corners would be pretty ineffective. Better, they might think, to spend their money on publishing a pamphlet explaining why Paul would be a great president. They might go on to realize that they weren't really good at writing such political material, so they use some of their money to hire a professional (call her a "campaign consultant," if you want), who would write a persuasive pamphlet. They might think that they could reach many more people if they used some of their money to buy space in a newspaper or time on television for an advertisement. The government could stop them from publishing the advertisement if it said they couldn't use their money to hire a writer or consultant, or to buy space or time for the ad. We know that the First Amendment means that the government can't punish them for publishing the ad, and so the First Amendment has to say *something* about government regulations of the use of money to support political activities. That's what it means to say that money is speech.

To say that the First Amendment has some bearing on whether money in politics can be regulated isn't to say that all such regulations are unconstitutional, only that the government has to have "pretty good" reasons for regulations that have the potential of limiting political speech addressed to the general public. And, according to the Supreme Court, the government's justifications for restricting campaign spending—a form of speech because money is speech—have to be better than its justifications for restricting contributions, because contributions might lead to corruption.

The second important point focuses on contributions to candidates and candidates' organizations. Sometimes campaign contributions are straightforward bribes. I give you $100,000 and you promise to vote for the bill I favor if you're elected. This is what the Court calls "quid pro quo corruption"—a direct exchange of money for a promise to vote as the donor said if the candidate won the election. I don't have to give the money directly to you, of course. I can give it to your campaign organization or your political party, with the same understanding that you'll pay me back (in policy) if you're elected. Quid pro quo corruption is illegal and hard to prove. Limits on campaign contributions can be aimed at preventing such corruption, although the limits would inevitably prevent contributions that weren't actually bribes: I might simply think that you're the best candidate around, and I might care a lot about getting the best candidates elected.

Large contributions can seem suspicious to voters who see you taking positions that coincide with my personal interests. That suspicion can lead people to lose trust in the government, which in turn makes it hard to get good public policy made or implemented—or at least so people who support restricting contributions think. Limits on contributions to candidates prevent the appearance of corruption as well as quid pro quo corruption. Yet it's not really clear why the government should be allowed to regulate contributions on the ground that some people mistakenly *think* that there's quid pro quo corruption going on. And rattling around in all of this is the most general question of all in constitutional law: How carefully should the Supreme Court review decisions made by elected legislators about contestable questions like these?

The language of corruption pervades campaign finance reform, but most often it's a metonym—a word describing quid pro quos and bribery standing in for some other concern vaguely related to that sort of corruption, ranging from making it easier for large contributors to get a politician's ear to worries about ordinary people getting turned off by a political system in which they don't have much say.

Third, there's the difference between spending by candidates and by "independent" organizations. It's harder to justify limits on spending under the First Amendment, because as we've seen spending money is what people do to get their ideas across, whether the ideas are their own, as with candidates, or the ones they endorse, as with my friends' spending on behalf of Ron Paul. The Supreme Court has been quite suspicious of limits on campaign spending. After the adoption of the Federal Election Campaign Act in 1971, the Court said that candidates who accepted public funding could be required to observe spending limits, which is one of the reasons the post-Watergate system for funding presidential candidates broke down: candidates discovered that they could raise much more than the public financing scheme gave them, and decided that the benefits of high spending exceeded the public relations benefits of taking public financing and spending less money. Now candidates can spend as much as they want if they raise money from people whose contributions are under the limits on contributions to candidates.

Limiting spending by groups other than candidates is much more difficult to justify. We've become familiar with corporate-sponsored "issue advertisements." These ads discuss some general public policy issue—tax rates, oil-drilling policy—from the perspective of the corporation paying for them. Such ads are no different from a First Amendment perspective from ads on the same topics by public interest groups like Campaign for Fiscal Responsibility or Earthwatch. Federal campaign finance law doesn't cover issue ads, and almost certainly couldn't.

Campaign finance law has tried to distinguish between issue ads and political ads by exempting issue ads but covering ads that contained "express advocacy" or "electioneering" about a particular candidate within one or two months of an election. Electioneering ads said: "Vote for [or against] Barbara Mikulski." As we saw in chapter 3, the Supreme Court said that the First Amendment allowed limits on electioneering ads only if the ads used the magic words "Vote for" or close equivalents. The result was the proliferation of electioneering thinly disguised as issue advertising: "Last month Senator Mikulski voted against oil drilling; call her to tell her that you're outraged at her vote." No magic words, but obviously an anti-Mikulski ad to anyone who saw it. Congress expanded the definition of "electioneering" in the McCain-Feingold Act, and the Supreme Court upheld the expanded definition.

Finally, most people don't write checks to a TV station's advertising division. They write their checks to a professional, who then prepares the ad and buys airtime. My friends who supported Ron Paul hired a campaign consultant. Turn the situation around, and we find existing organizations telling people, "Like you, we have no connections to Ron Paul, but like you we agree with his ideas. We're a really effective organization for getting those ideas across, and you ought to give your money to us instead of hiring someone perhaps less talented than we are." These are independent organizations that accept and then spend political contributions.

These organizations come in several flavors, with labels derived from the tax code. "501(c)(4)" organizations are supposed to be civic associations that promote social welfare in a non-partisan way. The League of Women Voters is the exemplary 501(c)(4) organization, with its voter registration drives and voter education programs.*

The other main type of independent campaign organization used to be the "527," political organizations that endorse and support candidates. Political action committees (PACs) are organized as 527s. Political action committees go back to the 1940s. Traditionally, they collected money and passed it on to candidates. The Republican and Democratic Governors Associations are 527s; so are corporate and union political action committees. Their PACs raise money from corporate managers and union members, then spend it advocating the election of favored candidates. Because of concern about corruption, the McCain-Feingold Act limited contributions to PACs, and by PACs to candidates. The standard anti-corruption arguments apply to these contributions: our worries about corruption resulting from a large contribution by Corporation Z's chief executive officer don't go away if the contribution comes from the Corporation Z Political Action Committee. It's probably worth noting that Democratic-leaning 527s have historically spent more than Republican-leaning ones, with Republican-leaning ones gradually closing the gap.

And then there are the "Super PACs." Here the tax code basically

---

* 501(c)(3)s—roughly, traditional charities—can engage in some partisan activities, but only if those activities are a small portion of what they do.

drops out of the picture. Super PACs raise money and spend it on their own. Before *Citizens United*, it wasn't clear whether or not Super PACs were subject to the same limitations on contributions as ordinary PACs. *Citizens United* and a follow-up lower court decision made it clear that people could give unlimited amounts to Super PACs because they were "independent" of candidates and so couldn't corrupt them. Money that used to go to ordinary PACs before McCain-Feingold now goes to Super PACs.

Super PACs have to register with the Federal Election Commission and disclose their contributors. These might lean red or blue, but some—like my Ron Paul supporters—are theoretically independent of parties and candidates. Justifying limits on spending by independent groups is quite difficult. One distraction lies in defining "independent." Some Super PACs are clear vehicles to support specific candidates. Some Super PACs are run by people who had served on the staffs of the candidate the Super PAC supports, and those people know—without needing a memo—what their favored candidate would like them to do. But, in some ways, that's just restating the problem. Suppose the "Friends of Ron Paul" really are independent, but they are political junkies. They see the themes Ron Paul is stressing in his own advertisements, and they read newspaper stories reporting what campaign insiders think a good strategy going forward would be. With no prior connections to Ron Paul's campaign and no coordination whatever, these people will—if they are moderately competent—behave just like the Super PACs. The First Amendment won't let you go after them simply for that.

Election law scholars worry that the shift from PACs to Super PACs makes a big difference, because it tends to substitute spending by independent groups for spending by our political parties, raising the possibility that "outsiders" can disrupt the parties' messaging. Because today's Super PACs really aren't independent, their concern is probably misplaced. The lack of independence, though, undermines the entire rationale for putting independent expenditures under the First Amendment's protection.

Does the First Amendment allow Congress to regulate contributions to and spending by independent organizations at all? The answer depends on whether the justifications for regulation are strong enough. The Court has said that the risk of quid pro quo corruption from contributions to independent groups is small. Candidates can actually appear at Super PAC fund-raisers. At such an event, the offhand "I appreciate your support" might actually mean just that, and not convey an implicit promise to repay the donor. The appearance-of-corruption problem is more serious, but if the group really is independent and doesn't coordinate with the candidate, maybe it's unreasonable for outsiders to think that somewhere deep inside the transaction is some corrupt exchange.

Campaign finance reformers do worry about quid pro quo corruption, but their deeper concerns are elsewhere. They start with a sense that there's just too much money sloshing around during political campaigns, although it's hard to see exactly why that's a problem. Probably the best argument is that campaigns have become so expensive that candidates spend so much time raising money that they can't spend enough time thinking about the policies they're called on to adopt. In response, critics of campaign finance regulations like to point out that Americans collectively spend about the same on political campaigns as we do on potato chips, and that candidates "work the phones" just as they work the train stations and local restaurants seeking support.

Campaign finance reformers also believe that candidates aren't competing on a reasonably even playing field and that spending limits equalize the competition. It's said that candidates who support policies favoring the rich get more money (from the rich, who have more money to give) than those who support policies favoring the poor. And incumbents typically get lots more money than challengers. Yet it's always been hard to explain why there should be an even playing field in political campaigns. No one really thinks that the Socialist Workers

Party's candidate should have the same resources as the Democratic Party's candidate—because, at the least, the money the candidate has to spend should have some rough correspondence to the candidate's support among the public. Why isn't the ability to raise money—for a Democrat in a deeply blue district, for a Republican in a red one—just a measure of that rough correspondence? Indeed, from the outset of the modern law of campaign finance regulation the Supreme Court has said that the regulations can't be justified by an interest in equalizing competition.

When you get to independent organizations, the problems become even harder. Start with my friends who think, really fervently, that Ron Paul has the very best ideas around about how the government should work. The first thing they do is "bundle"—send as much as the law allows them to Ron Paul's campaign directly. But suppose they have money and fervor left over. They want to do more to increase Paul's chances of winning. So they pool the rest of their money and buy advertisements saying that Paul's simply the best candidate. It's really hard to come up with an interpretation of the First Amendment that would allow the government to tell them they can't do that—that is, to impose limits on what they as citizens can spend to tell other people why they think everyone should vote for Ron Paul.

The best you can do is extend the idea of corruption, probably beyond the breaking point, to argue that when people see lots of money being spent by "independent" organizations like Citizens United, they're going to get suspicious that there's something nefarious going on—that somewhere behind the scenes the organization is getting some sort of quid pro quo. The "appearance of corruption" argument gets weaker the more it's extended.

Sometimes the idea of an equal playing field is restated as a problem about distorting public debate. Corporations and rich people flood the airwaves with ads supporting their positions. Campaign finance reformers say that this "drowns out" alternative views. It's never been clear exactly how. It's not as if rich people are shouting so loud that no one can hear the other side—really drowning out the alternatives. The idea must be that people who hear a lot about one position and rather little about another are likely to accept the first, more or less unthinkingly. That might be psychologically accurate, but it's not clear how to reconcile the psychology with First Amendment theories which generally assume that people are capable of thinking clearly about politics.

Drowning out might not be the reformers' real concern. Congress banned corporate and union contributions to politicians because it thought that power acquired in the economic arena shouldn't carry over to the political one. Maintaining the boundary between economics and politics is close to impossible. Conservatives like to use celebrity endorsements as an example: celebrities get their celebrity because they sing songs and act in movies people enjoy. They trade on their celebrity when they endorse political candidates. That's power in the entertainment domain leaching into the political one.

The line between economics and politics is hard to maintain even when we're worried only about money. Suppose I own shares in ExxonMobil. The corporation declares a dividend and sends me a check for $1,000. Nobody thinks I can't deposit the check in my personal account and then write a $1,000 check to a political candidate's campaign. I'm using ExxonMobil's economic power to generate resources I use in politics.

Restrictions on political spending—and on contributions to organizations that spend money on campaigns—have always hung by a thread from the First Amendment. *Citizens United* cut the thread.

What was left was the possibility of using public disclosure of spending as a way of controlling it. ExxonMobil's issue ads on oil drilling might not have anything to do with an active political campaign, or even with some proposal on Congress's plate at the moment. Knowing that ExxonMobil is sponsoring the ad helps viewers evaluate the claims the ad makes. Secrecy about an ad's origins reduces its contribution to public understanding. "Sponsored by ExxonMobil" provides information; "Sponsored by Americans for Energy Independence" doesn't.

That's why the Supreme Court has consistently said that Congress can require people who give money to campaigns or spend money on ads supporting candidates to disclose what they're doing. But sometimes disclosure might lead to real harm. The Court said that contributors to the Socialist Workers Party didn't have to disclose that they had done so, because the SWP showed that people who were "outed" as members faced real threats to their jobs and their safety.

Now BACK to Citizens United. Its challenge had two prongs. One was that Citizens United was a corporation—an ideological one, to be sure, but incorporated like ExxonMobil. Its budget was made up mostly of contributions from individuals, but with some contributions directly from for-profit corporations. Bossie *wanted* Citizens United to have those contributions so that he could bring a test case. As far back as 1986 the Supreme Court had said that ideological groups organized as corporations—the case involved the Massachusetts Citizens for Life— had a constitutional right to spend their money. Citizens United itself was protected by that decision, but Bossie wanted to expand it to cover contributions by for-profit corporations.

Federal statutes going back a hundred years prohibited corporations and unions from making campaign contributions from their treasuries, and modern campaign finance law extended that ban to contributions to independent organizations engaging in what the statutes called "electioneering communications." Bossie believed that the ban on corporate contributions to independent organizations like Citizens United was unconstitutional. He hired James Bopp to structure the case. After the Federal Election Commission decided that *Hillary: The Movie* was indeed an electioneering communication, Bopp went to court. As in *Wisconsin Right to Life*, Bopp made two arguments: the

McCain-Feingold Act didn't apply to a long-form documentary available primarily via video on demand, and if it did apply, the statute was unconstitutional. Citizens United argued that as an independent organization it had a right under the First Amendment to urge voters to vote for or against specific identified candidates—which would at least get rid of the silliness of the "Call Senator X" ads. The lower court disagreed with Bopp, and Citizens United appealed.

Bossie turned to Ted Olson for the Supreme Court case. Olson, who had been George W. Bush's Solicitor General, was a central figure at the intersection of the conservative legal establishment and the elite Supreme Court bar. Olson refocused the case on the question of whether *Hillary: The Movie* fit within the definition of "electioneering communications."

The Court heard oral argument on March 24, 2009. It didn't go well for the government. Malcolm Stewart, a career lawyer in the Solicitor General's Office, ran into trouble pretty early when Justice Alito asked him whether the government's theory would allow it to prohibit corporate contributions to an advocacy organization that sold a book urging people to vote against Senator Clinton. Stewart hemmed and hawed, but in the end answered honestly that the government could do that—even to the point of prohibiting the book's sale by a group organized as a corporation. Justice Alito said, "That's pretty incredible." So much time was consumed with questions about whether the regulations covered books that Stewart basically had no chance to explain why restricting spending by corporations might be justified.

Olson's decision to focus on whether the movie really was an "electioneering communication" turned out to be a strategic mistake, though only temporarily. When the justices voted on the case, Chief Justice Roberts was willing to buy Olson's argument, but no one else did. In the *Wisconsin Right to Life* case, he had Justice Alito on his side for a narrow decision, but with a couple more years of experience on the Court under his belt Justice Alito decided to join the other conservatives in dealing with the underlying constitutional challenge, in an opinion drafted by Anthony Kennedy finding that the First Amendment made it unconstitutional to restrict corporate contributions to finance the movie. The Chief Justice had been willing to use a statutory approach when he had one ally, but he wasn't ready to go it alone, and it looked as if Kennedy's opinion would carry the day.

Eventually it did, but not without some drama within the Court. Justice David Souter drafted a dissent, which excoriated the majority for disregarding the Court's usual procedures by deciding the important First Amendment question that Olson hadn't asked it to decide. Roberts acknowledged that Souter had a point, and perhaps more important worried that publishing Kennedy's opinion would make it look as if the Court was playing fast and loose with the rules, to the apparent advantage of Republican politicians. So he suggested that the case be set for reargument, with the parties asked to spend their time discussing the First Amendment.

On the last day of the Court's term the Court told the parties to come back and try again. Rearguments are rare, and usually they happen when the justices have had some problems working out an opinion that five can agree with. As a fig leaf, today's Court always adds something to the case when it calls for reargument. The reargument order here asked the parties to "address the question" of whether the Court should reconsider prior decisions holding that the extended "appearance of corruption" argument was good enough to justify restrictions on contributions to independent organizations. The new question wasn't a fig leaf this time. The flap over Kennedy's draft meant that the Court had to get the constitutional arguments out into the open. The Court also accelerated the hearing schedule in the case. Instead of waiting until the next term opened in October, it set the case for reargument just after Labor Day. Justice Kennedy used his existing draft as the template for the final opinion, but wrote a new opening: "In this case we are asked to reconsider" its prior decisions. Sure, it was asked to reconsider the decisions, but only because the Court told the parties to ask it to reconsider them. The caution of the Roberts Court's first term was gone.

The reargument went no better for the government than the initial one had. Justice Ginsburg asked Solicitor General Kagan, making her first oral argument, the question about books. She replied, to laughter, that the government's position had changed. Books weren't covered, and corporations could support their publication. Pamphlets were different, though. And then Justice Alito jumped in. What about Netflix, a free DVD, a book with the text of *Hillary: The Movie*? Kagan tried to rescue the point by emphasizing that the government had never gone (and, she thought, would never go) after books and the like. But that shouldn't matter under standard First Amendment theory. As Chief Justice Roberts said, "We don't put our First Amendment rights in the hands of bureaucrats." Kagan did try to explain the reasons for regulating corporate spending, but she had a hard time of it because of the position she was taking. Instead of saying that Congress wanted to equalize spending, which she knew the Court wouldn't accept, she said that Congress wanted to avoid distorting debate. But without some baseline—like rough equality—you can't talk about distortion, so she tried to use the word "distortion" to refer to something else. Chief Justice Roberts was especially critical of Kagan's position. Every time she mentioned distortion, he said that the government had basically abandoned the idea, and Kagan had to agree. In the end the Chief Justice asked specifically about whether the government didn't rely on the distortion rationale, and Kagan replied, "We do not rely at all on . . . anything about the equalization of a speech market. So I know that that's the way that many people understand the distortion rationale. . . , and if that's the way the Court understands it, we do not rely at all on that."

As in so many cases in the modern Supreme Court, the oral arguments really didn't make a difference. At most they confirmed the sense the conservatives had going in that the First Amendment ought to protect Citizens United and that any opinion upholding the regulation would undermine core free speech values. The Court had ordered reargument so that the five justices who already had agreed to Justice Kennedy's opinion could get the opinion issued without violating the Court's proprieties. The liberals had no hope of getting the five votes they needed to uphold the regulation. Justice Kennedy was a bear on the First Amendment, after all, and if they hadn't persuaded him in the first round, there was no way they were going to persuade him only a few months later. He was active in the discussion of the "books" question at the first argument, and his questions at the reargument revealed a deep skepticism about the government's effort to save the statute by insisting that it didn't cover all that many expenditures. The reargument may have shown the liberals that they were going to have to work hard on the definition of "corruption" to have any hope of writing a plausible dissent.

Justice Kennedy wrote the Court's opinion. He spent fifteen pages explaining why the Court couldn't fairly resolve the case by a narrow ruling. All the arguments he made were quite reasonable, but a judge who had wanted the Court to pursue a minimalist or narrow course could pretty easily have resolved some of them differently. I mention this not as a criticism of Justice Kennedy or his colleagues in the majority, but only to point out that they weren't compelled by the law to reach the broad conclusions they did.

Two holdings were at *Citizens United*'s core. The first—that corporations were persons covered by the First Amendment—attracted the public's attention. The second—that avoiding quid pro quo corruption was the only permissible reason for limiting spending by independent organizations—attracted the attention of campaign finance lawyers. The second holding, not the first, accounted for the apparently large increase in contributions to and spending by Super PACs during 2012. According to one source, the top ten Super PACs spent about $477 million in 2012, with conservatives outspending liberals by more than two to one, although, as the election's outcome showed, with little to crow about. Because Super PACs don't have to disclose much very quickly, we don't know yet how much of the money came from corporations (although it's worth noting that ninth on the list was the Service Employees International Union, which I assume didn't take any corporate money at all).

Mitt Romney caught a lot of flak for responding to a heckler's interjection about *Citizens United* by saying, "Corporations are people, my friend." Who has constitutional rights? People do. Decisions going back almost to the beginning of our constitutional system held that corporations could have constitutional rights too. The reason is that the corporations are one of the ways the law allows people to organize themselves to accomplish what they want. It would be silly to say that corporations weren't "persons" but partnerships were, or that unions, typically organized as unincorporated associations, were "persons" but the corporations they bargained with weren't.* Maybe corporations can't have a right to privacy because they are necessarily public. But they have rights against unreasonable searches of their property. It was no innovation for *Citizens United* to say that the corporations that gave it money had a constitutional right to do so. In that sense, they said, corporations were people.

Liberals treated the *Citizens United* decision as profoundly unwise policy. They worried that corporate giants like ExxonMobil would dominate political discourse. Their fears were overblown. *Citizens United* may have transformed campaign finance, but not because it allowed giant corporations to make political contributions. Within a

---

* I've met enough skepticism about the assertion that unions are typically unincorporated associations to confirm the point by examining the first page of the 2011 collective bargaining agreement between Ford Motor Company and the United Auto Workers, which indeed describes the UAW as an unincorporated association.

couple of years of *Citizens United* people began to understand that the problem with campaign finance was not corporations but rich people, the sugar daddies propping up the campaigns of Rick Santorum and Newt Gingrich during the 2012 primary campaign—spending "their own" money, not their corporations'.

Of course there are differences between a contribution from a personal checking account and one from a corporation's treasury. Some of the differences involve the tax laws. I "earn" income when ExxonMobil sends me a dividend check, so I have to pay taxes on it. What are the tax consequences of checks written by corporations? As we saw with the Koch brothers, sometimes there are no differences whatever. The Koch brothers have to pay the same taxes on the money Koch Industries contributes to campaigns that they would pay if Koch Industries were a partnership. That's what being a Subchapter S corporation means. From their point of view, there's no difference between making a contribution from Koch Industries and making it from their personal checking accounts.

That's almost exactly true as well for privately owned corporations with a relatively small number of investors, which are by number far the largest group of potential corporate contributors to campaigns. Take a typical privately held corporation, with three investors as the board of directors. If the investors are interested in making political contributions, they could vote as directors to declare a dividend and use the proceeds to make the contributions. What if they used the corporation's bank account? Their corporation would have to pay taxes on the contribution—or, more technically, it would have to pay taxes on the income it used to make the contribution—because spending on politics is not a deductible business expense. The only difference between a contribution from the corporation and one from the investors' checking accounts is that declaring a dividend takes some legal work that someone's going to have to pay for—and the modest possibility that the three investors

might agree to make a contribution from the corporate treasury but
one or two of them would renege if they had to make the contributions
from their own checking accounts.

I don't think anyone worries much about three-person corporations
making political contributions, although it's reasonably clear that most
corporate spending on politics—both before and after *Citizens United*—
came from such corporations. People worry about ExxonMobil and other
really large publicly held corporations throwing their financial weight
around. Those corporations, though, are quite a bit less free to make
contributions to support candidates than privately held ones. Again, such
spending isn't tax-deductible, which means that those contributions eat
away at the profits the corporations can report.

Deep in the weeds there is one real concern: corporations can deduct
as business expenses contributions made for the general activities of
groups like the Chamber of Commerce, on the theory that those contributions promote the corporation's business interests. In theory, general contributions to such groups can't be used for contributions by
the chamber to political campaigns or Citizens United–like groups,
but observers suspect that there are enough "wink-and-nod" arrange-
ments, in which the corporations pretend that they are giving money
for general operations but confidently expect the money to be used for
political campaigns, to worry about.

More explicit contributions from large public corporations to support a candidate or party are likely to be inhibited by business, not legal,
concerns. Shareholders might not agree with the political positions
taken by the candidates the corporation supports, particularly because
the contributions reduce the dividends they receive. And, of course,
many publicly held corporations sell directly to consumers, who have
been known to organize boycotts and pressure campaigns on companies they think are involved on the wrong side of some political issue.
Target was targeted, so to speak, for a large contribution it made to a
Republican candidate who opposed gay marriage. It's a nice question,

as lawyers put it, whether this sort of threat is enough like the one to the members of the Socialist Workers Party to justify insulating corporate contributions from disclosure. In his separate opinion in *Citizens United* Justice Thomas thought it was, but the eight other justices weren't worried. And whatever the ultimate legal position, boards of directors might well decide that the return on investment in politics isn't worth the hassle.

The 2012 report on business contributions to Super PACs cited earlier makes the point. It lists the twenty-five businesses making the largest contributions to Super PACs. There are a couple of large public corporations on the list—MGM Resorts International (at $300,000) and American Financial Group (at $400,000)—but most of the businesses on the list are privately owned. And the amounts are small compared to the multi-million-dollar contributions made by Sheldon Adelson to Newt Gingrich's campaign and Foster Friess to Rick Santorum's. The largest is $3 million from the privately held Contran Corporation, controlled by leveraged buyout specialist Harold Simmons. Notably, in 2004 Simmons gave $4 million to Swift Boat Vets and POWs for Truth. From his point of view, giving money from Contran's treasury was basically the same as writing a personal check. If you're worried about excessive spending on campaigns or distortions from spending, Simmons shows that it's billionaires you really have to worry about, not corporations (except, again, for political contributions hidden in contributions to the Chamber of Commerce).

Maybe corporations are people, but foreign corporations aren't American people. Picking up on a point Justice Stevens made in his dissent, President Obama criticized *Citizens United* in his 2010 State of the Union address because it "will open the floodgates for special interests—including foreign corporations—to spend without limit in our elections." The argument was simple. The Court's theory was that the First Amendment dealt with messages, not speakers. Justice Kennedy wrote, "The First Amendment protects political speech; and

disclosure permits citizens . . . to react to the speech of corporate entities in a proper way. This transparency enables the electorate to make
informed decisions and give proper weight to different speakers and
messages." People might not take an argument made by a corporation
seriously, but then too they might not take an argument made by a for-
eigner seriously either. The majority acknowledged the force of the point
with a feeble one-paragraph disclaimer that the statute didn't deal only
with "corporations or associations that were created in foreign countries or funded predominantly by foreign shareholders," and "assumed,
arguendo, that the Government has a compelling interest in limiting
foreign influence over our political process." The paragraph has all the
marks of a judge trying to avoid saying what his opinion really implies.

Conservatives got their knickers twisted over how impolite it was
to criticize the Court when some of its members were in the audience,
as if the justices were exalted figures you could bad-mouth anywhere
except in a room where they could hear you. Justice Alito could be seen
saying "Not so" when President Obama mentioned foreign corporations—another indication that Justice Kennedy's paragraph had been
carefully negotiated inside the Court. But President Obama was right
on the day he delivered the speech. As it can, the Court made President
Obama wrong a couple of years later, by upholding a statute prohibiting
foreigners from spending money on U.S. campaigns—although the
Court didn't make any effort to explain away *Citizen United*'s clear
implication that citizens' right to get information was as badly harmed
when they couldn't hear things foreigners said as when U.S. corporations were blocked from speaking by spending money.

Citizens United applies to unions too, and unions spend a lot of
money on politics. They're different from corporations in one important way. Sometimes workers are required by federal law to join unions
as a condition of keeping their jobs. The Supreme Court has held that
the First Amendment requires unions to refund to objecting union
members the portion of their dues that's used for political activities

rather than for activities related more directly to collective bargaining. The theory is that forcing people to "say" something with their money is just as bad under the First Amendment as stopping them from doing so. Unions claim, with some accuracy, that setting up the refund mechanisms is a lot of trouble and fairly expensive in itself.

The government tried to justify the ban on corporate contributions with a similar theory, which it labeled the "shareholder protection" theory. Just as some union members object to political uses of their money, so did some shareholders. Justice Kennedy rejected the shareholder protection theory. Shareholders might object to corporate spending on politics outside the one- or two-month limits built into the statute Citizens United challenged, so the regulation couldn't do much to protect them. And even if shareholders agreed with the spending unanimously, the challenged statute would bar the corporation from spending.

Of course the government had a response. Corporations could set up PACs to accept voluntary contributions from employees and shareholders. Justice Kennedy's riposte: "PACs are burdensome alternatives; they are expensive to administer. . . ." So are union refund mechanisms, but the latter seem to be constitutionally required while corporate PACs are constitutionally inadequate alternatives.

Driving Justice Kennedy's argument was something he quoted from an earlier decision. Shareholders could use "the procedures of corporate democracy." By that he meant that they could try to influence corporate policy in voting for directors. Specialists in corporate law know that it's essentially impossible for shareholders to change corporate policy through ordinary elections. More important, perhaps, the dissenting shareholders could simply sell their shares and avoid supporting speech with which they disagreed.

That looks like a real difference between unions and corporations. The law professor Benjamin Sachs has argued that the difference is an illusion. After all, no one's forcing the dissident union member to work at a union shop. Maybe a worker's alternatives were quite limited when the workforce was 35 percent or 40 percent unionized, but this "union density" is much lower today—around 7 percent in the private sector, though a higher 37 percent in the public sector, with wide geographic variations (2.6 percent in North Carolina, 24 percent in New York). On the shareholder side, many people are shareholders through their 401(k) retirement funds and through mutual funds chosen from a limited menu offered by their employers. Viewing things realistically, shareholders and union members might have roughly the same degree of choice—maybe a lot, maybe a little—about how "their" corporations and unions spend money on political campaigns.

The Court's discussion of the justifications for regulating campaign spending by independent organizations (and, necessarily, contributions to such organizations) was much more important than its treatment of corporations as persons. Justice Kennedy wrote: "Wealthy individuals and unincorporated associations can spend unlimited amounts on independent expenditures." That might have been dictum in *Citizens United*, but Justice Kennedy's logic led directly to a lower court holding that it was unconstitutional to limit contributions by anyone to groups that spent money independent of candidates. The Federal Election Commission recognized the argument's force and decided not to appeal that decision. Super PACs were the result.

Justice Kennedy's analysis proceeded from the assumption that "the First Amendment protects speech and speaker, and the ideas that flow from each." This implied that regulations which limited speech based on who the speaker was—a natural person or a corporation—had to have quite a strong justification. Then Justice Kennedy marched through the possible justifications and found them all inadequate.

Distorting the political process? Couldn't count, mostly because on analysis the anti-distortion argument turned out to be an argument favoring equalization of campaign spending, and the Court's precedents squarely reject equalization as a justification for spending restrictions.

As Justice Kennedy observed, the government, recognizing this, had basically abandoned the anti-distortion argument.

Corruption? The only kind of corruption that could count was quid pro quo corruption, and truly independent spending couldn't be part of a corrupt bargain.

Citizen disillusionment? Won't happen: "The appearance of influence . . . will not cause the electorate to lose faith in our democracy." That looks like a claim about what people actually believe, and maybe Justice Kennedy could have said that the government hadn't presented enough evidence to show that disillusionment would occur. That's not what he did, though. He made an argument sounding in logic to support an apparently empirical claim: "By definition, an independent expenditure . . . is not coordinated with a candidate. The fact that a corporation . . . is willing to spend money to try to persuade voters presupposes that the people have the ultimate influence over elected officials." That presupposition was "inconsistent with any suggestion that the electorate will refuse 'to take part in democratic governance' because of additional political speech made by a corporation or any other speaker." It's hard to know exactly what to make of this. Maybe Justice Kennedy—himself a former lobbyist and political lawyer— looked around his circle of acquaintances and saw no one disillusioned by large independent expenditures. Or perhaps he had some definition of disillusionment in mind that was itself independent of empirical facts, though what that definition might be is obscure.

The breakdown of the barriers between economics and politics? What barriers? "All speakers, including individuals . . . use money amassed from the economic marketplace to fund their speech." Kennedy quoted from an earlier dissent he had written: "Many persons can trace their funds to corporations, . . . in the form of dividends, interest, or salary."

Too much money in politics? No such thing. Under the First Amendment, the more the merrier. Restricting spending "prevents . . .

voices and viewpoints from reaching the public and advising voters on which persons or entities are hostile to their interests." The content of speech matters, not its amount.

Justice Kennedy had a fair amount of mopping up to do, but that's the core of *Citizens United*. The discussion of voter disillusionment aside, it's an entirely reasonable decision. There were reasonable arguments on both sides. In the old days, when people worried about judicial activism, their best argument was that the Supreme Court shouldn't set aside a congressional statute if you could develop reasonable arguments explaining how the statue was consistent with the Constitution. Not any more.

CITIZENS UNITED is on the books. What might come next?

First, better enforcement. *Citizens United* implied that independent Super PACs could accept unlimited contributions because the donations couldn't lead to quid pro quo corruption. David Bossie's Citizens United might have been a right-wing organization, but it really wasn't tied to any specific candidate. The First Amendment as interpreted in *Citizens United* would let you go after Super PACs that really were shams and that really did coordinate with the candidate to evade the contribution limits and so pose a risk of quid pro quo corruption. We haven't yet seen e-mails in which a candidate's campaign staff says to an independent organization, "I'd like you to buy time for an ad that deals with my position on oil drilling, to be shown in the following three markets," though such e-mails might exist. Often, though, we can be pretty sure that the Super PACs aren't really "independent" of the candidate they support. Restore Our Future was a Super PAC supporting Mitt Romney. It was organized and run by longtime Romney political operatives—his 2008 campaign treasurer, for example, and his chief campaign fund-raiser. Our Destiny was a Super PAC supporting Jon Huntsman; it got most of its money from former Governor

Huntsman's father. Despite Romney's lament that he wasn't "allowed to communicate with a Super PAC in any way, shape or form," it's a fantasy to think that these and other "candidate" Super PACs are really independent in the way *Citizens United* assumed.

The problem is that federal campaign finance law puts enforcement of the anti-evasion rules in the hands of the Federal Election Commission, three members of which must be Democrats, three Republicans. We often have gridlock when Congress is closely divided. The FEC is gridlocked by design.

Second, public financing. As a practical matter public financing is a non-starter, because the American public is unwilling to provide tax money to political candidates on the national or even the congressional level in anything like the amounts needed today. Public financing for presidential elections collapsed when candidates decided they could do better by raising money on their own. It "dots the landscape," as Justice Kagan put it, in scattered state and local elections. Even there, the Supreme Court has created a constitutional problem.

The government can't force candidates into a public financing system because money is speech: such a system *requires* that participants refrain from spending more than the system gives them. Suppose you are a serious candidate choosing between public financing and raising money on your own. One thing you'll worry about is that your opponent might stay out of the system and spend more than you are allowed to spend. Public financing systems try to address this by saying, "Here's the base amount we'll provide you. If your opponent stays out of the system and spends more than that, we'll add matching funds so that both of you have the same amount to spend."

Arizona had just such a system. The Court, dividing again along party lines, struck it down. The result was foreshadowed at the oral argument, when Chief Justice Roberts quoted from the state election agency's Web site that the system was designed to level the playing field. But, he said, haven't we made it clear that leveling the playing field—equalization—is not something governments can do?* In his opinion for the Court, the Chief Justice wrote, " 'Leveling the playing field' can sound like a good thing. But in a democracy, campaigning for office is not a game. It is a critically important form of speech." The conservative legal scholar Charles Fried had filed a brief pointing out that you could sensibly distinguish between leveling down—preventing the candidate with more resources from spending them—and leveling up, giving the candidate with fewer resources more. Leveling down prevents speech; leveling up encourages it. Or, as Justice Kagan put it in the most important opinion in her first year, the system "subsidizes and so produces *more* political speech" (italics in the original).

The Chief Justice didn't discuss the "leveling up" idea directly, because he argued that giving more money to the candidate with fewer resources actually did limit what the better-funded candidate would spend. The reason? Imagine that you're the richer candidate, and you have to decide whether to spend money on an advertisement knowing that your opponent will get a supplement to the base amount to match your spending. You might not buy the airtime for the ad because . . . Well, apparently because you're worried that your opponent might actually be able to respond to it with the additional money he'll get from the public financing system. According to the Court, this was a "burden" on your spending choices.

It's hard to know what to make of this. As Justice Kagan put it, "the very notion that additional speech constitutes a 'burden' is odd and unsettling." She treated the Chief Justice like a first-year law student who hadn't yet quite figured out how to make good legal arguments. His "world" had "gone topsy-turvy" in treating more speech as "a First Amendment injury." The case, she wrote, "may merit less attention than any challenge to a speech subsidy ever seen in this Court." Those

---

* In a misguided effort to save the statute, the agency scrubbed its Web site after the oral argument to remove the reference to leveling the playing field.

challenging the public financing system were "making a novel argument: that Arizona violated *their* First Amendment rights by disbursing funds to *other* speakers even though they could have received . . . the same financial assistance." She concluded: "Some people might call that *chutzpah*" (italics in the original).

Justice Kagan's rhetoric clearly stung the Chief Justice. She wrote: "We have never, not once, understood a viewpoint-neutral subsidy given to one speaker to constitute a First Amendment burden on another." Attempting to echo her, the Chief Justice responded: "None of those cases—not one—involved a subsidy given in direct response to the political speech of another, to allow the recipient to counter that speech." Justice Kagan was restrained enough to keep from responding, "That's just like saying that that other case is different because the car that hit the pedestrian there was blue, but the car in this case is green"—but she could have.

Chief Justice Roberts's opinion underplayed the strongest argument against Arizona's system. Arizona matched spending by independent groups supporting a privately financed candidate as well as the candidate's own spending above the limit. After *Citizens United* independent groups could spend whatever they wanted, with whatever messages they wanted. A privately financed candidate might really be overmatched under this system. She spends a little over the cap to get her distinctive message across, independent groups flood the airways with their own versions of a similar but not always identical message, and her opponent gets a subsidy adding to the tiny amount she spent over the cap the entire amount the independent groups spent to use for his distinctive message, with complete control over the message. That really might tilt the playing field in favor of the publicly financed candidate.

The Chief Justice's performance didn't burnish his reputation as a smart guy. But, of course, opinion quality matters less than the number of justices who join the opinion. Chief Justice Roberts got five to concur, and that was enough.

Third, maybe we'll amend the Constitution. The immediate political reaction by *Citizens United*'s critics was simple. If the Constitution as interpreted by the Supreme Court prohibits Congress from regulating corporate political spending, change the Constitution by amending it.

Writing a constitutional amendment to do the job isn't easy. "Move to Amend," which appears to be the major group lobbying for a constitutional amendment, proposes a "motion" that "money is not speech, and that human beings, not corporations, are persons entitled to constitutional rights." It's not clear that this "motion" is supposed to set out the terms of a constitutional amendment; it might be aimed at pushing members of Congress to write one. As written, the motion has the wrong target—corporations rather than rich people—and deals with too many constitutional rights, some of which corporations actually ought to have. A more precisely formulated proposal keeps the focus tight and the scope restricted: "Nothing in this Constitution shall prohibit Congress and the States from imposing content-neutral regulations and restrictions on the expenditure of funds for political activity by any corporation. . . ."

A proposal sponsored by nine Senate Democrats states: "Congress shall have power to regulate the raising and spending of money" in elections, including contribution and spending limits. Congress already has this power; the difficulty is that the First Amendment limits its power, and the proposal doesn't address the First Amendment. Independent senator Bernie Sanders of Vermont's proposal is a bit better from a technical point of view. Like the "motion to amend," it would limit constitutional rights to "natural persons," excluding corporations, and would directly prohibit corporations "from making contributions or expenditures in any election." It would deal with the "rich people" problem by authorizing legislatures to regulate and limit "all election contributions and expenditures," and it states that all regulations legislatures adopt, whether about campaign finance or anything else, would have to respect the freedom of the press. This means that a rich person who wants to influence elections would have to buy newspapers or television stations. Rupert Murdoch and Arianna Huffington have figured that out already, and I suspect that others would get on the bandwagon if Sanders's amendment were adopted.

But if writing an effective constitutional amendment is hard, getting it adopted is almost impossible. Two thirds of both the House and the Senate must approve the amendment and submit it to the states, where three quarters have to ratify it. Partisan division over campaign finance regulation makes that impossible, at least for the foreseeable future. There's a second path: calling a constitutional convention to propose amendments, which, again, three quarters of the states have to approve. That path has gotten some publicity recently. Yet liberals and conservatives unite in opposing a constitutional convention, because both sides fear that the other would dominate such a convention. For myself, that uncertainty is a feature, not a bug. The political activists who shape our politics, though, aren't about to get on board with convention proposals.

Were any of these amendments to be adopted, a hostile Court could "construe" it to do nothing to overturn *Citizens United*. Still the political forces impelling it would perhaps lead even today's Court to construe it as its drafters plainly intend. Or, more plausibly, were it adopted, the political terrain would have shifted pretty dramatically, and a quite different Court would then be in place. Indeed, the political energy that pushes amendment proposals forward might be important even if the proposals fail. With the fear of a convention hanging over their heads, for example, politicians might get creative about working around *Citizens United*.

On a less grand level than constitutional amendment, but perhaps more effective, is corporate law. Early in the modern history of campaign finance regulation, Victor Brudney spotted its weak point about corporations and offered a creative solution. Brudney moved from private practice in New York to Harvard Law School, where he taught corporation law. He had been a Supreme Court law clerk in the late

1940s, and retained an interest in constitutional law. In 1981 he wrote an article in the *Yale Law Journal* proposing that states change their law governing corporations to deal with corporate political spending. They should require that shareholders approve that spending—in each specific case, and by unanimous vote, according to the logic of Brudney's argument. The article had a seriocomic tone: comic because its proposal seemed so far-fetched and unnecessary, serious because Brudney had complete command of corporation law.

Citizens United revived interest among scholars in Brudney-like proposals. Details remained to be worked out: should the shareholder authorization be required each cycle or for each item of spending? Should there be a supermajority requirement? And, on the constitutional level, would building a provision specifically about speech into corporate law violate the First Amendment? Could newspapers and similar media corporations be exempted from the requirement without creating an unconstitutional form of discrimination among speakers? Newspapers are important vehicles for public discussion of politics—though perhaps less so these days with the rise of social media—and they are sometimes vehicles rich people use to promote their own interests. How would the Court interpret the First Amendment if faced with a statute building on Brudney's ideas? We'll probably never know because these proposals, which might actually be effective if implemented, are academic in a pejorative sense. There might be nothing really wrong with them, but they have no political traction at all.

Finally, there's the possibility of changing the Court rather than the Constitution. The dissents in *Citizens United* and *Arizona Free Enterprise Fund* laid out the path, with their implicit endorsement of some sort of equalization rationale for campaign finance regulation. What a doctrine geared to equalization would look like is unclear because the Court has set itself firmly against equalization ideas starting in 1976. Legislators and litigators have worked within that framework ever since, and so no one has tried to work out an equalization doctrine. The blank slate is something of an advantage, but only if justices are willing to go back to the beginning. The four dissenters might be. They struggled to fit their arguments within existing constitutional doctrine, offering metaphorical definitions of the anti-corruption interest that doctrine tolerated, but you can predict the sighs of relief they'd emit if they were able to shape their opinions around the idea of equalization.

One of our leading scholars of election law, Rick Hasen of the University of California–Irvine Law School, cautions against thinking that we can solve all the problems of our dysfunctional national political system by getting campaign finance law right. The sources of gridlock and hyperpartisanship lie much deeper than campaign finance rules. Still, reform has to start somewhere, and maybe getting people riled up enough about money's role in politics will make us more concerned about civics generally. We might then turn the energy let loose by the effort to reform campaign finance to go after things like the filibuster, partisan incivility, and politicians who worry more about getting elected than about doing the public's business. If one new Democratic appointee replaced one of the Court's Republican appointees, we might find Justice Kagan leading the new majority in that direction.

CAMPAIGN FINANCE regulations present genuinely difficult problems under First Amendment doctrine. *Citizens United* was almost entirely a doctrinal decision. Conservatives sometimes say that they are activists only in cases like *Heller*, the gun control case, when the Constitution as originally understood addressed a specific issue. Original understanding played only a passing role in *Citizens United*, though. There was a sideshow about what the framers would have thought about corporate contributions to political campaigns. And Justice Kennedy spent a long paragraph invoking the framers to show that they must have understood that the First Amendment prevented the government from "suppress[ing] the political speech by media corporations . . . the most important means of mass communications in modern times." As we saw in chapter 4, you can tug and haul originalism to make it do almost anything. The majority in *Citizens United* barely tried.

The partisan implications of campaign finance regulations are quite unclear. They probably favor congressional incumbents against challengers, though even that's not entirely clear. In presidential campaigns the regulations are probably a wash.* Yet partisans actually divide quite sharply over campaign finance regulations. Republicans don't like them, Democrats do. For all their attention to the ins and outs of First Amendment doctrine, in *Citizens United* all the justices voted as Republicans and Democrats.

Supporters of campaign finance regulations need to get from four to five. Doing that requires a change in the Court—and therefore depends on who gets to appoint the next justices to the Supreme Court. Appoint someone who agrees with today's dissenters, and the Court's intellectual balance might shift. John Roberts would still occupy the center chair, but the intellectual leader of the Court would be someone else. As I suggested at the start of this book, the prime candidate is Justice Kagan, and we might start talking about the "Kagan Court" instead of the "Roberts Court."

---

* Super PACs played a big role in the Republican primaries in 2012, perhaps giving the impression that *Citizens United* had a Republican "tilt." Super PAC spending on the Republican side wasn't matched by Super PAC spending on the Democratic side through mid–2012 because Democrats knew who their nominee was going to be.

EPILOGUE

Elections Matter

Every four years activists on the left and right try to get people excited over the possibility that the other side might get a chance to nominate a Supreme Court justice or two. The strategy is to try to scare people with the "one vote away" bogeyman. For Democrats, it's that the Court is just one vote away from overturning *Roe v. Wade*. For Republicans, the case that might be overruled is *Heller*. No one involved in presidential campaigns thinks that the "one vote away" strategy is worth a dime of advertising money. It doesn't change enough votes: few people who would have voted for Mitt Romney would vote for Barack Obama instead simply because they thought that Romney would nominate someone who would vote to overrule *Roe v. Wade*. But for politicians, turning out the base matters, and the "one vote away" strategy might have some—probably modest—effects on turnout. Presidential campaigns leave that argument to interest groups.

The Supreme Court played its usual role far in the background of the 2008 presidential campaign. With President Obama's reelection in 2012 the issue of potential appointments moved forward a bit. No one was sure that the president would even have a chance to nominate someone to the Court. There's some modest evidence that justices time their retirements with politics in mind: Republicans try to leave when there's a Republican president, for example. The court's oldest member is Ruth Bader Ginsburg, appointed by Democrat Bill Clinton. She has said that she would like to serve as long as Louis Brandeis—just shy of twenty-four years. That would take her to 2017, too late for President Obama to replace her. She looks incredibly frail, but that's been true for at least a decade, and her health is as good as you can expect for someone in her late seventies, who has overcome cancer twice. Like her colleagues, she's acutely aware that Justice O'Connor hasn't been happy in retirement, largely because her husband's health declined more rapidly than she had expected. Justice Ginsburg lost her spouse in 2010, and the parallel with Justice O'Connor might well occur to her. In any event, Justice Ginsburg's retirement wouldn't dramatically change the Court's ideological makeup, although replacing an oldish liberal with a younger one will give the liberals more time to gain a majority.

Replacing Justices Scalia or Kennedy, both of whom are in their mid-seventies, would of course make a difference. Justice Scalia has said that he certainly wouldn't like to leave and find himself replaced by someone dedicated to undoing his life's work. Justice Kennedy appears to revel in being the swing vote on the Court. President Obama really might not have a chance to make another appointment.

Still, age, illness, and chance can produce unexpected outcomes, so it might be worth thinking about President Obama's nomination strategy. Predictions about who a president will nominate to the Supreme Court are rarely as easy as the Sotomayor prediction. Politics and structures shape the pool of potential nominees, but who gets plucked from that pool results from the political context in which the president is operating when the opportunity to nominate arises. Politics and structures suggest pretty strongly that the next nominee will be a Protestant whose professional career was not on the east coast. Religion and region don't matter much any more, but the imbalances have become striking enough that a prudent president would take them into account next time.

Beyond that, President Obama would probably continue the Democratic demographic strategy. His judicial nominations during his first term give him a good pool of his "own people" to nominate. Right now there are three demographic constituencies that matter for party building.

Asian Americans are at the top of the list, in a position to add a first Supreme Court justice to the list of their group's accomplishments. Denny Chin, a federal court of appeals judge, leaps off the page. But Judge Chin is from New York, which at this point probably disqualifies him. A late arrival is Jacqueline Nguyen, appointed by President Obama first to a federal trial court in 2009 and then three years later to the court of appeals in California. She has the kind of compelling personal story we have become accustomed to: born in Vietnam, fleeing with her family in 1975, living in a refugee camp in the United States until the family settled in California. As a graduate of UCLA Law School, Judge Nguyen would break the Ivy lock on law school credentialing for the Supreme Court, and her experience as a prosecutor and state and federal trial judge fits her into the Sotomayor mold.

Liberal African Americans are bothered by the fact that Clarence Thomas is *the* African American on the Supreme Court. They would like to see a different voice, more representative of their views, from an African American Supreme Court justice. President Obama nominated Paul Watford to the Ninth Circuit in 2011. Watford graduated from UCLA Law School and clerked for the conservative Judge Alex Kozinski and the liberal Justice Ruth Bader Ginsburg. He was an appellate litigator in private practice for a decade before his nomination. Watford's credentials are nearly perfect, and his nomination, like Nguyen's, would break the Ivy League monopoly on justices' legal education. The Senate confirmed Watford by a vote of 61 to 34. The only opposition came from Republicans, who followed Senator Charles Grassley's lead in criticizing Watford for the work he had done as a volunteer lawyer in cases challenging as unconstitutional SB 1070, Arizona's law dealing with unlawful aliens, and challenging the method Kentucky used to administer lethal injections in carrying out the death penalty.

Another possibility is California Attorney General Kamala Harris, with an Asian-American mother and an African-American father. Her political role might make confirmation rocky, and she might have higher aspirations in politics anyway. Finally, gays provide important financial support for Democratic candidates. President Obama made some gestures in their directions with judicial nominations in his first term. Yet, one nominee for the federal trial court was confirmed by a strict party-line vote of 48–44, and a gay nominee for the specialized federal appeals court that deals with intellectual property issues withdrew from consideration after a long period in which the Senate did not take up the nomination. Nominating an out gay person to the Supreme Court would surely provoke an even larger political fight. There is an obvious candidate: Paul Smith, one of the most distinguished members of the specialized Supreme Court bar (as John Roberts was) and a former law clerk for Justice Lewis F. Powell.* Smith has also been active in gay rights organizations, serving as co-chair of the Lambda Legal Defense Fund. Smith might well have pretty strong support even from the small number of mainstream Republicans inside the Beltway, but his nomination would be like waving a red flag to social conservatives, and he's near the top end of the age qualification for a Supreme Court nominee. Even a failed Smith nomination might be worth it in party-building terms. But President Obama may think that the politics surrounding

---

* After his retirement, Powell said that he had never known a gay person.

the nomination of an out gay person would still be too contentious to be worth risking.

THE ROBERTS Court—or the Kagan Court—will be with us for several decades. We can't foresee all the issues it will deal with. Obamacare came out of nowhere. Maybe there will be blockbuster cases about human cloning or the use of drones in domestic law enforcement. The justices will deal with these cases using their judicial philosophies, as shaped by the political environment that led presidents to appoint them to the Court.

The dramatic three days at the end of June 2013, in which the Court decided important cases involving voting rights, affirmative action, and gay rights, were no exception.

Monday, June 24: In a surprisingly narrow decision, Justice Anthony Kennedy wrote an opinion sending a case involving affirmative action at the University of Texas back to a lower court, saying that the court should reconsider its decision and apply a more skeptical standard for evaluating affirmative action. Only Justice Ginsburg dissented.

Tuesday, June 25: Writing for a five-Justice majority that included Justice Kennedy, Chief Justice Roberts held unconstitutional a key provision of the Voting Rights Act, first adopted in 1965 and reaffirmed by Congress in 2006. The provision required some states to submit changes in their election laws to the Department of Justice for approval before the changes take effect, in the interest of avoiding racial discrimination. By singling out a handful of states, the Chief Justice wrote, the provision violated a structural principle that all states are equally sovereign, without sufficient contemporary justification.

Confirming the Court's generally pro-business leanings, Justice Alito delivered an opinion in another case the same day, upholding a developer's claim that its property might have been taken when a city said that it would give the developer a permit only if it paid to mitigate environmental problems elsewhere. The decision was again five-to-four along the expected conservative-liberal lines.

Wednesday, June 26: Justice Kennedy wrote an opinion holding unconstitutional a provision of the Defense of Marriage Act (DOMA), adopted in 1996, that denied federal benefits (and burdens) to marriages of gay and lesbian couples in states that recognize gay marriage. The other conservatives dissented. The Court ducked the central issue of whether the Constitution requires that states recognize gay marriages by finding technical flaws in a case presenting that issue. Chief Justice Roberts wrote for an odd coalition, joined by Justices Scalia, Ginsburg, Breyer, and Kagan. Justice Kennedy wrote the dissent on behalf of himself and Justices Thomas, Alito, and Sotomayor.

What can we make of these decisions? In the DOMA case Justice Scalia's dissent excoriated the majority for a "jaw-dropping . . . assertion of judicial supremacy over the people's Representatives in Congress and the Executive. It envisions a Supreme Court standing (or rather enthroned) at the apex of government . . . always and everywhere 'primary' in its role." That vision, for Justice Scalia, "aggrandizes" the Court's power and "diminish[es]" "the power of our people to govern themselves." He ended, "We might have let the People decide." Conservatives *and* liberals agreed with Justice Scalia about that. They just disagreed about which decisions reduced the people's power of self-government: for conservatives DOMA, for liberals the Voting Rights Act.

Evaluations issued over the next few days summarizing the term that had just ended understandably focused on the decisions issued in the term's final week. For commentators, the 2011–12 term was "the year of Obamacare," with Chief Justice Roberts playing the key—and perhaps statesmanlike—role in upholding the Affordable Care Act. The 2012-13 term was different somehow. Maybe it showed that the Court really was Anthony Kennedy's Court. Maybe it showed how the Chief Justice was a canny legal strategist, willing to bide his time until he could build a majority for his quite conservative positions. Just as the sharply divided Voting Rights decision had been foreshadowed by the NAMUDNO case (Chapter One), so the Texas affirmative action case might foreshadow a decision down the line finding affirmative action always unconstitutional.

Of course there's something to both of those takes on the 2012–13 term. But they miss trends that emerge only over a longer period. Monday and Tuesday were days vindicating the constitutional vision expressed in "The Constitution in 2000" (Chapter Two), developed in the Reagan Department of Justice and nurtured in the Federalist Society network in which the Chief Justice and Justices Scalia, Thomas, and Alito participated. Perhaps we should treat that pamphlet as the playbook for the Roberts Court, at least as long as Justice Kennedy is willing to go along.

Wednesday showed that sometimes he wouldn't, demonstrating how a justice's deviations from the core "conservative" or "liberal" line can make a real difference in important cases (Preface). As I noted earlier, gay rights is one of Justice Kennedy's signature issues. "The Constitution in 2000" was hostile to the idea that the Constitution protected gay rights, but that was mostly derived from its constitutional theory about the right to choose in connection with abortion. Justice Kennedy appears to have accepted the central holding of *Roe v. Wade*, though his opinion in the Partial Birth Abortion Act case (Chapter Three) shows that he's more grudging than his liberal colleagues in his understanding of the scope of the right to choose.

Chief Justice Roberts can be a canny legal strategist as long as Justice Kennedy is on the Court. But, of course, that's not forever—or even, probably, for a substantial portion of the rest of the Chief Justice's service. How might a conservative strategist calculate things knowing that the Court's composition might change? Certainly, hold off disasters like a finding that states have to recognize gay marriages. Maybe, plant seeds for future development. Maybe a Republican president will appoint Justice Kennedy's successor, and the seeds will grow into a forest of strongly conservative decisions. But maybe not, in which case the strategist will have wasted a chance to get something done. In which case his strategy should be: Take the money and run; get what you can while you have a majority.

All these uncertainties make it really hard, and probably foolish, to think like a strategist planning for the long term. The best course, and the one the Justices all follow, is to do your best to get five votes for the position you think most compatible with your overall vision of the Constitution.

Specific "postdictions" are a fool's game, but general ones based on the structures I have described in this book are not. The Court will remain balanced between politics and law, between being a Roberts Court and being a Kagan Court, until new appointees join the Court's family and reshape its dynamics.

NOTES

PREFACE

xi   Lithwick on Roberts and Kagan: Dahlia Lithwick, "Roberts v. Kagan: Will there be friction on the court?" http://www.newsweek.com/2010/07/30/roberts-v-kagan .print.html. The obscure case is *Robertson v. United States ex rel. Watson*, 130 S. Ct. 2184 (2010).

xiv   entitled to "survivors' benefits": *Astrue v. Capato*, 132 S. Ct. 2021 (2012).

xv   As one liberal blogger: Harold Meyerson, "The Court Will Rule—and Then?" available at http://prospect.org/article/court-will-rule–and-then (Nov. 14, 2011).

xviii   Lardner quotation: For the attribution, see http://www.barrypopik.com/ index.php/new_york_city/entry/the_race_is_not_always_to_the_swift_no_ the_battle_to_the_strong_but_thats_t/.

CHAPTER 1

2   "The outcome of this case": Randy Barnett, "Don't Put Your Faith in the Courts," The Volokh Conspiracy, http://www.volokh.com/2012/07/07/ randy-barnett-on-obamacare-don't-put-your-faith-in-the-courts.

2   proud "intellectual godfather": Kate Zernike, "Proposed Amendment Would Enable States to Repeal Federal Law," *New York Times*, Dec. 19, 2010, p. 14.

2   Development of argument against the Affordable Care Act: I rely here on James B. Stewart, "How Broccoli Landed on Supreme Court Menu," *New York Times*, June 13, 2012, and Andrew Koppleman, "Origins of a health care lie," *Salon*, May 31, 2012, available at http://www.salon.com/2012/05/31/ origins_of_a_healthcare_lie/.

7   growing marijuana at home: *Gonzales v. Raich*, 545 U.S. 1 (2005).

8   a well-regarded book: Randy E. Barnett, *Restoring the Lost Constitution: The Presumption of Liberty* (Princeton: Princeton University Press, 2004), 77.

11   off the wall: Jack M. Balkin, "From Off the Wall to On the Wall: How the Mandate Challenge Went Mainstream," *The Atlantic*, June 4, 2012,

available at http://www.theatlantic.com/politics/archive/2012/06/from-off-the-wall-to-on-the-wall-how-the-mandate-challenge-went-mainstream/258040/.

12 Randy Barnett's argument: See Andrew Koppleman, "Obamacare hater No. 1," *Salon*, June 20, 2012, available at http://www.salon.com/2012/06/20/the_brain_behind_the_healthcare_fight/.

13 "A train wreck": Toobin's comment was made on CNN; video available at http://www.youtube.com/watch?v=OYR543cpCSE.

14 Goldstein assessment: Tom Goldstein, "A tale of two great arguments," SCOTUSblog, March 27, 2012, available at http://www.youtube.com/watch?v=OYR543cpCSE.

14 What the oral arguments chiefly showed: The transcripts are available at http://www.supremecourt.gov/oral_arguments/argument_transcripts/11-398-Monday.pdf; http://www.supremecourt.gov/oral_arguments/argument_transcripts/11-398-Tuesday.pdf; http://www.supremecourt.gov/oral_arguments/argument_transcripts/11-393.pdf; and http://www.supremecourt.gov/oral_arguments/argument_transcripts/11-400.pdf.

15 started to prepare the battlefield: Obama is quoted in Kathleen Parker, "John Roberts on Trial," *The Washington Post*, May 22, 2012, A21. Leahy is quoted in an editorial, "Targeting John Roberts," *Wall Street Journal*, May 21, 2012, 16. Randy Barnett, "More on the Left's Threat to Delegitimate the Supreme Court If It Invalidates the ACA," May 22, 2012, available at http://www.volokh.com/2012/05/22/more-on-the-lefts-threat-to-delegitimate-the-supreme-court-if-it-invalidates-the-aca/, compiles other reactions among conservatives.

16 "In my first term": A video of his comments is at "President Obama at the 2012 White House Correspondents Dinner, http://videocafe.crooksandliars.com/heather/president-obama-2012-white-house-correspon.

20 Crawford reports on leaks: Jan Crawford, "Roberts switched views to uphold health care law," July 1, 2012, available at http://www.cbsnews.com/2102-3460_162-57464549.html?contributor=46834; Jan Crawford, "Discord at Supreme Court is deep, and personal," July 8, 2012, available at http://www.cbsnews.com/2102-3460_162-57468202.html?tag=contentMain;contentBody.

23 it "looked quite wrong": The case is described and sources cited in Mark Tushnet, *A Court Divided: The Rehnquist Court and the Future of Constitutional Law* (New York: W. W. Norton, 2005), 186–87.

23 Roberts on the "decisional process": Maura Reynolds, "Judge Roberts' View from the Bench," *Los Angeles Times*, Aug. 10, 2005, available at http://articles.latimes.com/2005/aug/10/nation/na-roberts10. I found the reference in Timothy P. O'Neill, "Harlan on My Mind: Chief Justice Roberts and the Affordable Care Act," available at http://ssrn.com/abstract=2127942.

25   Juvenile mandatory life without parole cases: *Miller v. Alabama*, 132 S. Ct. 2455 (2012). Martin Lederman suggested to me the importance of *Miller* to thinking about what happened in the ACA cases.

26   Ponnuru comment: Quoted from an audiotape reported in Orin Kerr, "More on the Supreme Court leak," The Volokh Conspiracy, July 3, 2012, available at http://www.volokh.com/2012/07/03/more-on-the-supreme-court-leak/.

26   Campos report on drafting process: Paul Campos, "Roberts wrote both Obamacare opinions," July 3, 2012, available at http://www.salon.com/2012/07/03/roberts_wrote_both_obamacare_opinions/.

29   Alicea comment: Joel Alicea, "Chief Justice Roberts and the Changing Conservative Legal Movement," Public Discourse: Ethics, Law and the Common Good blog, available at http://thepublicdiscourse.com/2012/07/5889?printer friendly=true. In the paragraphs that follow, quotations from other sources are taken from Alicea.

32   *The Constitution in the Year 2000*: Office of Legal Policy, *Report to the Attorney General: The Constitution in the Year 2000: Choices Ahead in Constitutional Interpretation* (Washington, DC, 1988). The discussion of the commerce and spending powers occurs at pp. 137–39.

34   *NAMUDNO* case: *Northwest Austin Municipal Utility District No. One v. Holder*, 557 U.S. 193 (2009).

37   the "awful" performance of Republican presidents: Marc A. Thiessen, "Why Are Republicans So Awful at Picking Supreme Court Justices?" *The Washington Post*, July 2, 2012, available at http://articles.washingtonpost.com/2012-07-02/opinions/35487845_1_conservatives-confirmation-hearings-supreme-court-justices.

41   Neal Katyal: "A Pyrrhic Victory," *New York Times*, June 28, 2012, available at http://www.nytimes.com/2012/06/29/opinion/in-health-care-ruling-a-pyrrhic-victory.html.

41   a "silver lining": Jonathan Adler and Nathaniel Stewart, "Positive Steps, Silver Linings," *National Review Online*, July 12, 20012, available at http://www.nationalreview.com/articles/309154/positive-steps-silver-linings-jonathan-h-adler.

41   David Cole lamented: "Why Can't We Celebrate When the Court Gets It Right?" NYRBlog, July 10, 2012, available at http://www.nybooks.com/blogs/nyrblog/2012/jul/10/why-cant-we-celebrate-supreme-court-victory/.

CHAPTER 2

44   Background on Bush nominations: My account draws heavily on Jan Crawford Greenburg, *Supreme Conflict: The Inside Story of the Struggle for Control of the United States Supreme Court* (New York: Penguin Press, 2007).

52   "We cannot ask a man": Quoted in Paul A. Freund, "Appointment of

Justices: Some Historical Perspectives," *Harvard Law Review* 101 (1988), 1146, 1162 (quoting George S. Boutwell, "Reminiscences of Sixty Years in Public Affairs," 29 [1902]). The underlying source is a generally weak one, so I think the statement should probably be treated as one said to have been made by Lincoln rather than attributed to him.

54   "that clown Rehnchburg": Nixon's statement is found on the so-called Watergate tapes, and has been widely cited. See, e.g., Peter Irons, *Brennan vs. Rehnquist: The Battle for the Constitution* (New York: Alfred A. Knopf, 1994), 46.

56   Reagan Justice Department pamphlet: Office of Legal Policy, *Report to the Attorney General: The Constitution in the Year 2000: Choices Ahead in Constitutional Interpretation* (Washington, DC, 1988).

59   Studies on executive branch experience: Michael Dorf, "Does Federal Executive Branch Experience Explain Why Some Republican Supreme Court Justices 'Evolve' and Others Don't?" *Harvard Law & Policy Review* 1 (2007), 458; Rob Robinson, "Executive Branch Experience, Supreme Court Nominees, and Increased Deference to the President in Separation of Powers Cases: Signaling or Socialization?" Paper prepared for the Midwest Political Science Association, Chicago, April 22–25, 2010, available at http://papers.ssrn.com/sol3/papers .cfm?abstract_id=1610257.

60   "Peekaboo" decision: *Free Enterprise Fund v. PCAOB*, 130 S. Ct. 3138 (2010).

61   Compliance Week story: http://www.complianceweek.com/supreme-courts-pcaob-decision-much-ado-about-little/article/189703/.

61   The Powell memorandum and its effects: The best description of the creation of, and difficulties associated with, conservative public interest law firms is Steven Teles, *The Rise of the Conservative Legal Movement: The Battle for the Control of the Law* (Princeton: Princeton University Press, 2008).

62   Lazarus published a pathbreaking article: Richard Lazarus, "Advocacy Matters Before and Within the Supreme Court: Transforming the Court by Transforming the Bar," *Georgetown Law Journal* 96 (2008), 1487.

63   Roberts nomination: "President Announces Judge John Roberts as Supreme Court Nominee," http://georgewbush-whitehouse.archives.gov/news/ releases/2005/07/20050719-7.html.

68   "What makes this harder is": O'Connor quoted in Jeffrey Toobin, *The Oath: The Obama White House and the Supreme Court* (New York: Doubleday, 2012), 209.

70   Study on candor during hearings: Dion Farganis and Justin Wedeking, " 'No Hints, No Forecasts, No Previews': An Empirical Analysis of Supreme Court Nominee Candor from Harlan to Kagan," *Law and Society Review*, vol. 45, no. 3 (2011), 525–58.

70   Academic literature on the "umpire" metaphor: A recent work that cites

much of the earlier literature is William Blake, "Umpires as Legal Realists," *PS* (April 2011), 271–76.

72 "There is absolutely no doubt in my mind": Obama speech at http://obama-speeches.com/031-Confirmation-of-Judge-John-Roberts-Obama-Speech.htm.

73 predictions: "The 75 Most Influential People of the 21st Century," *Esquire* magazine (October 2008), available at http://www.esquire.com/features/75-most-influential/obama-supreme-court-pick–1008. For a more qualified pre-election prediction, listing Sotomayor along with Elena Kagan, Seth Waxman, and Diane Wood, see Terry Carter and Stephanie Francis Ward, "The Lawyers Who May Run America," *ABA Journal* (November 2008), available at http://www.abajournal.com/magazine/article/the_lawyers_who_may_run_america_obama.

74 Republican delays of Sotomayor's promotion to court of appeals: Neil A. Lewis, "G.O.P., Its Eyes on High Court, Blocks a Judge," *New York Times*, June 13, 1998, A1.

75 Nixon's failed effort to nominate: A good discussion is Kevin J. McMahon, *Nixon's Court: His Challenge to Judicial Liberalism and Its Political Consequences* (Chicago: University of Chicago Press, 2011).

76 Academic study on Sotomayor's performance: Guy-Uriel Charles, Daniel L. Chen, and Mitu Gulati, " 'Not That Smart': Sonia Sotomayor and the Construction of Merit," http://papers.ssrn.com/sol3/papers.cfm?abstract_id=1907724.

76 Sotomayor strip search case: *N.G. and S.G. v. Connecticut*, 382 F.3d 225 (2nd Cir. 2004).

77 Sessions and Calabresi on empathy: Both quoted in Jesse Merriam, "The Stoics and Legal Conservatives: Strange Bedfellows or Just Strange Fellows?" *Law and Philosophy* 30 (2011), 201–02.

78 Frank Ricci case: *Ricci v. Destefano*, 557 U.S. 557 (2009).

79 Sotomayor's personal story: A good example, containing references to diabetes and the motorcycle chase, is Sheryl Gay Stolberg, "Sotomayor, a Trailblazer and a Dreamer," *New York Times*, May 27, 2009, A1.

80 "not that smart": Jeffrey Rosen, "The Case Against Sonia Sotomayor," *The New Republic*, May 4, 2009, available at http://www.tnr.com/article/politics/the-case-against-sotomayor?id=45d56e6f-f497-4b19-9c63-04e10199a085#.

80 "biography over brains": Dana Milbank, "But Will She Suit Up with the Washington Nine?" *The Washington Post*, May 27, 2008, A2.

82 Kagan confirmation hearings: A transcript is available at http://www.marylandindependentparty.org/for_discussion/Kagan_confirmation_hearings_transcript.html, and a video of the exchange at http://www.youtube.com/watch?v=Tku61sKhPGo.

83 Paul Campos wrote a highly critical profile: "Elena Kagan, Barack Obama,

and the American Establishment," http://www.lawyersgunsmoneyblog
.com/2010/07/elena-kagan-barack-obama-and-the-american-establishment
(July 21, 2010).

84 Kagan at Chicago and Harvard: In addition to personal knowledge, I rely
here on Paul Campos and Dahlia Lithwick, "Her Honor," http://nymag.com/
print/?/news/politics/elena-kagan-2011-12.

88 a "miracle": Kevin K. Washburn, "Elena Kagan and the Miracle at Harvard,"
Journal of Legal Education 61 (2011).

90 Kagan campaign finance opinion: *Arizona Free Enterprise Club's Freedom
Club PAC v. Bennett,* 131 S. Ct. 2806 (2011).

92 In a quite technical case: *Caraco Pharmaceutical Laboratories, Ltd. v. Novo
Nordisk A/S,* 132 S. Ct. 1670 (2012).

93 Kagan reportedly expressed: See Lithwick, "Her Honor," http://nymag.com/
print/?/news/politics/elena-kagan-2011-12.

93 DNA profile case: *Williams v. Illinois,* 132 S. Ct. 2221 (2012)

98 Argument in Montana case: *PPL Montana, Inc. v. Montana,* http://www
.supremecourt.gov/oral_arguments/argument_transcripts/10-218.pdf, 16.

98 Thomas on bankruptcy: John Schwartz, "Long Shot for Court Has Reputation for Compassion and Persuasion," *New York Times,* May 5, 2010, available
at http://www.nytimes.com/2010/05/06/us/06thomas.html.

99 Robert Jackson's "workable government": *Youngstown Sheet & Tube Co.
v. Sawyer* (The Steel Seizure Case), 343 U.S. 579, 643 (1952) (Jackson, J.,
concurring).

100 in a decision invalidating the legislative veto: *INS v. Chadha,* 462 U.S. 919,
959 (1983).

CHAPTER 3

102 Roberts and Thomas on the Court as family: Bill Mears, " 'Friendly' court
uneasy about changes on the bench," available at http://www.cnn.com/2009/
POLITICS/09/05/scotus.journal.court.change/.

103 "decorum and cordiality": Clare Cushman, *Courtwatchers: Eyewitness
Accounts in Supreme Court History* (Lanham, MD: Rowman & Littlefield,
2012), 150, referring to "report[s] from "[c]urrent Justices."

103 "a continuously running conversation": Tribute to former Justice Sandra
Day O'Connor, Supreme Court Historical Society, April 11, 2012, at http://
www.c-span.org/Events/Supreme-Court-Justices-Celebrate-Justice-Sandra-
Day-OConnor/10737429777/.

104 "more back-and-forth": Justice Thomas, quoted in Cushman, *Courtwatchers,*

152 (citing Brian Lamb, Susan Swain, and Mark Farkas, *The Supreme Court* [New York: Public Affairs, 2010], 94).

104   gave a commencement speech at Georgetown University: "Chief Justice Says His Goal Is More Consensus on Court," *New York Times*, May 22, 2006, A16.

105   "The Supreme Court has shown a surprising degree of unanimity": Bill Mears, "Roberts: 'The Hard Part is Coming Up,' " http://www.cnn.com/2006/ LAW/06/02/scotus.ahead/index.html?iref=newssearch.

105   "a more harmonious institution": Rodger Citron, "Process Makes Perfect: John Roberts' Marked, and Positive, Influence on the Supreme Court," http://www.slate.com/articles/news_and_politics/jurisprudence/2006/07/ process_makes_perfect.html.

105   New Hampshire abortion decision: *Ayotte v. Planned Parenthood of Northern New England*, 546 U.S. 320 (2006).

106   A group called Wisconsin Right to Life: *Wisconsin Right to Life v. Federal Election Commission*, 546 U.S. 410 (2006).

109   inmate in a Georgia prison: *United States v. Georgia*, 546 U.S. 151 (2006).

109   modest "federalism revolution": Discussed in Tushnet, *A Court Divided: The Rehnquist Court and the Future of Constitutional Law.*

111   Goodman's claims under the ADA: Recollection of Samuel Bagenstos, his attorney at the Supreme Court. Bagenstos reports that Goodman was released on parole in 2012.

111   Solomon Amendment case: *Rumsfeld v. FAIR*, 547 U.S. 47 (2006).

116   Texas redistricting case: *League of Latin American Citizens v. Perry*, 548 U.S. 399 (2006).

117   in a Clean Water Act case: *Rapanos v. United States*, 547 U.S. 715 (2006).

120   One academic study suggests: See Mark S. Hurwitz and Drew Noble Lanier, "Chief Justice Roberts and Consensus of the U.S. Supreme Court: A Cross-Time Comparison of Four Chief Justice Courts, 1953–2008," http://papers .ssrn.com/sol3/papers.cfm?abstract_id=1846663.

121   *Hudson* case: *Hudson v. Michigan*, 547 U.S. 586 (2006).

121   Kansas case: *Kansas v. Marsh*, 548 U.S. 163 (2006).

122   The third re-argued case: *Garcetti v. Ceballos*, 547 U.S. 410 (2006).

124   second *Wisconsin Right to Life* case: *Federal Election Commission v. Wisconsin Right to Life*, 551 U.S. 449 (2007).

127   "welcome news": Quoted in Linda Greenhouse, *Becoming Justice Blackmun* (New York: Times Books, 2005), 204.

127   *Casey* decision: *Planned Parenthood of Southeastern Pennsylvania v. Casey*, 505 U.S. 833 (1992).

131 Carhart cases: *Stenberg v. Carhart*, 520 U.S. 914 (2000); *Gonzales v. Carhart*, 550 U.S. 124 (2007).

135 Seattle and Louisville cases: *Parents Involved in Community Schools v. Seattle School District No. 1*, 551 U.S. 701 (2007).

140 Reactions of Robert Carter, Jack Greenberg, and William T. Coleman, Jr.: Reported in Adam Liptak, "The Same Words, but Differing Views," *New York Times*, June 29, 2007, A24.

141 Bowles case: *Bowles v. Russell*, 551 U.S. 205 (2007).

143 Ledbetter case: *Ledbetter v. Goodyear Tire & Rubber Co.*, 550 U.S. 618 (2007).

144 Ginsburg's oral statement: Transcript and audio available at http://www.oyez .org/cases/2000-2009/2006/2006_05_1074.

145 Military Commissions Act case: *Boumediene v. Bush*, 553 U.S. 723 (2008).

147 "walk the walk": Jan Crawford, "Discord at Supreme Court is deep, and personal," July 8, 2012, available at http://cbsnews.com/2102-3460_162-57468202.htm?tag=contentMain;contentBody.

CHAPTER 4

148 *Dictionary of Misinformation*: Tom Burnam, *The Dictionary of Misinformation* (New York: Thomas Y. Crowell, 1975), 218.

148 Bork: "The Advocates," *Life* magazine, vol. 14, no. 13 (November 1991), 98. He reiterated this view with only a slight hint at qualification four years later: "The Supreme Court has consistently ruled that there is no individual right to own a firearm. The Second Amendment was designed to allow states to defend themselves against a possibly tyrannical national government. Now that the federal government has stealth bombers and nuclear weapons, it is hard to imagine what people would need to keep in the garage to serve that purpose"—Robert H. Bork, *Slouching Toward Gomorrah: Modern Liberalism and American Decline* (New York: ReganBooks/HarperCollins, 1996), 166.

148 Burger article and interview: Warren E. Burger, "The Right to Bear Arms," *Parade* magazine, Jan. 14, 1990, 4; *MacNeil/Lehrer NewsHour*, Monday, Dec. 16, 1991.

149 the "Standard Model": The original use appears to be in Glenn Harlan Reynolds, "A Critical Guide to the Second Amendment," *Tennessee Law Review* 62 (1995), at p. 463.

149 NRA history and *Heller*'s background: I rely here on Adam Winkler, *Gun Fight: The Battle Over the Right to Bear Arms in America* (New York: W. W. Norton, 2011), 45–56, 63–68.

151 although surveys suggested: See, e.g, for an example, see "New Poll of NRA Members by Frank Luntz Shows Strong Support for Common-Sense Gun

Laws, Exposing Significant Divide Between Rank-and-File Members and NRA Leadership," July 24, 2012, available at http://e2.ma/message/p7lcb/hhkjgb.

151 Levinson article: Sanford Levinson, "The Embarrassing Second Amendment," *Yale Law Journal* 99 (1989), 637

152 the small-r republican version: I don't exempt myself from this point. My most widely cited article for a long time, "Following the Rules Laid Down," was a breathless retrieval of the small-r republican tradition as a vehicle for my criticism of prevailing methods of constitutional interpretation—*Harvard Law Review* 96 (1983), 781.

153 Tribe on gun rights: Laurence H. Tribe, *American Constitutional Law*, 3rd ed. (New York: Foundation Press, 2000), 901–02 n. 221.

155 "sympathetic people" and "the court of public opinion": Levy, quoted in Winkler, *Gun Fight*, 90.

159 "the [NRA's] improper strategic goals": Gura's motion quoted in ibid., 61.

163 Raoul Berger: See Raoul Berger, *Impeachment: The Constitutional Problems* (Cambridge, MA: Harvard University Press, 1972), and Raoul Berger, *Government by Judiciary: The Transformation of the Fourteenth Amendment* (Cambridge, MA: Harvard University Press, 1977).

164 History of originalism: Johnathan G. O'Neil, *Originalism in American Law and Politics: A Constitutional History* (Baltimore: Johns Hopkins University Press, 2005); Jamal Green, "Selling Originalism," *Georgetown Law Journal* 97 (2009), 657.

166 that women couldn't be lawyers: *Bradwell v. Illinois*, 83 U.S. 130 (1873).

166 you can ignore original expected applications: Jed Rubenfeld, *Revolution by Judiciary: The Structure of American Constitutional Law* (Cambridge, MA: Harvard University Press, 2005)

166 list of intellectual weaknesses: Thomas B. Colby, "The Sacrifice of the New Originalism," *Georgetown Law Journal* 99 (2011), 713.

166 prominent liberals were willing: See Jack M. Balkin, *Living Originalism* (Cambridge, MA: Harvard University Press, 2011).

167 "Richard Nixon once said": Gerard Magliocca, "Sigh . . . Originalism," posting to Balkinization, 9:06 am, Nov. 29, 2011, available at http://balkin.blogspot.com/2011/11/sigh-originalism.html.

168 *Heller* was a test: *District of Columbia v. Heller*, 554 U.S. 570 (2008).

169 examination of originalist materials: Mark Tushnet, *Out of Range: Why the Constitution Can't End the Battle Over Guns* (New York: Oxford University Press, 2007).

173 "The outcome can be laid at": *Texas v. Johnson*, 491 U.S. 397, 420 (1989) (Kennedy, J., concurring).

175   Bushrod Washington decision: *Corfield v. Coryell*, 6 Fed. Cas. 546, E.D. Pa.
       1823).

176   Supreme Court decision limiting the privileges and immunities clause: *The
       Slaughterhouse Cases*, 83 U.S. 36 (1873).

176   "I am not a nut": Antonin Scalia, Wriston Lecture at the Manhattan Institute
       for Policy Research, "On Interpreting the Constitution," Nov. 17, 1997 (tran-
       script available at http://www.manhattan-institute.org/html/wl1997.htm).

179   "green pastel redness": John Hart Ely, *Democracy and Distrust* (Cambridge,
       MA: Harvard University Press, 1980), 18.

180   sharp-bladed knives as "arms": Claton E. Cramer and Joseph Edward
       Olson, "Knives and the Second Amendment," available at http://ssrn.com/
       abstract=2070313.

180   nunchakus: *Maloney v. Rice*, 554 F.3d 56 (2nd Cir. 2009), vacated and
       remanded, 130 S. Ct. 3541 (2010).

181   Stevens's oral announcement in *Heller*: Available in audio at http://www
       .oyez.org/cases/2000-2009/2007/2007_07_290.

182   Judicial recusal case: *Caperton v. W.T. Massey, Inc.*, 556 U.S. 868 (2008).

184   Statute of Northampton: Discussed in Patrick J. Charles, "The Faces of the
       Second Amendment Outside the Home: History versus Ahistorical Standards
       of Review," *Cleveland State Law Review* 60 (2012). The eighteenth-century
       source is William Hawkins, *A Treatise of the Pleas of the Crown* (1716), ch.
       28, sect. 9, available in an edition published in 1824 at http://books.google
       .com/books?id=vZc0AAAAIAAJ.

CHAPTER 5

187   Newspaper stories: "Business Reigns Supreme," *The Washington Post*, July 1,
       2007, F3; Tony Mauro, "High Court Reveals a Mind for Business," *Legal Times*,
       July 2, 2007; Jeffrey Rosen, "Supreme Court, Inc.," *New York Times Magazine*,
       March 18, 2008, 38; Adam Liptak, "Justices Offer Receptive Ear to Business
       Interests," *New York Times*, Dec. 19, 2010, available at http://www.nytimes
       .com/2010/12/19/us/19roberts.html?pagewanted=all.

188   The political scientist Lee Epstein: Lee Epstein, William M. Landes, and
       Richard A. Posner, "Is the Roberts Court Pro-Business?" available at http://
       epstein.usc.edu/research/RobertsBusiness.pdf (Dec. 17, 2010). For a less
       statistical analysis reaching the same conclusion, see J. Mitchell Pickerill,
       "Something Old, Something New, Something Borrowed, Something Blue,"
       Santa Clara Law Review 49 (2009), 1063.

188   An overview of the 2011–12 term: Corey Ciocchetti, "The Constitution,
       the Roberts Court and Business: The Significant Business Impact of the

2011–2012 Supreme Court Term," available at http://papers.ssrn.com/sol3/papers.cfm?abstract_id=2073360.

188 liberal interest groups piled on: See Alan B. Morrison, "Saved by the Supreme Court: Rescuing Corporate America," Oct. 4, 2011, available at http://www.acslaw.org/publications/issue-briefs/saved-by-the-supreme-court-rescuing-corporate-america; Neil Weare, "U.S. Chamber Quietly Completes Undefeated 7–0 Term," June 29, 2012, available at http://theusconstitution.org/text-history/1503/us-chamber-quietly-completes-undefeated-7-0-term-suc cess-versus-solicitor-general.

189 conservative responses: Eric Posner, "Is the Supreme Court Biased in Favor of Business?" *Slate*, March 17, 2008, available at http://www.slate.com/blogs/con-victions/2008/03/17/is_the_supreme_court_biased_in_favor_of_business .html; Jonathan Adler, "Business, the Environment, and the Roberts Court: A Preliminary Assessment," *Santa Clara Law Review*, 49 (2009), 943; Ramesh Ponnuru, "Supreme Court Isn't Pro-Business, But Should Be," Bloomberg, July 5, 2011, available at http://www.bloomberg.com/news/2011-07-05/supreme-court-isn-t-pro-business-but-should-be-ramesh-ponnuru.html; Stephen Richer, "The Alleged Pro-Business Bias of the Supreme Court . . . Sigh . . . ," Forbes, Oct. 15, 2012, available at http://www.forbes.com/sites/stephen-richer/2012/10/15/the-alleged-pro-business-bias-of-the-supreme-court-sigh/.

190 Roberts on the "little guy": His comment came during his questioning by Senator Richard Durbin on Sept. 15, 2005.

194 Diana Levine case: *Wyeth v. Levine*, 555 U.S. 555 (2009).

196 Background of Gladys Mensing case: Jeremy Herb, "Generic Drug Labels at Core of Wrenching Case," *Minneapolis Star Tribune*, March 31, 2011, 1A. The case is *PLIVA v. Mensing*, 131 S. Ct. 2567 (2011).

198 Background of Alexis Geier case: "Much Rides on Air Bag Case," *Detroit News*, Dec. 5, 1999, 18; "Justices Hear Air Bag Case," *Detroit Free Press*, Dec. 8, 1999, 1E.

200 Scalia's description of Arizona's immigration crisis: *Arizona v. United States*, 132 S. Ct. 2492 (2012).

201 another Chamber of Commerce case: *U.S. Chamber of Commerce v. Whiting*, 131 S. Ct. 1968 (2011).

202 The global warming case: *Massachusetts v. EPA*, 549 U.S. 497 (2007).

205 The Concepcion case: *AT&T Mobility LLC v. Concepcion*, 131 S. Ct. 1740 (2011).

205 Description of Hulett firm: Taken from the firm Web site at http://hulett harperstewart.com/cases/.

207 "a classic abuse": Andrew Pincus, Letter to the Editor, "Get the facts straight in 'Concepcion,' " *National Law Journal*, July 23, 2012, 43.

209　Dukes case background: "Betty Dukes," available at http://www.walmart-class.com/staticdata/11Betty percent20Dukes.1027.pdf.

209　Toobin on *Dukes*: Jeffrey Toobin, "Betty Dukes v. Walmart," *The New Yorker*, June 20, 2011, available at http://www.newyorker.com/online/blogs/news desk/2011/06/betty-dukes-v-walmart.html.

210　Dukes case: *Wal-Mart Stores, Inc. v. Dukes*, 131 S. Ct. 2541 (2011).

212　Betty Dukes became a spokesperson: Dave Jamieson, "Betty Dukes, Renowned Dukes v. Walmart Plaintiff, Takes Her Fight Back to Capitol Hill," *Huffington Post Business*, available at http://www.huffingtonpost .com/2012/06/20/betty-dukes-walmart-supreme-court_n_1613305.html.

213　The "procedural" cases: A good presentation, with references to other works, is Miriam Gilles and Gary Friedman, "After Class: Aggregate Litigation in the Wake of *AT&T Mobility v. Conception*," *University of Chicago Law Review* 79 (2012), 623.

CHAPTER 6

215　"the most free speech court": Starr's comment is reported in Erwin Chemerinsky, "Not a Free Speech Court," *Arizona Law Review* 53 (2011), 723.

215　ACLU on campaign finance: The Web site is http://www.aclu.org/free-speech/ campaign-finance-reform.

215　Study of Roberts Court free speech decisions: Monica Youn, "The Roberts Court's Free Speech Double Standard," available at http://www.acslaw .org/acsblog/the-roberts-court's-free-speech-double-standard. The study is discussed in Adam Liptak, "Study Challenges Supreme Court's Image as Defender of Free Speech," *New York Times*, Jan. 7, 2012, A25.

216　When Chief Justice Roberts wrote: *Herring v. United States*, 555 U.S. 135 (2009).

216　Xavier Alvarez case: *United States v. Alvarez*, 132 S. Ct. 2537 (2012).

216　List of Congressional Medal of Honor recipients at http://www.cmohs.org/ living-recipients.php.

216　Rick Strandlof's case: A detailed portrait of Strandlof is Kelsey Whipple, "Will the Real Rick Strandlof Please Stand Up?" *Denver Westword News*, July 26, 2012, available at http://www.westword.com/2012-07–26/news/ rick-strandlof-stolen-valor-and-identity/.

217　Stolen Valor organization: http://www.stolenvalor.com/target.cfm.

218　Walter Chaplinsky case: *Chaplinsky v. New Hampshire*, 315 U.S. 568 (1942).

219　crush video case: United States v. Stevens, 130 S. Ct. 1577 (2010).

222　Fred Phelps case: *Snyder v. Phelps*, 131 S. Ct. 1207 (2011).

223　Falwell case: *Hustler Magazine, Inc. v. Falwell*, 485 U.S. 46 (1988).

224   Vermont's prescription data-mining case: *Sorrell v. IMS Health Services, Inc.*, 131 S. Ct. 265 (2011).

225   known as "detailers": For a description of how detailers work, see Carl Elliott, *White Coat, Black Hat: Adventures on the Dark Side of Medicine* (Boston: Beacon Press, 2010), chap. 3.

226   Supreme Court decision: *Valentine v. Chrestensen*, 316 U.S. 52 (1942).

226   Chrestensen as P. T. Barnum: Tom Gerety, "The Submarine, the Handbill, and the First Amendment," *Cincinnati Law Review* 56 (1988), 1167.

226   Virginia convicted Jeffrey Bigelow: *Bigelow v. Virginia*, 421 U.S. 809 (1975). The case is discussed in Greenhouse, *Becoming Justice Blackmun*, 116–19.

227   Ralph Nader and other consumer advocates: *Virginia Board of Pharmacy v. Virginia Citizens Consumer Council*, 425 U.S. 748 (1976).

228   The Court settled on a doctrinal formulation: From *Central Hudson Gas & Electric Corp. v. Public Service Commission*, 447 U.S. 557 (1980).

233   study of television news: Elliott E. Slotnick and Jennifer A. Segal, *Television News and the Supreme Court: All the News That's Fit to Air?* (New York: Cambridge University Press, 1988), esp. pp. 223 and 226.

233   "Disgusting But Not Illegal": *New York Times*, Aug. 1, 2010, available at http://www.nytimes.com/2010/08/02/opinion/02mon2.html.

233   "Even Hurtful Speech": *New York Times*, March 2, 2011, available at http://www.nytimes.com/2011/03/03/opinion/03thu2.html.

233   "The Right to Even Ugly Free Speech": *The Washington Post*, March 3, 2011, A4.

234   "a commendable reinforcement": *The Washington Post*, June 29, 2012, available at http://articles.washingtonpost.com/2012-06-29/opinions/354 62431_1_stolen-valor-act-california-court-justice-kennedy.

234   The editorialists thought: "The High Court's Misguided Decision on Violent Video Games," *The Washington Post*, June 27, 2011, available at http://articles.washingtonpost.com/2011-06-27/opinions/35234055_1_violent-video-games-depictions-of-animal-cruelty-minors.

236   "poor and puny anonymities": *Abrams v. United States*, 250 U.S. 616, 629 (1919) (Holmes, J., dissenting).

239   "BONG HiTS 4 JESUS case": *Morse v. Frederick*, 551 U.S. 393 (2007). James C. Foster, BONG HiTS 4 JESUS: *A Perfect Constitutional Storm in Alaska's Capital* (Fairbanks, Alaska: University of Alaska Press, 2010), provides details on the case's background.

241   "material support" decision: *Holder v. Humanitarian Law Project*, 130 S. Ct. 2705 (2010).

241   Humanitarian Law Project: Its Web site is at http://hlp.home.igc.org but does not appear to have been updated since 2010.

244   "outside salesmen" decision: *Christopher v. SmithKline Beecham Corp.*, 132
      S. Ct. 2156 (2012).

245   FDA decision on tobacco advertising: *FDA v. Brown & Williamson Tobacco
      Corp.*, 529 U.S. 100 (2000).

245   Massachusetts tobacco advertising decision: *Lorillard Tobacco Co. v. Reilly*,
      533 U.S. 525 (2001).

246   how unions could raise money: *Knox v. Service Employees International Union,
      Local 1000*, 132 S. Ct. 2277 (2012). Justice Sotomayor, joined by Justice
      Ginsburg, agreed with the narrow result the majority reached, so technically
      the Court didn't divide on partisan lines. But Justice Sotomayor specifi-
      cally criticized Justice Alito for reaching out to cast doubt on the "opt out"
      approach the Court had previously taken to the problem.

246   A recent academic study on speech and justices' tilt: Lee Epstein, Christopher
      M. Parker, and Jeffrey A. Segal, "Do Justices Defend the Speech They Hate?:
      In-Group Bias, Opportunism, and the First Amendment." Paper prepared for
      presentation at the 2012 Annual Meeting of the American Political Science
      Association, New Orleans, LA.

CHAPTER 7

247   2012 presidential campaign spending: Rick Cohen, "Look Who's Spending:
      Election 2012 Super PAC Rundown," Nov. 29, 2012, available at http://www
      .nonprofitquarterly.org/policysocial-context/21421-look-whos-spending-elec
      tion-2012-super-pac-rundown.html.

248   The Koch brothers: For an extended portrait, see Jane Mayer, "Covert
      Operations: The Billionaire Brothers Who Are Waging a War Against
      Obama," *The New Yorker*, Aug. 30, 2010, p. 44. For a response, see Mat-
      thew Continetti, "The Paranoid Style in Liberal Politics," *The Weekly
      Standard*, April 4, 2011, p. 24. On the Subchapter S status of Koch
      Industries, see John McCormack, "Koch Industries Lawyer to White
      House: How Did You Get Our Tax Information?" *The Weekly Standard*
      Blog, Sept. 20, 2010, available at http://www.weeklystandard.com/blogs/
      koch-industries-lawyer-white-house-how-did-you-get-our-tax-information-1.

248   effects of *Citizens United*: A good presentation of *Citizen United*'s effects is
      Matt Bai, "How Much Has Citizens United Changed the Political Game?"
      New York Times Magazine, July 17, 2012, available at http://www.nytimes
      .com/2012/07/22/magazine/how-much-has-citizens-united-changed-the-polit
      ical-game.html.

249   David Bossie and *Citizens United*: On Bossie, see Francis X. Clines, " 'Pit
      Bull' Congressman Gets Chance to Be More Aggressive," *New York Times*,

March 9, 1997, 22; Eric Schmitt, "A Top Aide Resigns," *New York Times*, May 10, 1998, 42. The Citizens United Web site, describing its activities, is at http://www.citizensunited.org/.

254   501(c)(4)s, 527s, and Super PACS: A good introduction is Richard Briffault, "Super PACs," *Minnesota Law Review* 96 (2012), 1629.

254   spending by 527s: The statistics are taken from "527s: Advocacy Group Spending," http://www.opensecrets.org/527s/.

256   Americans collectively spend about the same: For one version, see *Cato Handbook for Congress*, "Restrictions on Political Speech," http://www.cato.org/pubs/handbook/hb105-18.html, which compares the $3.2 billion of political spending in 1991–92 to the $4.5 billion spent annually on potato chips.

259   Socialist Workers Party disclosure case: *Brown v. Socialist Workers '74 Campaign Committee*, 459 U.S. 87 (1982).

260   *Citizens United* transcripts of oral argument: Available at http://www.supremecourt.gov/oral_arguments/argument_transcripts/08-205.pdf (initial argument); http://www.supremecourt.gov/oral_arguments/argument_tran scripts/08-205[Reargued].pdf (reargument).

261   For the Court's internal deliberations I rely on Jeffrey Toobin, "Money Unlimited," *The New Yorker*, May 21, 2012, 36.

263   According to one source: 2012 report on business contributions to Super PACs at: http://www.demos.org/sites/default/files/imce/AuctioningDemoc racy-DataAppendix-Final.pdf. I thank John Coates for directing me to this report.

264   UAW-Ford agreement: http://www.soldiersofsolidarity.com/files/related newsandreports2011and12/2011_uaw_ford_contract.pdf.

267   it "will open the floodgates": 2010 State of the Union address quoted and the reaction discussed in Mark A. Graber, "A Tale Told by a President," *Yale Law and Policy Review Inter Alia*, http://yalelawandpolicy.org/blog/2010/06/30/ tale-told-president, 13–14 (including references to the reaction).

268   upholding a statute prohibiting foreigners: *Bluman v. Federal Election Commission*, 132 S. Ct. 1087 (2012).

269   lower court decision after *Citizens United*: *SpeechNow v. Federal Elections Commission*, 599 F.3d 686 (DC Cir. 2010). Before *Citizens United*, there was a plausible argument that 527s could accept unlimited contributions, but actually doing so was quite risky, and no court had allowed such contributions.

269   The law professor Benjamin Sachs: "Unions, Corporations, and Political Opt-Out Rights After *Citizens United*," *Columbia Law Review*, 112 (2012), 800.

270   "union density": Figures taken from Bureau of Labor Statistics, "Union Members Summary" for 2011, http://www.bls.gov/news.release/union2.nr0.htm.

273 Despite Romney's lament: Michael D. Shear, "Romney Says 'Super PACs' Have Been a 'Disaster,' " *New York Times—The Caucus*, Dec. 20, 2011 (available at http://thecaucus.blogs.nytimes.com/2011/12/20/romney-says-super-pacs-have-been-a-disaster/. (I owe the quotation to Richard Briffault, "Super PACs," noted above).

273 Arizona had just such a system: *Arizona Free Enterprise Club's Freedom Club Pac v. Bennett*, 131 S. Ct. 2806 (2011)

276 Writing a constitutional amendment: In order, http://movetoamend.org/; http://www.opencongress.org/bill/112-hj78/text; http://www.scribd.com/doc/71154073/A-Constitutional-Amendment-to-Reform-Campaign-Finance; and http://thomas.loc.gov/cgi-bin/query/z?c112:S.J.RES.33.

277 Victor Brudney spotted: Victor Brudney, "Business Corporations and Stockholders' Rights Under the First Amendment," *Yale Law Journal*, 91 (1981), 235.

279 Hasen comments: Richard L. Hasen, "Fixing Washington," *Harvard Law Review* 126 (2012), 550.

EPILOGUE

284 Grassley on Watford: Senator Grassley's criticisms were contained in a statement made in the Senate Committee on the Judiciary and reiterated during the confirmation debate. For the statement, see http://www.grassley.senate.gov/news/Article.cfm?customel_dataPageID_1502=38826.

ACKNOWLEDGMENTS

In addition to the material identified in the Notes, I have drawn only on events open to the public which I attended, with the exception of some aspects of my description of Justice Kagan's academic career. In the interests of full disclosure, I note that Eugene Meyer has been extremely kind to my idiosyncratically conservative daughter, which undoubtedly makes my view of the Federalist Society more ambivalent than it might otherwise be. I participated in a moot court for one of James Bopp's Supreme Court arguments, though I don't remember which one. Dane von Breichenruchardt attended two short courses on recent Supreme Court decisions I taught. While I was teaching at the University of Wisconsin and Georgetown University, I was "secretary"—the bureaucratic administrator—of the Conference of Critical Legal Studies. And the press release announcing my appointment to the Harvard faculty was a topic of questions submitted to Justice Kagan by Oklahoma Senator Tom Coburn after her oral testimony at her confirmation hearings.

My colleague and friend Louis Michael Seidman read several chapters, and cautioned me against making insupportable claims about what one or another justice might have been thinking. Richard Hasen read a draft of the chapter on campaign finance, and kept me from making some basic errors. Some mistakes may remain in that chapter and elsewhere, for which I am solely responsible. Occasionally I have simplified legal doctrines in ways that might seem mistaken to specialists, with the goal of ensuring that non-specialists can understand the doctrines without being misled about their core ideas.

My agent Sydelle Kramer encouraged me to keep the idea of writing a book about the Roberts Court in mind, until I decided that the Roberts Court had been around long enough to take up her idea. Alane Salierno Mason provided terrific editorial guidance in shaping the book and helping me identify its most important themes. Ann Adelman's copyediting substantially improved the book as well.

INDEX